The Fishmonger Cookbook

The Fishmonger Cookbook

By Dorothy Batchelder

From a New England neighborhood fish market —
an expert's guide to selecting, preparing, cooking, & serving
the very best fish & seafood.

YANKEE BOOKS

Emmaus, Pennsylvania

Dedication

To my children—Jennifer, Rick, and Becca—
whose love makes it all worthwhile.

Originally published by Yankee Publishing Incorporated

Printed in the United States of America

Interior design and illustrations by Debra Wright
Cover design by J Porter
Cover painting by Carol Inman

Library of Congress Cataloging-in-Publication Data

Batchelder, Dorothy, 1943–
    The fishmonger cookbook.
    Includes index.
    1. Cookery (Fish)   2. Cookery (Seafood)   I. Title
TX747.B344   1988   641.6'92   88–17356
    ISBN 0–89909–359–0 paperback

Distributed in the book trade by St. Martin's Press

2 4 6 8 10 9 7 5 3 1 paperback

Acknowledgments

My thanks and appreciation to all the fishmongers, past and present; to those people who have helped make the store such a great success — especially Thalia Large, Angela Ruth Pendleton, Robert Walter, Ellen Brisch, Cheryl Williams, and Rebecca Olson; to Howard Richardson, a man of extraordinary talents; to my parents, Sam and Peggy, who raised a Dorothy who wanted to wear not ruby slippers but a pair of shiny black rubber boots; and to my editor, Sandy Taylor, for her determination to get this book published.

Contents

Introduction

Ten years ago, when I bought The Fishmonger, located in a residential area in West Cambridge, Massachusetts, it was the only market in that part of town selling fresh fish. The business had only the bare essentials; I had to buy a display case, sink, and cutlery, and then stock up on quality seafood. Although I knew nothing at all about the food industry, good luck, timing, and my instincts all seemed to point out that this was the business for me. My three children were in school, and I needed a profession outside the home to support us. So I decided to teach myself how to be a fishmonger by observing the experts.

The male-dominated Boston Fish Pier was the place I went to learn, but it was a difficult environment for a newcomer, especially a woman. In the beginning, there was prejudice to overcome and trust to win. I hoped that if I paid my bills on time and tried not to be too indecisive, I would get by and eventually be accepted. As I look back, there was one event that turned the tide, so to speak.

The B&M Fish Company is a small brokerage firm near the Boston Fish Pier. Owned by the Merino family, it was run by Larry, a vocal, hard-working fellow who manned the telephone, taking daily orders, and Tony, his large, cigar-smoking brother, who cut fish all day and never said a word to me. One morning, Larry noticed my concern about getting my feet and running shoes wet in a store that was overflowing with fish guts and scales. But he said nothing and went about his business. The next day, when I arrived to select my fish, waiting for me among the haddock was a new pair of shiny black rubber boots. Attached to them was a note saying, "For Dorothy, my sweetheart, Larry."

Over the years, with the help of other fishmongers, I have learned how to select the freshest seafood and how to cut and filet fish. In fact, now I can bone fish internally, leaving the head and tail intact, to present a neat, compact package for stuffing.

As my business grew, The Fishmonger became a market not only for fresh seafood but also for carry-out foods such as homemade soups, chowders, salads, pasta sauces, fish cakes, and dinners of various kinds. At first it was a great way to use up the leftover fish bought the day before, but after a year, I had the buying so precise that we never had anything left over. So I began purchasing additional fish just for the take-out menu.

Every week now, approximately one thousand people come through The Fishmonger's door, from affluent professionals to blue-collar workers, each asking what the freshest seafood is and some how it should be cooked. I'm trying to wean them away from the old standbys and encourage them to sample underutilized, less familiar fish such as hake, wolffish, and mako shark, for these are the fish of the future. The more traditional kinds, such as haddock and halibut, are becoming scarce and, as a result, more costly.

After countless conversations about seafood and recipes, I decided to record this information so that other people could discover the variety of fish available to them. I've arranged the book alphabetically for ease of finding the individual seafood. Each entry includes a brief introduction to the fish or shellfish. I explain how to judge its freshness, what the best cooking methods are, and whether any other fish can be substituted for it. This introduction is followed by a selection of recipes. One thing I point out to my customers and emphasize in this book is that fish is not something you should spend hours preparing. Instead, it generally requires only brief cooking — especially when using a microwave oven. And fresh fish will never smell up your house or taste fishy.

In addition to being quick and easy to prepare and basically economical (there's little waste), seafood is also nutritious and even better for your health than previously thought. Recent medical research regarding heart disease has shown that fish oils, especially the omega-3 variety, help to break down the cholesterol in your bloodstream and reduce the chance of heart attack. Fish such as mackerel, tuna, herring, shad, salmon, anchovies, and bluefish are good sources of omega-3. Today, nutritionists are recommending that people eat 3½ ounces of fish two or three times a week. Shellfish, always thought to be high in cholesterol, are low in comparison to chicken or beef.

Given the widespread concern over salt consumption, I have tried to use it sparingly in my recipes. Add more or less according to your own preference, or leave the salting entirely to the individual diners.

When a recipe calls for butter, I specify un-salted, but salted also will work. If you prefer to use a commercial brand of mayonnaise rath-er than the homemade recipe I have included, the best substitution is Hellmann's. Do not use salad dressing.

Foods high in fat, such as heavy cream or sour cream, are found in some of my recipes, but there are just as many preparations using less caloric ingredients, and in many instances I suggest a low-fat substitution such as yogurt. *The Fishmonger Cookbook* isn't intended to be a diet cookbook, but I have tried to include something for everyone, whether you count calories, watch your cholesterol, or simply love to eat.

Dorothy Batchelder
The Fishmonger
252 Huron Avenue
Cambridge, MA 02138
(617) 661-4834

Anchovies

Anchoa mitchilli

Eight species of anchovies live in the Atlantic waters. These small sea fish grow to no more than six inches in length, and their color ranges from bright silver on the belly to a dark greenish blue or almost black on the back. The anchovy differs from the herring (sardine) in its projecting snout and deeply cleft mouth, which extends back almost to the gills, and its large black eyes. Anchovies travel in densely packed schools along the surface of the water and frequently are found swimming with herring. They feed on small ocean organisms and spawn in fresh water.

Commercially, anchovies are marketed in the canned form and are used most often as a garnish. They are familiar on pizza, in antipasti, as a butter for broiled fish, and as a canapé. When using canned varieties, make sure you soak them in milk or water to cover to get out as much excess salt as possible.

When fresh (and uncured), anchovies have a light gray flesh and are delicious grilled or fried in olive oil.

Anchovy-Mint Sauce

MAKES 1½ CUPS

Fresh mint provides a unique complement to this sauce, which can be served over pasta or used as a dip for raw vegetables.

2-ounce tin anchovy filets,
  drained
4 cloves garlic, minced
¼ cup fresh mint leaves
¾ cup olive oil

2 tablespoons capers,
  squeeze-drained and
  chopped
½ cup pitted black olives,
  chopped
½ cup chopped fresh parsley

In food processor fitted with metal blade, combine anchovies, garlic, and mint just a few seconds but until well mixed. With motor running, add oil in steady stream until incorporated. Pour sauce into glass bowl and stir in capers, olives, and chopped parsley. Allow to sit at room temperature 15 minutes so flavors blend before serving.

Pasta with Anchovy-Onion Sauce

SERVES 4

Specialty food stores sell a good grade of anchovy that is not as salty as those sold in supermarkets.

6 anchovy filets
4 tablespoons olive oil
2 cups chopped onion
1 tablespoon minced garlic
¼ cup chopped fresh parsley
1 teaspoon chopped fresh
  thyme (½ teaspoon dried)

2 tablespoons chopped fresh
  basil (1 tablespoon dried)
1 cup tomato purée
¼ cup dry white wine
1 pound pasta
Freshly ground black pepper
  to taste

Soak anchovies in water to cover for 30 minutes to remove salt. Pat dry and cut each filet into four pieces. Heat oil in saucepan and add chopped onion and minced garlic. Sauté until soft and translucent, about 4 minutes.

Add anchovies, parsley, thyme, and basil. Stir in tomato purée and white wine, and simmer sauce for 30 minutes. Cook pasta al dente and serve topped with sauce and generous grinding of black pepper.

Anchovy Butter

MAKES ½ CUP

Serve this over grilled swordfish or bluefish for a wonderful tart/salty flavor.

4 anchovy filets, tinned	1 tablespoon fresh lemon
Milk	juice
8 tablespoons unsalted butter, softened	

Soak anchovy filets in milk to cover for 30 minutes. Dry on paper towel and chop very fine with sharp knife until paste consistency. Add to softened butter and stir in lemon juice, blending until mixed thoroughly. Use immediately or form into log shape, wrap in plastic wrap, and freeze for later use, slicing off a portion as needed.

Tapenade (Anchovy Dipping Sauce)

MAKES 1½ CUPS

This recipe comes from southern France and is a zinger of a dip for raw vegetables or a dressing for cold pasta salad.

Two 2-ounce tins anchovy filets, drained	1 teaspoon dry mustard
7-ounce can tuna	2 tablespoons fresh lemon juice
¾ cup pitted black olives	¼ cup olive oil
3 cloves garlic, minced	
¼ cup capers, squeeze-drained and chopped	

Soak anchovies in water to cover for 30 minutes to remove excess salt. Drain and pat dry with paper towel.

In food processor fitted with metal blade, purée anchovies, tuna, olives, garlic, capers, mustard, and lemon juice. Blend until smooth and no chunks are left. With motor running, add oil in steady stream until incorporated and sauce is thick and fluffy. Transfer to serving dish and serve at room temperature.

Bagna Cauda
(Hot Anchovy-Garlic Dip)

MAKES 1 CUP

This traditional Italian sauce can be served with raw vegetables or over broiled fish.

4 tablespoons unsalted
   butter
½ cup crème fraîche (recipe
   follows) or 1 cup heavy
   cream boiled until reduced
   to ½ cup

4 cloves garlic, minced
2 ounces anchovy filets,
   finely chopped

In heavy saucepan, melt butter. Add crème fraîche and garlic, and cook over low heat about 5 minutes, making sure not to burn. Add chopped anchovies and cook 5 minutes longer, just at a simmer. Transfer to flameproof container and keep warm over candle or place on small electric hot tray.

CRÈME FRAÎCHE

½ cup heavy cream (not
   ultrapasteurized)

¼ cup buttermilk

Whisk heavy cream and buttermilk together in bowl, then cover with plastic wrap and let stand at room temperature (around 70°) 4-6 hours, or until thickened. Transfer to jar with tight-fitting lid and refrigerate 4 hours. Flavor becomes more tart with time. Keeps up to 4 weeks.

Black Sea Bass

Centropristis striata

Black sea bass is often confused with black-fish, or tautog, but it is a true bass. Its diet consists chiefly of crabs, shrimps, and mollusks. When buying fresh whole black sea bass, look for those that are firm to the touch and have bright, clear eyes and red gills.

The flesh of black sea bass is white and has a rather large flake. Its sweet, delicate taste is cherished by many native Cape Codders. It can be cooked in a number of ways, including baked, sautéed, and steamed.

Baked Black Sea Bass with Rosemary   SERVES 4

It is best to cook this fish whole because you get so much more of the flesh than when it is fileted. Black sea bass has a very low oil content, so its taste is not as strong as that of bluefish.

3-pound whole black sea bass	2 tablespoons olive oil
2 tablespoons dried rosemary	2 tablespoons unsalted butter
Salt	½ cup dry white wine

Clean fish, removing scales, innards, and gills but leaving head and tail intact. Rub 1 tablespoon of the rosemary inside body cavity and sprinkle with a little salt. Rub outside of fish with oil and sprinkle with salt and remaining rosemary. Dot with butter and drizzle wine over all. Put in shallow baking pan and bake in preheated oven at 350° for 20-30 minutes. Transfer to platter by slipping 2 spatulas underneath fish at head and tail. Pour juices from pan over fish and serve.

Black Sea Bass Seviche   SERVES 4

Sibby Thorndike was my best friend when I was growing up. At age 16, we convinced our parents to take us to a dude ranch in Wyoming, where we were able to ride the open range with cowboys. Now Sibby lives in Panama, where seviche is a native dish — a far cry from the beans and dogs we had on the range.

1-pound black sea bass filet	2 hot chili peppers, seeded
½ cup fresh lime juice	and sliced
⅓ cup olive oil	1 red onion, sliced
2 cloves garlic, minced	Lettuce leaves
2 tablespoons chopped fresh	1 avocado, sliced, for garnish
cilantro leaves	Sliced tomatoes for garnish

Remove and discard skin from filet and cut into 1-inch pieces. In large bowl whisk together lime juice, oil, and garlic. Stir in cilantro and chili peppers. Add fish, making sure it is submerged in marinade. Add more lime juice if needed. Lay onion slices on top, cover bowl with plastic wrap, and refrigerate 12 hours.

With slotted spoon, remove solids from marinade and serve on bed of lettuce with avocado and tomato slices and additional cilantro for garnish.

Black Sea Bass with Olives and Capers   SERVES 2

2-pound whole black sea	2 tablespoons capers,
bass	squeeze-drained
Flour	¼ cup chopped scallions
2 tablespoons unsalted	Juice and rind of ½ lemon
butter	¾ cup dry white wine
2 tablespoons olive oil	Chopped fresh parsley for
½ cup pitted black olives,	garnish
sliced	

Clean fish, removing innards and scales but leaving head and tail intact. Rinse and pat dry with paper towel. Dust outside with flour.

In ovenproof saucepan or Dutch oven, heat butter and oil, and brown fish evenly on both sides, about 2 minutes per side. Remove fish to plate. Add olives, capers, scallions, lemon juice and rind, and wine to pan and bring to simmer. Lay fish on top, spoon on some juices, and bake, covered, in preheated oven at 400° for 15-20 minutes, or until fish flakes when tested with fork at its thickest part.

Transfer fish to platter, spoon on juices, and garnish with chopped parsley.

Steamed Black Sea Bass in Black Bean Sauce

SERVES 2-3

Fermented black beans are black beans that have been salted and then dried. They should be rinsed before using. The tinned kind need only to be drained.

2-pound whole black sea bass	¼ teaspoon salt
2 slices gingerroot	1 teaspoon minced garlic
2 tablespoons rice wine	Black Bean Sauce (recipe follows)

Clean fish of scales, gills, and innards, leaving head and tail intact. Rinse and pat dry with paper towel. With sharp knife, make long diagonal slashes across flesh every 2 inches. Place fish in flat-bottom glass dish.

Flatten gingerroot with cleaver to release aroma and combine in bowl with wine, salt, and garlic. Rub over fish and refrigerate 1 hour.

Place fish on rack over boiling water. Cover and cook 15-20 minutes, or until fish flakes when tested with fork at its thickest part. Transfer to platter and spoon on sauce.

BLACK BEAN SAUCE

2 tablespoons peanut oil	1 teaspoon minced garlic
2 tablespoons fermented black beans	¼ cup chicken broth
1 tablespoon minced scallions	2 tablespoons rice wine
	1 teaspoon sugar

Heat oil in saucepan over high heat. Add beans, scallions, and garlic, and fry 30 seconds, or until beans are fragrant. Combine broth, wine, and sugar, and add to beans. Cook 5 minutes.

Blackfish
(*see* Tautog)

Bluefish

Pomatomus saltatrix

Bluefish are a fast-swimming, voracious fish that travel in huge migratory schools up and down the East Coast from Nova Scotia to Florida. They can grow to 50 pounds in deep tropical waters, but the average size is between 5 and 15 pounds.

Bluefish have razor-sharp teeth that click together as they begin their feeding frenzy, so the term "snapper" (no relation to red snapper) has been applied to them. Technically, a snapper is a young bluefish of 3 to 6 pounds. Snapper blues are the most desirable to eat because they have a sweeter flavor that comes from their diet of crustaceans, mollusks, and various inshore fish. When freshly caught, they have a rich blue color with a distinctive metallic sheen. Larger blues (10 pounds and over) feed on mullet, herring, and menhaden, which create a strong, oily taste. "Choppers" are baby blues under 3 pounds and are best cooked whole.

Bluefish is sold whole or fileted; allow 1 pound per person for the whole fish, ½ pound

How to Filet Bluefish

Place the fish so the backbone is toward you. Run your finger down the bone structure of the head until you feel the flesh begin. Insert a boning knife here and make an incision straight down the back to the tail.

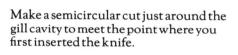

Make a semicircular cut just around the gill cavity to meet the point where you first inserted the knife.

With one hand, pull the flesh back while you continue to cut the flesh from the bones, working over the center backbone, around to the belly side, and on down to the tail.

Turn the fish over, again positioned with the backbone toward you. This time, however, insert the knife at the tail end and repeat the cutting procedures described in the preceding illustrations.

To skin bluefish, grasp the tail end of the skin with one hand, pulling taut as you push the knife down the length of the filet, separating the flesh from the skin.

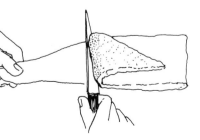

21

for filets. When buying bluefish in the round (whole), make sure they are firm to the touch and straight, not floppy. Their eyes should be bright and clear, and they should have rosy red gills. Bluefish are easy to filet (see p. 21), and they can be a money-saver if bought whole. Use the bones in your garden as fertilizer, but be sure to dig them down deep enough so as not to attract cats, dogs, or wildlife.

Because bluefish are fast swimmers, they have a large amount of muscle hemoglobin in their flesh, which makes it dark in color. Their pronounced flavor, sometimes described as "gamey tasting," comes from the darker concentration of meat down the center on the skin side. This can be removed by making a shallow cut along both sides of the filet, taking care not to cut through the flesh completely.

When cooking bluefish, it is a good idea to neutralize the oils and fat by using vegetables such as tomatoes and onions or citrus fruits such as lemons and limes. Bluefish should be either baked, broiled, fried, or grilled. I don't particularly like bluefish in chowder because it tends to dominate the flavor, but some die-hard New Englanders love it this way, so decide for yourself.

* * * * * * * *

A word of caution: PCBs — polychlorinated biphenyls — are chemicals that were used extensively by electric companies. In 1977 the federal government barred their use because research disclosed that prolonged ingestion of meat, fish, and eggs containing PCBs could result in liver damage, reproductive disorders, skin lesions, and, in tests on laboratory animals, cancer. PCBs have been found in the milk of nursing mothers who have eaten foods containing PCBs.

Fish with a high fat content, such as bluefish

and striped bass, are especially likely to contain PCBs. Nonfatty fish such as flounder, haddock, cod, and pollock are unlikely to accumulate excessive amounts. When using bluefish, remove the skin and discard the fatty, darker portion of the flesh that runs down the center of the filet. Eat small bluefish (under 10 pounds) rather than large ones, and, like most things in life, eat them in moderation. At The Fishmonger, I will not sell bluefish to a pregnant woman or nursing mother.

The Fishmonger Smoked Bluefish Spread

SERVES 8-10 AS APPETIZER

Smoked bluefish has a distinctive flavor and makes an excellent spread for hors d'oeuvres. This recipe is a favorite with my customers.

¾ pound smoked bluefish
1 pound cream cheese, cut into small pieces
2 heaping teaspoons Pommery mustard
1 teaspoon prepared horseradish
2 tablespoons sour cream
2 tablespoons fresh lemon juice

2 tablespoons minced red bell pepper
2 tablespoons minced Bermuda onion
2 tablespoons chopped fresh parsley
Cayenne pepper to taste (optional)

Remove skin from bluefish, check for bones, and discard darker flesh along center of filet. Break apart fish and put in food processor fitted with metal blade. Add cream cheese, mustard, horseradish, sour cream, and lemon juice, and mix well until blended. Transfer mixture to mixing bowl. Add red bell pepper, onion, and parsley, and combine. Add cayenne pepper for spicier taste. Serve with crackers or raw vegetables.

Pickled Bluefish

SERVES 4-6

This refreshing summer salad is great for a buffet. Various seasonal vegetables can be used to change the color and texture.

2 pounds bluefish filets, skinned	1 tablespoon fennel seed
4 cloves garlic, minced	1 tablespoon black peppercorns
3 Bermuda onions, sliced	½ cup dry white wine
4 carrots, julienned	¼ cup balsamic vinegar
1 green bell pepper, seeded and cut into thin strips	1 bay leaf, crumbled
1 red bell pepper, seeded and cut into thin strips	¼ teaspoon salt
5 tablespoons olive oil	Chopped fresh basil and sliced tomatoes for garnish

Bake bluefish in buttered baking dish in preheated oven at 400° for 15 minutes. Remove from oven and set aside to cool.

Combine garlic, onions, carrots, and bell peppers. Heat oil in sauté pan and sauté vegetables with fennel seed and peppercorns until vegetables are soft.

Remove from heat and add wine, vinegar, bay leaf, and salt. Stir to combine. Pour mixture over cooked bluefish and refrigerate 6 hours. To serve, garnish with fresh basil and tomatoes.

Gravad Fiske (Cured Bluefish)

SERVES 10-12

Serve this as a buffet item at a cocktail party. It is similar to Gravlax, which is made with fresh salmon and dill, but costs about one third as much. The salt and sugar actually cook the fish and leach out the juices. The weighting and turning help speed the process. The fish is done when it feels firm to the touch and doesn't spring back when pressed down with your finger. The tail end will cure faster because it is thinner, so test at the thickest part.

2 bluefish filets (1½ pounds each), with skin	¼ cup fresh rosemary leaves or fresh dill
½ cup salt	2 tablespoons green peppercorns (optional)
1 cup sugar	

Check bluefish filets for bones. Mix salt and sugar together in glass bowl. Coat outside of one bluefish filet with ¼ cup of the sugar-salt mixture and lay, skin side down, in glass or pottery dish.

Spread all but ¼ cup of the remaining sugar-salt mixture on both flesh sides of filets. Spread rosemary leaves evenly over each filet. Put green peppercorns on top if desired and put flesh sides of filets together like a sandwich. Spread remaining ¼ cup sugar-salt mixture on skin of the top filet. Lay plastic wrap and foil on top of fish and weight with bags of sugar or rice. Refrigerate 2 days, turning and draining off excess liquid each 24 hours.

To serve, put one filet on wooden cutting board and use sharp knife to slice diagonally across the grain at an angle. Serve with Mustard-Rosemary Sauce or Horseradish Sauce and pumpernickel or dark rye bread.

MUSTARD-ROSEMARY SAUCE

½ cup chopped fresh rosemary
⅓ cup Dijon mustard
3 tablespoons dark brown sugar

1 ½ teaspoons dry mustard
1 ½ cups olive oil or corn oil

Combine all ingredients in mixing bowl and whisk until smooth.

HORSERADISH SAUCE

⅔ cup sour cream
2 tablespoons prepared horseradish
1 tablespoon minced fresh chives

Freshly ground black pepper and cayenne pepper to taste

Combine first 3 ingredients in mixing bowl and blend well. Season with black and cayenne peppers.

Bluefish and Green Bean Salad   SERVES 6

This satisfying salad makes an ideal supper on a sultry summer evening. You can substitute asparagus, broccoli, or snow peas for the beans.

2 pounds bluefish filets	6 radishes, sliced
1 pound green beans, stringed and ends trimmed	12 pitted black olives, sliced
1 cup Garlic Vinaigrette (recipe follows)	1 red bell pepper, thinly sliced
1 pound red-skinned potatoes	Salt and pepper to taste
	3 tomatoes, quartered
	2 hard-boiled eggs

Remove skin from bluefish, check for bones, and place in buttered baking dish. Bake in preheated oven at 400° for 15-20 minutes.

Blanch beans in boiling water for 30 seconds. Drain immediately and plunge in ice water to stop cooking. Drain again, toss with 3 tablespoons vinaigrette, and set aside. Boil potatoes until just done. To test, cut one in half and insert knife blade or skewer, which should go through the potato easily. Plunge in ice water, drain, and toss with 3 tablespoons vinaigrette. Set aside.

When fish is done, break into pieces and let cool in large dish. Add beans, potatoes, radishes, olives, and bell pepper. Toss mixture carefully with remaining dressing. Season with salt and pepper, and garnish with tomato quarters and hard-boiled eggs, cut into wedges.

GARLIC VINAIGRETTE

2 cloves garlic, minced	1 tablespoon Dijon mustard
¼ teaspoon salt	¾ cup olive oil
3 tablespoons white wine vinegar	

With mortar and pestle, mash garlic to paste. Blend in salt. Place in clean bowl and whisk in vinegar and mustard. Add oil in thin stream, whisking constantly until all is incorporated.

Marinated Bluefish with Tangy Green Sauce

SERVES 6

This tart and tasty dish is topped with shrimp as a garnish.

3 pounds bluefish filets,
  skinned
10 cranks of freshly ground
  black pepper
4 cloves garlic, smashed with
  flat blade of knife
1 tablespoon chopped fresh
  oregano

½ teaspoon ground cumin
½ cup fresh lemon juice
½ cup fresh lime juice
Tangy Green Sauce (recipe
  follows)
12 large cooked shrimp

Cut bluefish into 6 equal pieces and place in glass dish. Combine pepper, garlic, oregano, cumin, and lemon and lime juices. Pour over fish pieces, stir to combine, and let marinate in refrigerator 3 hours. Transfer to baking dish and bake in preheated oven at 400° for 20 minutes.

Remove fish from oven and turn heat to broil. Coat each piece of fish with Tangy Green Sauce and broil 3 minutes, or until lightly browned. Garnish with cooked shrimp that have been cut in half lengthwise.

TANGY GREEN SAUCE

¾ cup whole almonds
3 cloves garlic, minced
Juice and grated rind
  of 1 lemon
3 tablespoons chopped fresh
  parsley

3 tablespoons capers,
  squeeze-drained
¾ cup olive oil
Salt and cayenne pepper to
  taste
¼ cup red wine vinegar

Toast almonds in preheated oven at 400° for 10-15 minutes, or until browned. Put all ingredients except vinegar in food processor fitted with metal blade and mix until puréed. With processor running, slowly add vinegar until all is incorporated.

Bluefish Baked Whole
with Rice, Raisin, and Pine Nut Stuffing

SERVES 6

On my fortieth birthday, Joel Sohn, an old friend, gave me a stuffed bluefish. It was not the kind you eat but one you hang on the wall as a trophy. It received notoriety by being used in an American Express commercial.

5-pound whole bluefish	Freshly ground black pepper
3 tablespoons olive oil	to taste
1 cup minced onion	½ teaspoon cinnamon
½ cup whole pine nuts	¼ teaspoon nutmeg
1 cup long-grain rice,	½ cup raisins or currants
uncooked	(previously soaked in water
2½ cups fish stock (see p.	and drained)
180) or chicken broth	½ cup chopped fresh parsley

Have your fishmonger gut fish and remove scales, gills, and center backbone, keeping head and tail intact.

Heat oil in pan and sauté onion until translucent. Add pine nuts and rice, and sauté until rice is shiny. Add fish stock, black pepper, cinnamon, and nutmeg, and bring to boil. Lower heat to simmer, cover, and cook until liquid is absorbed. Stir in raisins and chopped parsley, and remove from heat. Spoon stuffing into body cavity, secure with twine, and bake in ovenproof dish in preheated oven at 400° for 20-30 minutes.

Baked Stuffed Bluefish

SERVES 6

Buying a fish whole can save you money, but for this recipe you also can use two filets of the same size or one large filet cut in half horizontally. In either case, place the stuffing between the filets, tie with twine, and bake 10 minutes to the inch, measured at the thickest part.

5-pound whole bluefish (or 2	2 teaspoons chopped fresh
filets, 1¼ pounds each)	rosemary (¾ teaspoon
1 lemon	dried)
6 tablespoons unsalted	1 tablespoon capers, squeeze-
butter	drained
1 cup minced onion	½ cup dry red wine
1 green bell pepper, chopped	3 cups prepared stuffing mix
2 ribs celery, diced	½ cup dry white wine
2 carrots, peeled and diced	Lemon slices for garnish

Have your fishmonger gut fish and remove scales, gills, and center backbone, keeping head and tail intact. Rinse fish and pat dry with paper towel. Squeeze juice of 1 lemon over flesh inside fish.

Melt 4 tablespoons of the butter in pan and sauté onion, bell pepper, celery, and carrots until tender. Add rosemary, capers, and red wine, and simmer 2 minutes. Add stuffing mix and stir to moisten. (The fish will exude some of its own juices while it bakes, so do not make stuffing too moist.) Remove pan from heat. Spoon stuffing mixture in body cavity and tie fish with heavy twine to keep stuffing from falling out. Make foil nest on baking sheet and place stuffed fish on top. Dot with remaining 2 tablespoons butter and pour white wine over top. Bake in preheated oven at 400° for 15 minutes, reduce temperature to 350°, and cook 20 minutes more, or until fish flakes easily when tested with fork. Serve whole fish on platter garnished with lemon slices.

Baked Bluefish with Minted Yogurt   SERVES 2

My mother had a wonderful herb garden, and as a child, I was so proud to be able to identify the mint among all the other herbs. Here it is combined with yogurt to make a delicious, low-calorie sauce.

1-pound bluefish filet, skinned and cut into 2 equal pieces
2 tablespoons olive oil
1 medium zucchini, thinly sliced

1½ cups peeled, seeded, and chopped tomatoes
1 cup yogurt cheese*
3 tablespoons plain yogurt
¼ cup chopped fresh mint

Check bluefish for bones, rinse, and pat dry with paper towel. Heat oil and sauté zucchini for 3 minutes over medium heat. Add tomatoes and cook 2 minutes more. Spread mixture in baking dish large enough to hold fish pieces.

Combine yogurt cheese, yogurt, and mint. Dip both pieces of bluefish in mixture and lay on top of zucchini-tomato mixture. Spread remainder of yogurt mixture over fish and bake in preheated oven at 400° for 15 minutes, or until done.

* To make yogurt cheese, let 1¼ to 1½ cups plain yogurt drain in sieve for 4 hours or longer. It should have the consistency of cream cheese and hold its shape.

Bluefish with Mustard Sauce and Mussels

SERVES 4

Bluefish and blue mussels make a wonderful combination. Each has a distinctive taste, yet the mustard sauce pulls it all together.

2 pounds bluefish filets, skinned
2 tablespoons olive oil
1 ½ pounds mussels, washed and debearded (see p. 141)

½ cup water
½ cup dry white wine

MUSTARD SAUCE

2 tablespoons unsalted butter
1 large shallot, minced
1 tablespoon flour
½ cup mussel broth
1 cup heavy cream

3 tablespoons Pommery mustard
Salt and pepper to taste
2 tablespoons chopped fresh parsley for garnish

Cut bluefish into 4 equal pieces. Oil baking dish and place bluefish pieces in dish, spacing them slightly apart. Brush with oil and cover with foil. Bake in preheated oven at 350° for 15-20 minutes.

Steam mussels by bringing water and wine to simmer in sauté pan. Add cleaned mussels and cook 5 minutes, or until shells open and orange mussels show. Drain in sieve, saving broth to use in mustard sauce. When mussels are cool enough to handle, set aside a few in their shells for garnish. Remove remainder from shells.

While fish is baking, also make sauce. Melt butter, add shallot, and cook until soft. Whisk in flour and cook over medium heat for 2 minutes. Mix mussel broth with cream and add to flour mixture in slow, steady stream, whisking as you go. Whisk in mustard, stir in shucked mussels, and season with salt and pepper.

Pour sauce over cooked bluefish and garnish with chopped parsley and reserved mussels.

Sautéed Bluefish Cheeks

SERVES 2

Bluefish have meaty cheeks that are sweet, tender, and delicious. To remove the cheeks, feel for the soft, fleshy cavity under each eye and insert a sharp filet knife at a 20-degree angle to the bone. Cut around the cavity in a circle, keeping the angle of entry the same.

¾ pound bluefish cheeks
Juice of 1 lemon
1 egg, beaten
½ cup flour or cornmeal
¼ teaspoon salt

¼ teaspoon pepper
4 tablespoons unsalted
butter
Chopped fresh parsley for
garnish

Place bluefish in bowl, pour on lemon juice, and toss to coat. Dip in beaten egg and dust with flour mixed with salt and pepper. Melt butter in pan and sauté cheeks, turning often, for 5-7 minutes, or until evenly browned and done. Transfer to heated platter and garnish with chopped parsley. Serve immediately.

Butterflied Bluefish Grilled in Foil

SERVES 4-5

Small "snapper" blues are easy to manage on the grill. Their taste is usually sweeter than that of the larger bluefish because they eat squid and small fish.

4-pound whole bluefish
Salt and pepper to taste
2 tablespoons unsalted
butter
½ cup dry white wine
2 cloves garlic, minced

2 scallions, chopped
1 tablespoon chopped fresh
tarragon (1 teaspoon
dried)
2 teaspoons chopped fresh
thyme (¾ teaspoon dried)

Remove head and gills from bluefish, leaving tail intact. Remove center backbone down to tail, but do not cut through skin. Rinse and pat dry with paper towel. Season with salt and pepper. Lay fish open, skin side down, on large piece of heavy-duty foil, allowing enough extra foil to fold up into pouch. Combine butter, wine, garlic, scallions, tarragon, and thyme in saucepan and heat until blended. Brush half the sauce on inside flesh of bluefish, fold fish together, and pour remaining sauce on top. Crimp edges of foil together to make tight envelope, place on grill 3 inches from coals, and cook 15-20 minutes. Remove from foil and serve.

Broiled Bluefish Marinated in Scandinavian Mustard Sauce

SERVES 2

My daughter Rebecca brought this recipe home from Denmark, where she lived for a summer with a Danish family. They served it with herring, yet bluefish seems more appropriate here.

1-pound bluefish filet, skinned
3 tablespoons white vinegar
2 tablespoons Dijon mustard
2 tablespoons sugar
¼ teaspoon ground cardamom

¼ teaspoon freshly ground black pepper
⅓ cup olive oil
Fresh dill sprigs for garnish

Put bluefish in glass dish. Combine vinegar, mustard, sugar, cardamom, and pepper in stainless steel bowl and add oil in steady stream, whisking constantly until all is incorporated. Pour sauce over bluefish and marinate in refrigerator 2 hours.

Preheat broiler or grill and cook filet 15 minutes, or until fish flakes easily when tested with fork at its thickest part. Garnish with dill sprigs and serve immediately.

Broiled Bluefish Teriyaki

SERVES 2

This also can be grilled over charcoal or mesquite chips. If so, leave the skin on the filets, as it will hold the fish together when cooking and make it easier to remove the fish from the grill. Alternatively, you can place a piece of foil with holes poked in it on the grill to allow the smoke to flavor the fish.

1-pound bluefish filet
1 teaspoon dry mustard
1 tablespoon hot water
1 teaspoon cornstarch
1 tablespoon dry sherry
2 tablespoons soy sauce
¼ cup chicken broth

1½ teaspoons sugar
1 teaspoon finely minced gingerroot
1 tablespoon chopped fresh parsley for garnish
Lemon wedges for garnish

Check fish for bones and set aside. Mix mustard with hot water and let sit 10 minutes. Dissolve cornstarch in sherry and set aside. Combine mustard mixture, soy sauce, chicken broth, sugar, and gingerroot in small saucepan and simmer over low heat. Increase heat and add sherry-cornstarch mixture, stirring constantly until mixture thickens and becomes clear. Remove from heat.

Preheat broiler. Brush fish with teriyaki sauce and broil 5 minutes. Brush with sauce again and cook 5 minutes more. Check for doneness with fork. Brush with sauce once again just before serving. Garnish with chopped parsley and lemon wedges.

Broiled Bluefish with Garlic Mayonnaise   SERVES 4

When garlic is boiled, it loses its bite and is easier to digest. Here it adds a sweet but subtle flavor.

2 pounds bluefish filets, skinned
2 tablespoons unsalted butter
10 cloves garlic, unpeeled
1 egg yolk
1 tablespoon fresh lemon juice

½ cup olive oil
½ cup corn oil
Salt and cayenne pepper to taste
Lemon wedges and chopped fresh parsley for garnish

Place bluefish filets on broiler pan lined with foil. Dot with butter. In small saucepan boil garlic in water to cover for 15 minutes, or until soft. Drain and peel off skins.

Broil bluefish under preheated broiler for 12 minutes, or until almost done. Meanwhile, blend garlic, egg yolk, and lemon juice in food processor fitted with metal blade. Combine oils in bowl. With processor running, add ½ cup of the combined oils at a time in slow, steady stream until all is used up and mayonnaise consistency is formed. Season with salt and cayenne, and add more lemon juice if desired.

Remove bluefish from broiler, spread garlic mayonnaise evenly on top, and return to broiler for 2-3 minutes, or until lightly browned and fish is done. Garnish with lemon wedges and parsley.

Clams

Hard-shell clam or bay quahog
(*Mercenaria mercenaria*)
Soft-shell clam (*Mya arenaria*)
Sea clam (*Spisula solidissima*)

The clams we sell at The Fishmonger fall into three categories: hard-shell, soft-shell, and sea clams.

Hard-shell clams, or quahogs, are found from Newfoundland to Florida and are sold by size. The smallest are the "littlenecks," named after Littleneck Bay, New York. They are the most prized and bring the most money at the market. Littlenecks can be eaten raw on the half shell, baked as an appetizer, steamed in stews, or cooked in a sauce for pasta. Medium-size quahogs are called "cherrystones" and also can be eaten raw, steamed, or baked. The largest hard-shell clams are used in chowder and stuffing; hence the names "chowders," "chowder hogs," and "stuffies" have been applied to them. These quahogs have much tougher and muskier flesh. They generally are steamed open, and the bodies are chopped or diced for soups. Another size quahog that falls between cherrystones and chowders are called "topnecks." Sometimes these are used as a substitute for cherrystones.

Never buy hard-shell clams that are cracked or already open because they will have lost their natural juices and could be spoiled. Only buy those that are tightly closed.

The soft-shell clam is found from Canada to Cape Hatteras, with Maine the leading producer. Its shell is easily broken and does not close tightly. The long neck hangs out from one end, and if you touch it, it coils back inside the shell. This is a good way to test for freshness. Also known as "steamers," "belly clams," "longnecks," and "Ipswich clams" (the latter named after a town in Massachusetts), these clams are used for frying and steaming. "Steamers," as we call them at The Fishmonger, are found in the tidal bays and sandbars of many beaches. When harvested, they are raked up from the sand and mud, which gets lodged within their shells, so they should be rinsed thoroughly before cooking. Another way to rid them of grit is to dip them in some of their cooking broth after steaming.

Be leery of buying steamers from less than reputable dealers, as these are the clams most often affected by the "red tide." Clams are filter feeders and can ingest large amounts of dinoflagellate phytoplankton, which is harmless to the clam but poisonous to humans. Marine biologists and fish and game personnel carefully monitor shellfish harvesting and close beds when toxin levels become too high. All legal soft-shell clams have to pass through an inspection plant and receive tags of certification, but some dealers try to get around this. Do not buy clams without proper certification.

Sea clams are found in offshore waters sometimes as deep as 200 feet or more. These are large clams, too big to use whole, and are usually minced or chopped by processors. They are a lot less expensive than the others and are used in clam chowder, fried clam strips, and deviled clams. Found from Canada to North Carolina, they are sold mainly as frozen processed meats.

Hard- and soft-shell clams are usually sold

alive by the pound, bushel, or quart. When buying hard-shell clams, figure on about six littleneck clams per person and about four cherrystones per person; with soft-shell clams, figure on 1 pound per person, which amounts to a little less than a quart. For sea clams, about ½ pound per person will be adequate since these are generally used in stuffings and pasta sauces.

Clams Casino   SERVES 6 AS APPETIZER, 3 AS MAIN COURSE

Baked clams are one of my favorite dishes to serve with cocktails. They can be prepared ahead of time and baked as the guests arrive.

36 littleneck clams, unshucked	2 tablespoons fresh lemon juice
8 slices bacon	1 tablespoon Worcestershire sauce
¼ cup minced onion	2 dashes of Tabasco
¼ cup minced red bell pepper	¾ cup bread crumbs
¼ cup minced green bell pepper	Lemon wedges for garnish
2 sticks unsalted butter, softened	

Wash and scrub clams to remove sand and set aside. In skillet fry bacon until crispy and drain on paper towels. Using 2 tablespoons bacon fat, sauté onion and bell peppers until soft, about 3 minutes.

In bowl combine butter, lemon juice, Worcestershire sauce, Tabasco, crumbled bacon, and sautéed vegetables. Mix thoroughly and refrigerate.

Open clam shells (see p. 37), leaving meats in bottom shells and discarding tops. Top each with heaping teaspoon of butter mixture. Sprinkle with bread crumbs. Bake in preheated oven at 400° for 10 minutes, or until browned and bubbly. Serve with lemon wedges and provide forks and lots of napkins.

How to Open a Clam

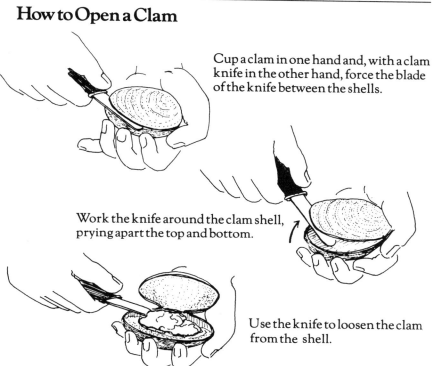

Cup a clam in one hand and, with a clam knife in the other hand, force the blade of the knife between the shells.

Work the knife around the clam shell, prying apart the top and bottom.

Use the knife to loosen the clam from the shell.

Baked Clams with Garlic   SERVES 4 AS APPETIZER

Many years ago, while living in Washington, D.C., the one store where I opened a charge account was Cannon's Fish Market in Georgetown. It was well supplied and reminded me of home.

24 littleneck clams
8 tablespoons unsalted
  butter
3 cloves garlic, minced

2 tablespoons chopped fresh
  parsley
1 tablespoon fresh lemon
  juice

Wash and scrub clams to remove sand and grit, then open them (see above), leaving clams in bottom shells and discarding tops. Put in baking dish.

Melt butter in saucepan, add garlic, and cook until soft. Add parsley and lemon juice, and stir to combine. Top each clam with mixture, using all of it.

Bake clams in preheated oven at 400° for 10 minutes until bubbly. Transfer to plates, spoon juices over top, and serve with French or Italian bread for soaking up juices.

The Fishmonger Clam Chowder SERVES 10-12

This chowder combines three types of clams — steamers, cherrystones, and sea clams. Each has a different flavor and texture, and their natural sea salt adds the right amount of seasoning. Customers tell me this chowder is "the best."

12 cherrystone clams,
   unshucked
4 pounds steamer clams
1 cup water
½ cup dry white wine
Pinch of dried thyme
3 or 4 Idaho potatoes, peeled
   and diced
¼ pound bacon, diced
¼ pound salt pork, diced
3 cups chopped onions

2 teaspoons dried thyme
2 teaspoons freshly ground
   white pepper
¼ cup flour
6 cups bottled clam juice
2 pints minced sea clams
   (about 2 pounds)
3 cups milk
4 cups light cream
Chopped fresh parsley for
   garnish

Wash and scrub cherrystones and steamers to remove sand and grit. In pot heat water, wine, and pinch of thyme to simmer. Add cherrystones and steam until open. Remove clams from broth, remove meat from shells, and chop. Set aside. Add cleaned steamers to pot and steam 3-5 minutes, or until open. Remove from broth, remove meats from shells, and pull off thin black skin covering clam neck and side. Leave steamers whole and dip in clean water to remove any excess shell and sand. Reserve with chopped cherrystones.

Cook diced potatoes in boiling water until just done. (The potatoes should have a firm, not soft, texture.) Drain and reserve.

In soup kettle, fry bacon and salt pork over medium-high heat until fat is rendered, about 3-4 minutes. Add onions and cook until soft. Stir in 2 teaspoons thyme and white pepper. Add flour and stir to blend.

Heat clam juice in separate pot and add by the cupful to onion mixture, stirring after each addition. Bring to simmer, then add minced sea clams and cook 10 minutes. Add potatoes, cherrystones, and steamers to soup kettle. Strain broth from cooked clams through sieve lined with cheesecloth or two layers of paper towels. Add to chowder along with milk and cream, and heat until hot, but do not boil. Serve garnished with chopped parsley.

Manhattan Clam Chowder

To make a concentrated, flavorful broth, it is important to steam clams in as little liquid as possible. The clams themselves will release their own juices, so you will end up with more liquid than when you started.

36 cherrystone clams, unshucked
2 cups water
1 cup dry white wine
3 tablespoons unsalted butter
1 cup chopped onion
2 ribs celery, chopped
2 tablespoons chopped fresh thyme (2 teaspoons dried)

½ teaspoon dried marjoram
1 bay leaf, broken in half
¼ teaspoon cayenne pepper
¼ cup tomato paste
28-ounce can tomatoes
1 pound Idaho potatoes, cut into 1½-inch cubes
1 cup heavy cream
¼ cup minced fresh parsley

Wash and scrub clams to remove any sand and grit. Bring water and wine to boil and add clams. Bring back to boil, then lower heat to simmer and cook until clams open, about 5 minutes. Transfer clams to bowl and strain juices through fine sieve lined with cheesecloth or two layers of paper towels. (This is to catch shell particles, which can make a good chowder dreadful.) Remove clams from their shells and chop into bite-size pieces.

In soup kettle melt butter and sauté onion and celery until soft, about 4 minutes. Add thyme, marjoram, bay leaf, and cayenne, and mix to combine. Stir in tomato paste and tomatoes that have been broken apart with your hands. Add strained clam broth and bring to boil. Reduce heat and simmer 20 minutes.

Meanwhile, cook potatoes in separate pot in boiling water until just done. They should be firm, not soft, so they hold up in the chowder. While potatoes cook, add clams to soup kettle along with heavy cream. Heat but do not boil. Add potatoes and parsley, then serve.

Fried Clams*   SERVES 2

Woodman's, which claims to have invented the fried clam, is located in Essex, Massachusetts, and is one of my favorite places to eat. One special trip there was with my brother Ted one New Year's Day, with the snow stacked up outdoors and the steamers and lobsters keeping the inside warm and wet, smelling just like the ocean in summer.

2 cups shucked soft-shell clams	1 egg
¾ cup flour	2 tablespoons milk
½ teaspoon salt	½ cup bread or cracker crumbs
¼ teaspoon pepper	½ cup cornmeal
Vegetable oil for frying	Tartar Sauce (recipe follows)

Drain clams of any liquid and pat dry with paper towel. Make sure black skin around neck and along body is removed.

Combine flour, salt, and pepper, and dust clams with this mixture. Shake clams in sieve to get off excess flour so they won't turn gummy. Heat 2 inches of oil in heavy skillet until hot.

Mix egg with milk and crumbs with cornmeal. Dip clams in egg mixture, then in crumb mixture, and fry in hot oil, being careful not to cook too many at a time. Drain on paper towels and serve immediately with Tartar Sauce.

TARTAR SAUCE

1 cup mayonnaise (see p. 283)	1 tablespoon capers, squeeze-drained and chopped
2 tablespoons fresh lemon juice	2 tablespoons chopped fresh parsley
1 tablespoon chopped pickle, dill or sour	

Whisk all together until well blended.

* Fried clams will not be greasy if you follow a couple of rules. First, get the oil hot enough. It's good to test the oil first with a piece of bread, which should brown quickly. Second, fry the clams in small batches to avoid overcrowding. If you want to avoid deep-frying altogether, sauté the clams in 4 tablespoons unsalted butter and 4 tablespoons olive oil.

Clam Fritters

MAKES 36

On numerous past family vacations to Great Exuma in the Bahamas, my children would always ask for Nora's conch fritters. We'd dive for the conch, and Nora, the cook, would whip up a fresh batch. Not having the same kind of conch up north, I persevered and came up with this recipe, which is great for cocktails or as a first course.

1 pint minced sea clams
(about 1 pound)
2 tablespoons unsalted
butter
⅓ cup chopped onion
¼ cup minced green bell
pepper
¼ cup minced red bell
pepper
¼ cup minced celery

1½ cups flour
2 teaspoons baking powder
½ teaspoon dried thyme
1 egg
¾ cup milk
½ teaspoon Tabasco
Vegetable oil for frying
Fritter Dipping Sauce (recipe
follows)

In saucepan cook clams until juices are rendered and clams are chewy. Drain well, pressing out excess juice; discard juice.

In skillet melt butter over medium heat and add onion, bell peppers, and celery. Cook until soft, about 3 minutes. Remove from heat and set aside.

In bowl combine flour, baking powder, and thyme. In another bowl beat egg, add milk and Tabasco, and whisk well. Add to flour mixture and stir to combine. Add pepper and onion mixture, and combine well. Stir in cooked clams.

In heavy skillet pour oil to depth of 2 inches. Heat until hot. Drop fritters by the tablespoonful into hot oil, cooking only six at a time so as not to overcrowd. Fry 2 minutes, turning to brown all sides. Remove with slotted spoon and drain on paper towels. Serve with dipping sauce and accompany with toothpicks.

FRITTER DIPPING SAUCE

¾ cup ketchup
½ cup mayonnaise (see p.
283)
2 tablespoons prepared
horseradish

1 tablespoon fresh lemon
juice
1 tablespoon minced shallots
½ teaspoon Tabasco

Combine all ingredients in bowl and whisk until well blended. Refrigerate until ready to use.

The Fishmonger White Clam Sauce   SERVES 6

This sauce is heavy on the garlic, probably my favorite aroma, and sells quickly at The Fishmonger, as customers buy three or four pints at a time to keep in the freezer. Fresh steamers or littleneck clams could be used for extra flavor; you can never have too many clams.

2 pints minced sea clams
  (about 2 pounds)
3 tablespoons unsalted
  butter
3 tablespoons olive oil
5 cloves garlic, minced
1 cup chopped onion
Juice and grated rind of 1
  lemon
½ teaspoon crushed red
  pepper flakes
1 teaspoon dried thyme
¼ teaspoon Tabasco
1 bay leaf, crumbled

1 tablespoon chopped fresh
  basil (1 teaspoon dried)
1 teaspoon dried oregano
Pinch of saffron
¼ cup flour
4 cups bottled clam juice
1 cup dry white wine
1 tablespoon cornstarch
1 tablespoon dry white wine
2 pounds linguine
¼ cup chopped fresh parsley
½ cup freshly grated
  Parmesan cheese

Cook clams in saucepan until juices are rendered. Drain clams, discarding broth. (I find this juice to be quite tasteless, and it adds little to the sauce.)

Heat butter and oil in large saucepan. Add garlic and onion, and sauté 3-4 minutes, or until soft. Add lemon juice and rind, red pepper flakes, thyme, Tabasco, bay leaf, basil, oregano, and saffron. Stir to blend. Add flour and blend well.

Heat bottled clam juice and 1 cup wine in separate saucepan to simmer and add to flour mixture by the cupful, stirring constantly. Simmer 30 minutes, uncovered.

Combine cornstarch and 1 tablespoon wine, and add to sauce, stirring until thickened. (It should just coat metal spoon.) Add cooked clams to sauce, and heat through. Cook linguine al dente and drain. Remove sauce from heat, add parsley and Parmesan cheese, and stir to blend. Pour over pasta and serve with toasted Italian garlic bread.

The Fishmonger Red Clam Sauce   SERVES 4-6

This thick, rich sauce is packed with clams. Store any leftovers in the freezer for later use.

2 pints minced clams (about
   2 pounds)
⅓ cup olive oil
3 tablespoons unsalted
   butter
1 large onion, finely chopped
6 cloves garlic, minced
32-ounce can peeled
   tomatoes, drained (reserve
   juice)
3 anchovy filets
½ cup tomato paste
2 cups bottled clam juice

½ cup dry red wine
1 bay leaf
1 tablespoon fennel seed
1 teaspoon crushed red
   pepper flakes
2 teaspoons dried oregano
2 tablespoons chopped fresh
   basil (2 teaspoons dried)
½ teaspoon dried thyme
1½ pounds pasta
½ cup freshly grated
   Parmesan cheese
½ cup chopped fresh parsley

Cook minced clams in saucepan until firm. Drain off juices, reserving 2 cups. Set clams aside to cool.

In another saucepan heat oil and butter over medium-high heat, add onion and garlic, and sauté until onion is soft. In food processor fitted with metal blade, purée drained tomatoes, anchovy filets, and tomato paste for 10 seconds. Combine reserved tomato juice, bottled clam juice, and wine in saucepan and boil until reduced to thick paste, being careful not to burn.

Add bay leaf, fennel seed, red pepper flakes, oregano, basil, and thyme to onion-garlic mixture and cook 2 minutes. Add puréed tomato mixture and reduced tomato-clam paste, and simmer 30 minutes. Add cooked clams and heat until warmed through. Meanwhile, cook pasta al dente and drain. Remove sauce from heat, discard bay leaf, stir in Parmesan cheese and parsley, and serve over pasta.

Clams with Ginger and Scallions SERVES 4

Serve this with boiled rice and steamed fresh vegetables when you don't feel like going out to dinner but have a craving for Chinese food.

24 littleneck clams, unshucked	2 tablespoons dry white wine
3 tablespoons peanut oil	2 tablespoons soy sauce
4 scallions, thinly sliced	1 tablespoon rice vinegar
1 tablespoon minced gingerroot	1 teaspoon sugar
1 tablespoon minced garlic	2 teaspoons sesame oil
1 hot chili pepper, sliced	2 teaspoons cornstarch
	2 teaspoons water
	½ cup chopped fresh cilantro

Wash and scrub clams to remove sand and grit. In wok heat peanut oil and add scallions, gingerroot, garlic, and chili pepper. Stir-fry quickly until fragrant, about 1 minute. Add clams and heat until shells open slightly.

Combine wine, soy sauce, vinegar, sugar, and sesame oil in bowl. Add to clams and heat to simmer. In cup mix cornstarch and water. Add to wok, stirring until sauce thickens. Fold in cilantro and serve.

Clams with Tomatoes and Cilantro SERVES 4

Cilantro is an herb frequently used in Mexican dishes. It is aromatic and distinctive but not for everyone's taste. Here it is included only as a garnish so as not to dominate the flavor of the sauce.

24 littleneck clams	⅛ teaspoon crushed red pepper flakes
2 tablespoons olive oil	¼ cup chopped fresh basil
1 cup chopped onion	Freshly ground black pepper to taste
3 cloves garlic, minced	1½ pounds linguine
1 red bell pepper, cored, seeded, and cut into strips	2 tablespoons chopped fresh cilantro
2 cups peeled, seeded, and chopped tomatoes	

Wash and scrub clams to remove sand and grit. In large saucepan heat oil over medium heat. Add onion, garlic, and red bell pepper, and cook 5 minutes, or until soft. Add tomatoes, red pepper flakes, basil, and black pepper, and sauté 3 minutes. Add clams, cover, and steam 8-10 minutes, or until clams open. Meanwhile, cook linguine al dente and drain. Ladle sauce over pasta and garnish with chopped cilantro.

Clams with Mushrooms for Pasta   SERVES 4

Clams are a wonderful addition to pasta sauces. Here they are cooked in their shells, so it is very important to scrub the clams thoroughly so the sauce does not become gritty. Chunks of chicken or hot sausage could be added to make this even heartier.

24 littleneck clams, unshucked	1 bay leaf, crumbled
½ cup peeled, seeded, and chopped tomato	½ pound mushrooms, sliced
¾ cup chopped onion	¼ cup heavy cream
¾ cup chopped green bell pepper	2 tablespoons cognac
2 tablespoons dry red wine	¼ teaspoon crushed red pepper flakes
1 clove garlic	½ cup dry white wine
2 teaspoons olive oil	2 tablespoons olive oil
½ teaspoon ground cumin	2 teaspoons minced shallots
2 dashes of Tabasco	1½ pounds pasta
	Chopped fresh parsley for garnish

Scrub and wash clams to remove sand and grit, and set aside. Put tomato, onion, and bell pepper in food processor fitted with metal blade and combine 5 seconds. Add red wine, garlic, 2 teaspoons oil, cumin, Tabasco, and bay leaf, and blend 10 seconds, or until a coarse purée.

In skillet combine mushrooms, cream, cognac, and pepper flakes, and simmer 5 minutes, or until reduced and thickened. Whisk in vegetable purée. Add white wine, 2 tablespoons oil, and shallots, and bring to simmer. Add clams and coat with sauce. Cover and simmer 10 minutes, or until clams open. Meanwhile, cook pasta al dente and drain. Serve pasta topped with sauce and garnished with chopped fresh parsley.

Cod (Atlantic)

Gadus morhua

Cod are found throughout the North Atlantic and as far south as Virginia. They are bottom dwellers, inhabiting the submarine plateaus on the continental shelf where the water is cool and rich in food.

Cod is marketed whole, in steaks, or fileted, as well as salted or smoked. Cod roe is a delicacy in the spring and is sold fresh as "spawn" or smoked and canned. Many New Englanders use cod tongues and cheeks in chowder.

At the Boston Fish Pier, Atlantic cod is graded by weight. A "scrod" cod weighs no more than 4 pounds; "markets" weigh between 4 and 10 pounds; "large" cod weigh 10 to 25 pounds; and extra-large, or "whale," cod weigh 25 pounds or more. (The term "scrod" is misleading. It is not the name of a fish species but instead is used to denote a certain size. Scrod can be a small cod, haddock, or pollock.)

Fresh whole cod is firm to the touch, has bright eyes, and is red around the gills. The flesh has a slightly pink tinge and is firm and compact. Freshly caught cod must rest 12 to 24 hours before being cut. Often I have bought whole cod that has been "too fresh to cut," as the natural rigor mortis has not set in. If cut during this stage, the flesh might tear, with the end result being mushy, unattractive filets.

Cod is a very lean, mild-tasting fish that is well suited for broiling, poaching, baking, or frying. It does not grill well because it has a tendency to flake and fall apart while cooking. Fish that can be substituted for cod are haddock, pollock, and hake.

The Fishmonger Provençal Fish Soup   SERVES 6-8

This spicy soup will fill you up but not out. Some of our customers call it simply "red soup."

2 pounds cod filets
4 tablespoons olive oil
2 cloves garlic, minced
2 cups sliced leeks, white
    part only, thoroughly
    rinsed and drained
1 tablespoon dried basil
Pinch of saffron
2 teaspoons fennel seed
1 bay leaf
½ teaspoon crushed red
    pepper flakes

32-ounce can peeled whole
    tomatoes, including juice
8 cups fish stock (see p. 180)
1 cup dry white wine
1 tablespoon sugar
½ teaspoon salt
Juice and grated rind
    of 1 orange
2 tablespoons tomato paste

Cut filets into 2-inch chunks and set aside. Heat oil in large stock pot, add garlic, and cook until golden. Add leeks and cook 4 minutes, or until soft. Then add basil, saffron, fennel seed, bay leaf, and red pepper flakes, and cook 1 minute. Add tomatoes, broken into pieces with your hands, fish stock, wine, sugar, and salt. Heat to simmer. In separate bowl mix together orange juice and rind and tomato paste. Add to soup, blend well, and simmer 15 minutes. Stir in fish pieces and cook until fish flakes, about 5 minutes. Remove bay leaf and serve at once.

Taramosalata

MAKES 3 CUPS

This variation of a recipe from Greece, where smoked carp roe is traditionally used, can be served as a dip, spread, or salad dressing.

1 pair smoked cod roe (about ¾ pound)	Freshly ground black pepper to taste
1 pound cream cheese, softened	½ cup olive oil
Juice and grated rind of 1 lemon	½ cup cold heavy cream
1 large clove garlic, minced	2 tablespoons minced scallion greens

Peel and discard membrane of cod roe. Break up eggs into food processor fitted with metal blade. Add cream cheese broken up into chunks. Add lemon juice and rind, minced garlic, and pepper. Blend 15-20 seconds. With processor running, add oil in slow, steady stream. Then slowly add cream and blend just a few seconds, making sure not to overmix. Fold in scallion greens and serve as dip with warm pita bread triangles.

Codfish Loaf

SERVES 4

This is my substitute for meat loaf. You can use any vegetables, but carrots add a bit of color to a very white dinner.

1¼-pound cod filet	½ pound green beans, trimmed
3 tablespoons unsalted butter	4 egg whites
½ cup minced scallions	Salt and pepper to taste
3 tablespoons flour	Dill sprigs for garnish
1 cup milk, scalded	Herbed Butter Sauce (recipe follows)
Dash of cayenne pepper	
2 carrots, julienned	

Check filet for bones and cut into 1-inch pieces. In saucepan melt butter and cook scallions until soft. Stir in flour and cook roux 2 minutes. Add scalded milk, whisking until blended. Add cayenne and cook sauce over low heat until thickened. Set aside to cool.

Blanch julienned carrots in boiling water for 2 minutes. Drain and rinse under cold water; reserve. Blanch beans in boiling water for 3 minutes. Drain and rinse under cold water; reserve.

In food processor fitted with metal blade, purée cod pieces and add egg whites one at a time, blending well after each addition. Add three quarters of cooled sauce and blend. Season with salt and pepper.

Spoon one third of fish mixture into buttered glass 1½-quart loaf pan. Smooth top with spatula and arrange half the blanched beans lengthwise. Cover beans with remaining sauce and arrange carrots on top. Cover with another third of fish mixture, then arrange remaining beans on top. Add remaining third of fish to cover. Tap pan several times to eliminate air pockets and allow sauce to settle. Put loaf pan in baking pan and add enough hot water to reach two thirds of the way up loaf pan. Cover top with buttered piece of waxed paper and bake in preheated oven at 350° for 1 hour. Loaf is done when knife inserted in center comes out clean. Transfer to rack and let cool 5 minutes. Run sharp knife around edges of pan, place heated platter on top, and turn over so loaf will be in center of platter. Garnish with sprigs of fresh dill and serve with Herbed Butter Sauce.

HERBED BUTTER SAUCE

1 cup fish stock (see p. 180) or bottled clam juice
⅓ cup minced scallions
¼ cup dry white wine
¼ cup heavy cream
1 tomato, peeled, seeded, and chopped
2 tablespoons chopped fresh dill
2 tablespoons finely chopped fresh parsley
1 tablespoon unsalted butter, softened
1 tablespoon flour
6 tablespoons cold unsalted butter, cut into 6 pieces
2 tablespoons fresh lemon juice
Salt and pepper to taste

In stainless steel saucepan, combine fish stock, scallions, wine, and heavy cream. Reduce to 1 cup by boiling over high heat. Add tomato, dill, and parsley, whisking to blend. Knead together 1 tablespoon softened butter and flour until blended. Add to liquid, whisking until thickened.

Remove pan from heat and whisk in 6 tablespoons cold butter, 1 tablespoon at a time, until all is incorporated. Add lemon juice and season with salt and pepper. Spoon over codfish loaf and transfer remainder to heated serving bowl.

Cod Baked in Sour Cream

SERVES 2-3

For a low-calorie version of this recipe, use plain yogurt in place of the sour cream.

1 pound cod filet
1 cup sour cream
1 tablespoon chopped fresh
  dill (1 teaspoon dried)
1 tablespoon chopped fresh
  parsley (1 teaspoon dried)
½ teaspoon dry mustard

¼ teaspoon ground ginger
½ teaspoon grated lemon
  rind
Juice of ½ lemon
½ teaspoon salt
Paprika

Check fish for bones. Mix sour cream with dill, parsley, mustard, ginger, lemon rind, lemon juice, and salt. Dredge fish filets in sour cream mixture and lay in buttered baking dish. Pour remaining sauce on top, dust with paprika, and bake in preheated oven at 400° for 15 minutes, or until fish flakes easily when tested with fork.

Cod Curry

SERVES 4-6

Curry is a combination of spices, with turmeric providing the dominant yellow color. The exact amount of each one used can be changed according to personal preference.

2 pounds cod filets
1 teaspoon paprika
1¼ teaspoons turmeric
4 tablespoons olive oil
3 medium onions, finely
  chopped
2 cloves garlic, minced
½ teaspoon chili powder
½ teaspoon ground cumin
½ teaspoon mustard seed
¼ teaspoon cinnamon

¼ teaspoon ground cloves
¼ teaspoon ground
  cardamom
4 medium tomatoes, peeled,
  seeded, and chopped
2 tablespoons chopped fresh
  cilantro
½ cup water
Salt to taste
1 cup plain yogurt

Cut filets into 4 serving pieces. Combine paprika and 1 teaspoon of the turmeric and rub over fish. Heat oil in sauté pan, add fish, and sauté until browned. Remove fish to buttered ovenproof dish.

Fry onions and garlic in same sauté pan, adding more oil if necessary. Add chili powder, cumin, mustard seed, cinnamon, cloves, cardamom, and remaining ¼ teaspoon turmeric. Cook, stirring, for 2 minutes. Add tomatoes, cilantro, and water, and simmer 5 minutes. Season with salt and add yogurt, stirring to blend. Cover fish with curry sauce and bake in preheated oven at 350° for 15-20 minutes.

Cod with Oyster Sauce   SERVES 4

The rich flavor of the oysters and their "liquor" adds a touch of class to mild-tasting cod.

1½-pound cod filet
1 cup milk
2 tablespoons unsalted
  butter

Salt and pepper to taste

OYSTER SAUCE

½ pint shucked oysters and
  their liquor
¼ cup dry white wine
3 tablespoons unsalted
  butter
3 tablespoons flour
1 cup light cream, scalded

1 tablespoon chopped fresh
  parsley
1 teaspoon fresh lemon juice
Salt and cayenne pepper to
  taste
Paprika

Soak cod in milk for 1 hour. Drain, place in buttered baking dish, dot with butter, and sprinkle with salt and pepper. Bake in preheated oven at 400° for 10-15 minutes.

Meanwhile, make sauce. Poach oysters in their liquor and the wine in small, stainless steel saucepan until oysters just begin to curl; do not overcook. Strain through sieve and reserve liquid. Boil liquid until reduced to about ½ cup.

In clean saucepan melt butter, add flour, and cook, stirring, for 1 minute over medium heat. Add reduced wine-oyster liquid and scalded cream. Whisk until smooth and thickened. Add parsley and lemon juice, and season with salt and cayenne. Just before serving, add poached oysters and stir to warm. Spoon over cooked cod, sprinkle with paprika, and serve.

Grilled or Broiled Codfish Steaks SERVES 4

It's fun to get the grill out in the middle of winter and make this recipe. Although cod is scarce and costly at this time, it is cheaper to buy the fish cut into steaks. These are usually made from the large "whale" cod.

Two 1-pound cod steaks
Salt to taste
8 tablespoons unsalted
  butter
2 tablespoons grated onion
3 tablespoons fresh lemon or
  lime juice and grated rind

¼ cup bottled chili sauce
1 tablespoon chopped fresh
  tarragon (1 teaspoon
  dried)
1 teaspoon paprika
2 tablespoons chopped fresh
  parsley

Rinse steaks of any entrails and blood, pat dry, and salt lightly. Melt butter in saucepan and add onion, lemon or lime juice and rind, chili sauce, tarragon, paprika, and parsley. Bring to simmer and cook 3 minutes, or until flavors have blended. Brush steaks liberally with butter sauce and grill or broil 5 minutes per side, basting frequently. Serve accompanied by extra warmed sauce.

Stuffed Cod with Zucchini and Tomatoes SERVES 4

This is a welcome dish at summer's end when the garden is overflowing with ripe tomatoes and zucchini.

1½ pounds cod filets (2
  equal-size pieces)
Juice and grated rind
  of 1 lemon
Salt and pepper to taste
4 tablespoons unsalted
  butter
2 cups chopped onions
1 cup cooked rice
3 tablespoons chopped fresh
  parsley

¼ cup sliced almonds
1½ cups peeled, julienned
  zucchini
2 cups peeled, seeded, and
  chopped tomatoes
1 tablespoon chopped fresh
  basil (1 teaspoon dried)
1 tablespoon chopped fresh
  dill (1 teaspoon dried)

Rub fish with 1 tablespoon of the lemon juice, sprinkle with salt and pepper, and set aside. In skillet melt 2 tablespoons of the butter and cook half the chopped onions until soft. Add cooked rice, parsley, lemon rind, 1 tablespoon lemon juice, almonds, and salt and pepper to taste. Stir over low heat until well mixed.

Place one piece of cod in buttered baking dish. Spoon vegetable-rice mixture down the middle and lay other piece of cod on top, in opposite direction.

In clean skillet melt remaining 2 tablespoons butter and cook remaining onions and julienned zucchini until soft. Add tomatoes, basil, and dill. Season with salt and pepper. Simmer until tomatoes are soft, about 5 minutes. Pour over fish and bake in preheated oven at 400° for 20 minutes, or until fish flakes easily when tested with fork.

Deep-Fried Codfish Balls   SERVES 6

These codfish balls can be made in advance and frozen, then reheated in a hot oven. If you want to avoid deep-frying, shape into cakes and fry in butter. Good for Sunday breakfast.

1 ½ pounds salt cod	Dash of dry mustard
2 pounds Idaho potatoes	1 egg
2 tablespoons unsalted butter	2 tablespoons heavy cream
¼ teaspoon pepper	Flour
Dash of ground ginger	Oil for frying

Cut salt cod into 1-inch pieces and soak in water to cover for 24 hours, changing water two times to remove excess salt used in curing. In saucepan heat 2 quarts water to boil, add soaked and drained salt cod pieces, and simmer 15-20 minutes. Drain and cool. Squeeze well to remove excess moisture and pull apart into small flakes, removing any bones and skin. Place salt cod in bowl and set aside.

Cook potatoes until tender, drain, and mash with butter until smooth. Add pepper, ginger, and mustard, and mix well. Beat egg with cream and add to potatoes, stirring to incorporate. Add flaked codfish and mix well with your hands. Form mixture into balls about the size of a quarter and roll in flour.

In saucepan heat 2 to 3 inches of oil to 375° and drop balls into oil, cooking for 1 minute, or until browned. Drain on paper towels and serve with lemon wedges and cocktail sauce if desired.

Poached Codfish Steaks

SERVES 4

This is the ideal way to cook cod because it keeps the fish moist and adds no calories if you omit the wine. You can use filets, but choose the thicker part. Keep the liquid at a low simmer so the fish won't fall apart.

4 small codfish steaks (8 to 10 ounces each), 1 inch thick	1 cup chopped onion
	6 whole peppercorns
	1 sprig fresh parsley
1 cup dry white wine	¼ teaspoon dried thyme
4 cups water	½ teaspoon salt
1 carrot, peeled and sliced	

Rinse steaks and set aside. Put remaining ingredients in nonreactive skillet large enough to hold fish in single layer. Bring to boil and cook 5 minutes. Turn down heat, place fish in poaching liquid, and bring to simmer. Cover and poach 8-10 minutes depending on thickness of steaks. Remove from liquid, pull off skin, and remove center bone so that 2 nice chunks of fish can be served per person. Accompany with Red Pepper–Cilantro Sauce (see p. 76), Herbed Curry Sauce (see p. 141), or Neapolitan Sauce (see p. 93).

Cod in Spinach with Mornay Sauce

SERVES 4

Spinach is best cooked in as little water as possible to retain its natural dark-green color and pleasant flavor. Avoid using an aluminum pan, which gives spinach an acidic taste and grayish color.

1 ½ pounds cod filets	½ cup dry white wine
1 tablespoon chopped shallots	1 pound fresh spinach, rinsed and stems removed
2 tablespoons chopped onion	

MORNAY SAUCE

3 tablespoons butter	1 egg yolk
3 tablespoons flour	Pinch of nutmeg
1¾ cups milk, scalded	Salt and freshly ground black pepper to taste
⅓ cup heavy cream	
1 cup grated Gruyère cheese	

Cut cod into 4 equal pieces. Butter a baking dish and sprinkle bottom with shallots and onion. Arrange cod pieces on top and pour wine over fish. Cover with foil and bake in preheated oven at

400° for 15 minutes, or until fish flakes easily when tested with fork.

Meanwhile, steam spinach for 2 minutes. Drain, squeeze out excess moisture, and coarsely chop leaves.

Make Mornay Sauce by melting butter in saucepan. Add flour and cook 1 minute. Combine milk and cream, and add to roux in steady stream, whisking constantly. Add cheese, blending until melted, and bring to bubbling boil, stirring constantly. Remove from heat and whisk in egg yolk and nutmeg. Season with salt and pepper. Return to low heat to keep warm until ready to serve.

Place spinach in oval baking dish and lay cooked cod on top. Strain fish cooking liquid into small saucepan, reduce by three quarters, and add to Mornay Sauce. Spoon sauce over fish and broil briefly, until browned. Serve immediately.

Cod with Herb Sauce   SERVES 4

When I was a child, the fish market my mother went to was open only on Thursdays and Fridays. It smelled awful, and I couldn't wait to get out of there. The fish we bought would be wrapped in many layers of old newspaper for us to take home.

1½ pounds cod filets	1 teaspoon chopped fresh
3 tablespoons unsalted	oregano (½ teaspoon
butter	dried)
1 small clove garlic, minced	1 teaspoon chopped fresh
2 scallions, sliced	thyme (½ teaspoon dried)
2 tablespoons flour	1½ cups milk, scalded
1 teaspoon chopped fresh	Salt and pepper to taste
marjoram (½ teaspoon	
dried)	

Place cod in buttered ovenproof dish, dot with 1 tablespoon of the butter, and bake in preheated oven at 400° for 15 minutes.

Meanwhile, melt remaining 2 tablespoons butter in saucepan. Add garlic and scallions, and cook 2 minutes. Stir in flour and cook 1 minute more. Mix herbs together in mortar and grind with pestle, then add to flour mixture. Gradually add scalded milk, whisking constantly until sauce thickens and is smooth, about 5 minutes. Season with salt and pepper. Serve warm over cod filets.

Crab

Blue crab *(Callinectes sapidus)*
Jonah crab *(Cancer borealis)*
Red crab *(Geryon quinquidens)*
Sand crab *(Ovalipes ocellatus ocellatus)*
Snow crab *(Chionoecetes oplilio)*

A number of crab species are available in New England markets, including the long-time favorite, king crab. But I have included only those of commercial value found along the East Coast: blue crab, Jonah crab, red crab, sand crab, and snow crab.

The blue crab, whose scientific name means "beautiful swimmer," is tinted blue on its claws and lives in both salt and fresh water from Cape Cod to Florida. As a hard-shell crab, the meat is marketed as "lump" meat (solid pieces from the body of the crab often used in cocktails and salads), "flake" meat (smaller pieces from the body), and "claw" meat (less tasty and attractive than the other two). Blue crab has a firm, hearty meat that holds up very well when cooked. It is expensive and can be purchased pasteurized in 1-pound cans, which should be refrigerated.

The soft-shell blue crab is one that has just molted or lost its shell. The Chesapeake Bay area is the major place for harvesting the blue crab during the molting stage, which takes place from mid-May through September. When buying soft-shell crabs, look for those with translucent, pearly gray-blue shells, white bellies, and pink tips on the claws. They should be plump and springy to the touch, with no trace of hardness. Soft-shell crabs are cooked whole — sautéed, fried, or grilled — and the entire crab is eaten.

Jonah crabs are in abundance from Georges Bank to North Carolina. They are caught as part of the offshore lobstering industry, as they crawl into the traps in search of food. If you were to buy live crabs in New England, they would probably be Jonah crabs. Their claws are big and desirable. Often they are sold as a substitute for the more desirable stone crab of Florida, but there is little comparison in taste. The Jonah has more claw than arm and more black on its pincers. Jonah claws are sold as "cocktail claws" or "crab fingers."

Red crabs reside on the edge of the continental shelf and are abundant from Maine to North Carolina. They are marketed as "red crab cocktail claws" and are sold cooked, cracked, and frozen. The red crab has the ability to regrow its claws and can be returned to the sea declawed, hopefully to survive. Red snow crab claws are not from the same crab but are very similar.

Freshly picked sand, or lady, crabmeat, arrives daily at The Fishmonger from Maine. Its meat is sweet and delicate and is sold in ½-pound containers — enough to make a salad for two.

The snow crab belongs to the spider crab family. It has long spidery legs and a body covered with dense hairs. This product is sold canned by the ounce or in 5- or 15-pound frozen blocks. Marketed as fancy, salad, shredded, or even sawdust meat, there are many grades of this crab. It lacks the sweet flavor of fresh crab, but it is tasty in a soup, quiche, or casserole.

A word about surimi, which is now being marketed as "sea legs" or "imitation crabmeat." Surimi is a paste made from a white fish, usually pollock, which is then flavored either artificially or with real seafood. The Japanese developed the technology by extracting the flesh from the fish, mincing and washing it several times, then mixing it with stabilizers such as sugar and sorbitol, which give it a long shelf life when frozen. Processors in this country thaw the surimi and mix it with binders such as flour or egg whites and add color and flavor to make it look and taste like crabmeat. The one thing in its favor is that it is inexpensive and can be used as a supplement to pricier shellfish.

Mushrooms Stuffed with Crabmeat

SERVES 8-10 AS APPETIZER

These can be cooked the night before a party, then warmed briefly right before serving.

½ pound fresh crabmeat
¼ cup mayonnaise (see p. 283)
⅓ cup chopped black olives
2 tablespoons chopped fresh parsley
½ teaspoon minced garlic
2 tablespoons chopped scallions
24 large mushroom caps, wiped with damp cloth
2 tablespoons finely grated Cheddar cheese
⅓ cup bread crumbs

Flake crabmeat into small bowl and check for shell particles and cartilage. In another bowl mix together mayonnaise, olives, parsley, garlic, and scallions. Add crabmeat and mix with fork. Stuff into mushroom caps. Combine cheese and bread crumbs, and sprinkle over top. Place mushrooms in greased shallow baking pan and bake in preheated oven at 400° for 15 minutes.

Crab and Corn Chowder

Where I grew up in Massachusetts, a group of families would gather on Sundays during fall and winter to walk in the woods or along the beaches, watching for birds and simply enjoying nature. Hence, "The Chowder and Marching Society" was formed. Our outings always sparked our appetites and we looked forward to the chowders that families alternated bringing along to feed the entire group. This was one such dish.

½ pound fresh crabmeat	4 tablespoons flour
2 cups cooked corn kernels (about 4 ears)	2 cups milk
	¼ teaspoon cayenne pepper
2 cups chicken broth	Dash of nutmeg
4 tablespoons unsalted butter	1 cup heavy cream
	Salt and pepper to taste
½ cup sliced onion	Paprika

Flake crabmeat into bowl and check for shell particles and cartilage. Put corn kernels and ½ cup of the chicken broth into food processor fitted with metal blade. Pulse 3 times.

Melt butter in soup pot, add onion, and cook until soft. Stir in flour and cook 1 minute. In separate pan heat remaining 1½ cups chicken broth and milk to tepid and add to onion mixture, stirring as you add. Add puréed corn and simmer 10 minutes. Stir in cayenne, nutmeg, and heavy cream, and bring to simmer. Add crabmeat and season with salt and pepper. Ladle into individual bowls, sprinkle with paprika, and serve.

Deviled Crabs and Scallops SERVES 4

Traditionally, this mixture is stuffed back into reserved crab shells and presented heated. Scallop shells are easier to clean and reuse, however, and you can find them at most kitchen supply stores.

1 pound fresh crabmeat	½ cup minced celery
½ pound scallops	½ cup minced scallions
5 tablespoons unsalted butter	½ cup mayonnaise (see p. 283)
½ cup minced onion	2 teaspoons Worcestershire sauce
¼ cup minced green bell pepper	Juice of 1 lemon
¼ cup minced red bell pepper	¼ cup minced fresh parsley
	¼ cup fine bread crumbs

Pick through crabmeat to check for shell particles and cartilage. Remove feet from scallops (see p. 192) and cut to uniform size if there are large ones. In skillet melt 3 tablespoons of the butter over medium heat and sauté onion, bell peppers, celery, and scallions about 4 minutes, or until soft. In another skillet sauté scallops in 1 tablespoon of the butter for 3-5 minutes, or until cooked. Add crabmeat and stir to combine.

In large bowl combine mayonnaise, Worcestershire sauce, lemon juice, and parsley. Add scallop-crab mixture and stir. Add onion mixture and combine. Divide mixture among 4 scallop shells. Dust with bread crumbs and use remaining 1 tablespoon butter to dot each shell. Bake in preheated oven at 400° for 10-15 minutes, or until bubbly and warm throughout.

Crabmeat Salad SERVES 4

When my father and I would go sailing in Maine, by lunchtime he would always have a hankering for crabmeat. We would sail along the coast in search of an open fish market, then satisfy our hunger with a luscious salad or crabmeat cocktail.

1 pound fresh crabmeat	2 tomatoes, quartered
Lettuce leaves	2 hard-boiled eggs, sliced
1 avocado, peeled, seeded, and sliced	Chili-Mayonnaise Sauce (recipe follows)

Flake crabmeat into bowl, removing any shell particles or cartilage. Arrange lettuce leaves on platter and mound crabmeat in middle. Garnish with avocado, tomatoes, and eggs. Pass sauce in bowl.

CHILI-MAYONNAISE SAUCE

2 scallions, chopped
3 tablespoons chopped red
   bell pepper
1 teaspoon minced garlic
2 tablespoons capers,
   squeeze-drained and
   chopped

2 tablespoons prepared
   horseradish
1 cup mayonnaise (see
   p. 283)
½ cup chili sauce
½ teaspoon crushed red
   pepper flakes

Combine all ingredients in bowl and whisk until well mixed. Spoon over salad to taste. Also good on shrimp salad or as dip for cold cooked lobster.

Stir-Fried Crab with Ginger and Scallions

SERVES 2 AS FIRST COURSE

Use any big-bodied crab for this recipe. With a cleaver or large chef's knife, cut crab in half through the stomach. Remove the gills, cut off the legs and claws, and cut the body into ½-inch slices. Crack the claws with the back of the knife.

2-pound whole crab
3 tablespoons peanut oil
12 scallions, sliced into
   2-inch lengths
2 tablespoons julienned
   gingerroot
2 cloves garlic, minced
1 cup bottled clam juice

2 tablespoons rice wine
1 tablespoon soy sauce
1 tablespoon bottled oyster
   sauce
1 tablespoon cornstarch
1 tablespoon water
2 teaspoons sesame oil

Clean crab and cut into pieces as described above. In wok heat peanut oil and stir-fry scallions, gingerroot, and garlic. Add crab pieces and stir lightly. Combine clam juice, rice wine, soy sauce, and oyster sauce, and add to wok. Bring to boil, cover, and cook 5 minutes, or until crab shell is pink and meat is white.

Remove crab, scallions, gingerroot, and garlic to platter. Reduce liquid to one half by boiling. Combine cornstarch and water, add to reduced liquid, and cook until sauce thickens. Stir in sesame oil, pour over crab, and serve.

How to Clean a Soft-Shell Crab

Lift the pointed edge on each side of the crab, remove the spongy gills with your fingers, and discard them.

Remove the crab eyes with your fingers or cut them off with scissors or a knife.

Lift the shell between the eye sockets, remove the sand sack (a translucent jellylike mass), and discard it.

Grilled Soft-Shell Crabs   SERVES 4

Charcoal or mesquite adds a wonderful smoky flavor to these crabs. Using a wire grill makes it much easier to turn this many crabs.

12 soft-shell crabs	1 tablespoon fresh lemon
4 tablespoons unsalted	juice
butter	¼ teaspoon nutmeg
½ cup chopped scallion	½ teaspoon soy sauce
greens	Dash of Tabasco

Clean crabs (see above). In saucepan melt butter, add scallion greens, and sauté 1 minute. Add lemon juice, nutmeg, soy sauce, and Tabasco, and blend.

Place crabs on wire grill and brush generously with sauce. Grill over charcoal 4 minutes per side, or until crabs are pink and crispy. Serve accompanied by extra sauce.

Sautéed Soft-Shell Crabs SERVES 2

Many of my customers are frightened of cooking these crabs themselves. They would rather order them out at a restaurant. At the store, we clean them on request, so they are usually quite dead by the time the customer gets them home.

6 soft-shell crabs	4 tablespoons unsalted
Flour for dredging	butter
Salt and pepper to taste	Lemon wedges for garnish

Clean crabs just before cooking (see p. 62). Pat dry thoroughly with paper towel, then lightly dust with flour seasoned with salt and pepper.

In skillet melt butter over medium heat until bubbly, add crabs, top side down, and cook 3 minutes. Turn on their stomachs and cook another 3 minutes. Serve immediately with lemon wedges and Tartar Sauce (see p. 40).

Deep-Fried Soft-Shell Crabs SERVES 2

As with all deep-frying, make sure the oil is hot enough before frying the crabs. Test with a bread cube, which should turn brown in a few seconds.

6 soft-shell crabs	½ teaspoon salt
½ cup flour	¼ teaspoon freshly ground
1 cup fresh bread crumbs	black pepper
1 egg	Vegetable oil
¼ cup milk	

Clean crabs (see p. 62). Pat dry with paper towel. Spread flour and bread crumbs on separate plates. In bowl whisk together egg, milk, salt, and pepper.

Dip one crab at a time into flour, then into egg mixture, and then into bread crumbs. Refrigerate 20 minutes before cooking. Pour oil to depth of 2 inches in heavy skillet, heat until hot, then add crabs. Cook 3-4 minutes, drain on paper towels, and serve.

Cusk

Brosme brosme

Cusk is a member of the cod family (Gadidae). The cusk's fins have white edges and form one continuous line down its upper back. Of a solitary nature, cusk never mass together in schools. They grow rather slowly and have a slow rate of metabolism.

Cusk can be used in place of monkfish or wolffish, for the flesh is firm and white. A series of small pin bones is found in the middle of the filet, and it is best to cut these out before cooking. The flesh contains a moderate amount of oil and is well suited to grilling, broiling, or baking. Because it holds together well, cusk also can be used in soups or stews.

Cusk and Shrimp with Fresh Tomato Sauce

SERVES 4

The addition of cusk makes this dish much more affordable.

1 pound cusk filets
16 large shrimp
6 tablespoons olive oil
4 cloves garlic, minced
2 pounds fresh tomatoes, peeled, cored, seeded, and chopped
1 cup fresh basil leaves, firmly packed

¼ cup fresh parsley sprigs
½ cup dry white wine
½ teaspoon salt
Freshly ground black pepper to taste
1 teaspoon sugar

Cut filets into 1-inch pieces. Peel and devein shrimp (see p. 221) and set aside with cusk.

In sauté pan heat oil to bubbling, add garlic, and sauté until golden, about 3 minutes. Add tomatoes, stir, and cook 5 minutes. Coarsely chop basil and parsley, and add to tomatoes. Stir in wine, salt, and pepper. Simmer 20 minutes. Add sugar and cusk, and cook 10 minutes. Add shrimp and cook until pink, about 3 minutes. Serve over pasta and accompany with garlic bread.

Cusk Grilled on Skewers

SERVES 4-6

Just about any fresh herb will work in this marinade. Use what is left over for basting the fish while it grills and right before serving.

2 pounds cusk filets	Cherry tomatoes
½ cup fresh lime juice	Green bell pepper, seeded
½ cup olive oil	and cut into chunks
½ cup sliced scallions	Bermuda onion, cut into
Freshly ground black pepper	chunks
to taste	
1 tablespoon chopped fresh	
cilantro, rosemary, mint,	
basil, or thyme	

Cut filets into 1½-inch pieces. Whisk together lime juice, oil, scallions, black pepper, and fresh herb. Pour over fish and let marinate 1 hour in refrigerator.

Put fish on skewers, alternating with tomatoes, bell pepper, and onion. Grill over charcoal until done, about 5 minutes, turning and basting with excess marinade.

Broiled Cusk
with Lemon-Basil Butter

SERVES 4

When making a compound butter, the butter should be softened, not melted, because melting breaks down the solids (curds and whey) that occur naturally when butter is made.

1 ½ pounds cusk filet
2 tablespoons unsalted
  butter
4 tablespoons unsalted
  butter, softened
2 teaspoons grated lemon
  rind
2 teaspoons fresh lemon
  juice

1 teaspoon minced shallot
½ teaspoon minced garlic
2 tablespoons chopped fresh
  basil (2 teaspoons dried)
¼ teaspoon salt
¼ teaspoon freshly ground
  black pepper

Place cusk on broiler pan lined with foil. Dot with 2 tablespoons butter and broil 3 inches from heat for 7-10 minutes.

Put 4 tablespoons softened butter in small bowl and use fork to beat in lemon rind and juice, shallot, garlic, basil, salt, and pepper until well incorporated. When fish is done, dot with lemon-basil butter and serve immediately. Wrap extra butter in plastic wrap and store in freezer for later use.

Baked Cusk with Macadamia Sauce   SERVES 4

Macadamia nuts were brought to the United States in the mid-1800s by Australian John Macadam. Today, through clever advertising, they are plentiful and reaching more homes. The flavor of these mild, creamy-tasting nuts can be enhanced by toasting them in a pan until lightly browned.

1 ½ pounds cusk filet
2 tablespoons unsalted
   butter

1 teaspoon dried thyme
¼ cup dry white wine

MACADAMIA SAUCE

1 tablespoon unsalted butter
2 tablespoons chopped
   shallots
⅓ cup dry white wine

¾ cup heavy cream
¾ cup toasted unsalted
   macadamia nuts, finely
   ground in food processor

Place cusk in buttered ovenproof dish. Dot with butter, sprinkle with thyme, and pour wine over all. Bake in preheated oven at 350° for about 15 minutes, or until fish is opaque in center.

Meanwhile, make sauce. In saucepan melt butter over medium heat. Add shallots and cook until soft. Add wine and bring to simmer, reducing liquid to 4 tablespoons. Stir in cream and return to boil, stirring constantly for 3-5 minutes, or until thickened. Add ground nuts and stir to incorporate. Spoon over cooked fish, garnish as desired, and serve immediately.

Eel

Anguilla rostrata

Eels are easily recognized by their snakelike appearance. As they approach sexual maturity, their eyes get bigger and their bellies take on a bright silver color, at which stage they become known as silver eels. Found from Greenland to the West Indies, they breed in the Sargasso Sea between Bermuda and Puerto Rico.

Eels should be alive when bought, but if you can't bear the thought of killing, gutting, and skinning them yourself, ask your fish market to do so. Allow half a pound per person.

Eels have firm white flesh with a delicious flavor that is more like chicken than fish. The flesh has a high fat content and can be broiled, baked, sautéed, fried, grilled, or simmered. If you grill eel, do not remove the skin. Eel for bouillabaisse is best fileted first, as the bones are an unwelcome addition.

Italian Eel Stew   SERVES 4

Manny and Tony of Fresh Water Fish Company on the Boston Fish Pier have their tanks brimming with eels for the week before Christmas, when members of the local fishing community buy it for traditional preparations.

2 pounds eel, skinned and
  gutted
¼ cup olive oil
2 tablespoons unsalted
  butter
1 cup chopped onion
2 cloves garlic, minced
2 bay leaves, crumbled
6 sprigs parsley, leaves only

10 pitted green olives, sliced
3 ounces prosciutto, diced
1 hot chili pepper, seeded
  and chopped
6 tablespoons dry white wine
2 tomatoes, peeled, seeded,
  and chopped
½ cup boiling water
Salt to taste

Cut eel into 2-inch-long pieces. In skillet heat oil and butter, add onion and garlic, and cook over medium heat until soft, about 3 minutes. Add eel pieces, cover, and cook over low heat 5 minutes, turning often so all sides are cooked. Add bay leaves, parsley, olives, prosciutto, and hot pepper. Stir and cook 5 minutes. Add wine, tomatoes, and water. Cover and cook 20 minutes. Season with salt. Serve in bowls accompanied by garlic bread.

Eel Cooked in Soy Sauce

SERVES 4

On a recent trip with Earthwatch (an organization that sponsors world-wide educational expeditions for the lay person), I went to Hong Kong and China to help Skip Lazelle and Numi Goodyear catch reptiles. While there, I became fascinated with the local fishmongers and their catch: live eels swimming in plastic buckets, live turtles in mesh bags, and live, twitching shrimp, all ready to be purchased.

2 pounds eel, cleaned and skinned	3 tablespoons soy sauce
2½ tablespoons cornstarch	1 tablespoon sugar
7 tablespoons peanut oil	1 tablespoon rice wine
3 cloves garlic, crushed	2 teaspoons sesame oil
6 scallions, cut into 1-inch pieces	2 cups fish stock (see p. 180)
2 tablespoons julienned gingerroot	½ teaspoon crushed red pepper flakes
	2 teaspoons rice vinegar
	1 tablespoon water

Cut eel into 1½-inch-long pieces. Dust with 1½ tablespoons of the cornstarch.

Put 4 tablespoons of the peanut oil in wok over medium-high heat. Add garlic and cook 1 minute. Add eel, frying in batches until golden brown, about 3 minutes. Drain eel on paper towels.

Transfer garlic to small dish and set aside. Clean and dry wok, reheat, and add remaining 3 tablespoons peanut oil. Add scallions and gingerroot, and stir-fry 1 minute. Add soy sauce, sugar, wine, sesame oil, fish stock, red pepper flakes, and vinegar, and heat to simmer. Put garlic pieces and eel into mixture and simmer 20 minutes. Remove eel to platter. Thicken sauce with mixture of remaining 1 tablespoon cornstarch and 1 tablespoon water. Pour over eel and serve with boiled rice and steamed bok choy.

Fried Eel with Mustard Sauce   SERVES 4

Although strong in flavor, the hot mustard sauce does not overwhelm the rich taste of the eel.

2 pounds eel	2 tablespoons unsalted
2 eggs	butter
¼ teaspoon salt	2 tablespoons olive oil
¼ teaspoon cayenne pepper	Mustard Sauce (recipe
1 ½ cups bread crumbs	follows)

Have eel skinned, then cut into 2-inch-long pieces. Beat eggs with salt and cayenne. Dip eel pieces in egg mixture, then roll in bread crumbs.

Heat butter and oil in skillet and add eel pieces, frying until browned, about 5 minutes per side. Serve with Mustard Sauce on the side.

MUSTARD SAUCE

3 tablespoons dry mustard	5 tablespoons boiling water
½ teaspoon paprika	1 tablespoon olive oil
6 drops Tabasco	

Combine mustard, paprika, and Tabasco in bowl. Whisk in boiling water and oil until thoroughly blended.

Steamed Eel Stew   SERVES 6

The eels are cooked with their bones and skin still intact. Once they are done, the skin can be removed easily and the flesh eaten right off the bones.

2 eels (about 1 ½ pounds	1 cup rice wine
each)	½ teaspoon salt
6 scallions, sliced	1 tablespoon chopped fresh
4 slices gingerroot, julienned	cilantro
5 cups water	

Cut eels into 1½-inch pieces. In saucepan combine scallions, gingerroot, water, wine, and salt. Bring to simmer, add eel, and simmer 30-40 minutes. Serve steaming hot in soup bowls, garnished with chopped cilantro.

Flounder
(or Sole)

Summer flounder
(Paralichthys dentatus)
Winter flounder
(Pseudopleuronectes americanus)
American plaice
(Hippoglossoides platessoides)
Witch flounder
(Glyptocephalus cynoglossus)

There is no "true sole" of commercial value in New England waters. Excepting the authentic Dover sole imported here from England and France, all fish marketed here as sole are actually species of flounder, a flatfish with a rounded shape.

When young, flatfish look like most other fish until they are about one inch long. Then an eye migrates, the body flattens, and one side turns dark and the other side light. From this point the fish swims eyes up and blind side down. It is a master of camouflage, blending into its habitat on the bottom of the ocean.

The summer flounder ranges from Maine to the Carolinas. Also called "fluke" or "plaice," its eyes are on the left side of its body. A large flounder averaging 5 to 10 pounds, it moves inshore during the summer to spawn; during the winter, it lives offshore in deeper waters. Its flesh is white and lean with a large flake.

The winter flounder, which ranges from Labrador to the Chesapeake Bay, is known as "black-back" flounder when it weighs less than 3½ pounds and "lemon sole" when it is more than 3½ pounds. These right-handed flounders (their eyes and guts are on the right side) move inshore to spawn in the winter and spring and live offshore in the summer. The thickest and meatiest of the flatfishes, barring halibut, they have lean, sweet flesh. The black-back flounder has dark, threadlike strands throughout its flesh, and I consider it the best tasting of all the flounders.

American plaice comes to us from Canada and is sold as either flounder or sole, depending on the needs of the market on a particular day. Also called "dab" or "sand dab," it is the most common flounder in fish markets and is the least expensive at the pier. It is a right-handed flounder with a large mouth like a halibut. Its flesh is uniform in color, with a light yellow hue and a pink tinge; it is mild tasting and sweet. Filets are usually small, averaging no more than 8 ounces each.

Witch flounder is more commonly called "gray sole." A right-handed flounder with a small mouth, it is found from Canada to Cape Hatteras. Most flounders are round and stocky, but the witch flounder is 2½ to 3 times longer than it is broad. It has the whitest flesh of all flounders, and its long, thin filets are excellent for rolling. It is light textured with a delicate taste.

Flounder is sold whole; dressed with the head, tail, guts, and skin removed; or fileted. It can be pan-fried or sautéed, poached, stuffed, and baked — the varieties are endless. Handle it carefully while cooking because the filets are fragile and tend to break apart.

Body, Mind, and Sole

SERVES 6

One of the pleasures of fish is its simplicity, as shown by this recipe, given me by Andrea Bell, a former cooking instructor in Cambridge.

2 pounds gray sole filets
4 tablespoons unsalted
 butter
Juice of 1 lemon
1 tablespoon curry powder

4 tablespoons soy sauce
2 cloves garlic, minced
2 tablespoons chopped fresh
 parsley for garnish

Check filets for bones. Melt butter in large skillet. Add lemon juice, curry powder, soy sauce, and garlic. Heat, mixing well, until bubbly. Lay filets in skillet and sauté 2 minutes. Carefully turn over filets without breaking. Cook another 2 minutes, or until fish flakes when tested with fork. Transfer to warm plates, spoon sauce over filets, and garnish with chopped parsley.

Broiled Gray Sole with Ginger

SERVES 2

When you're tight for time or too hungry to wait long for dinner, fix this.

¾ to 1 pound gray sole
2 tablespoons unsalted
 butter

3 tablespoons dry white wine
Salt and pepper to taste

FRESH GINGER SAUCE

1 tablespoon olive oil
1 clove garlic, minced
1 tablespoon peeled and
 julienned gingerroot

1 tablespoon rice vinegar
1 tablespoon soy sauce
½ teaspoon sugar
1 teaspoon cornstarch

Lay sole in one layer in buttered baking dish so filets do not overlap. Dot with butter, sprinkle with wine, and season with salt and pepper. Broil in preheated oven for 3-4 minutes, or until fish flakes easily when tested with fork.

Meanwhile, make sauce. Heat oil in small saucepan over medium heat and sauté garlic and ginger for 2 minutes, stirring constantly.

In bowl combine vinegar, soy sauce, sugar, and cornstarch, and mix thoroughly. Add to ginger-garlic mixture and whisk until thickened, about 2 minutes. Place sole on plates, spoon sauce over top, and garnish as desired.

Mushroom-Stuffed Flounder with Tarragon Sauce

SERVES 6-8

Tarragon Sauce embellishes many fish dishes. Reserve and freeze any leftover sauce for another use.

3 pounds flounder filets
1 pound mushrooms
3 tablespoons unsalted
   butter
4 shallots, minced
1 tablespoon dried tarragon

¼ cup port
⅓ cup heavy cream
2 tablespoons flour
Salt and pepper to taste
½ cup water
½ cup dry white wine

TARRAGON SAUCE

6 tablespoons unsalted
   butter
2 shallots, minced
1 tablespoon dried tarragon
4 tablespoons flour
4 cups fish stock (see p. 180),
   reduced to 1 cup

2½ cups light cream
2 tablespoons dry white wine
Salt and cayenne pepper to
   taste

Pat flounder dry with paper towel and set aside while preparing mushroom stuffing. Mince mushrooms in food processor fitted with metal blade. Melt butter in large skillet, add shallots and tarragon, and sauté 5 minutes. Stir in mushrooms and cook over medium-low heat until mushrooms start to exude juice. Add port and cream, and turn heat up to medium to reduce liquid, cooking about 10 minutes, or until mixture becomes bubbly and less moist. Add flour and stir over low heat until well blended. Season with salt and pepper. Transfer to bowl and refrigerate until ready to use.

Place 1 to 2 tablespoons of stuffing on each flounder filet and roll up. With overlapped ends on bottom, place filets in buttered baking dish, side by side. Combine water and wine, and pour over fish. Cover dish tightly with lid or foil and cook in preheated oven at 350° for 20 minutes.

Meanwhile, make Tarragon Sauce. Melt butter over medium heat, add shallots and tarragon, and cook until shallots are soft, about 3 minutes. Stir in flour and cook 2 minutes over low heat. Gradually add reduced fish stock and cream, and cook until sauce thickens. Add wine and any extra mushroom stuffing for flavor. Season with salt and cayenne. When fish is done, transfer to platter, spoon on sauce, and serve.

Gray Sole in Carrot-Sherry Sauce   SERVES 2

Ellen Brisch, a Fishmonger chef, and Mrill Ingram prepared this for 350 people attending a conference at Earthwatch, a nonprofit organization that sponsors educational expeditions around the world. Earthwatch president Brian Rosborough praised the dish, saying he wished every team out in the field could eat so well.

¾ pound gray sole filets
(2 equal pieces)
2 tablespoons fresh lemon
juice
¼ cup dry white wine
2 tablespoons water

½ bay leaf, crumbled
Pinch of thyme
Carrot-Sherry Sauce (recipe
follows)
Chopped fresh chives or
scallion greens

Check filet for bones and set aside. In nonreactive skillet combine lemon juice, wine, and water, and bring to simmer over medium-low heat. Add bay leaf and thyme.

Fold filets in half and lay in liquid. Cover skillet to keep in steam and gently simmer filets 4-6 minutes, or until they flake easily when tested with fork. Carefully remove with wide spatula, place on platter, and keep warm in low oven while making sauce. Ladle sauce on top and garnish with chopped chives.

CARROT-SHERRY SAUCE

1 tablespoon unsalted butter
1 carrot, finely grated (about
¼ cup)
2 tablespoons dry sherry

2 teaspoons flour
¼ cup heavy cream or crème
fraîche (see p. 16)

Melt butter in saucepan over medium heat. Add carrot and cook 3 minutes. Stir in sherry and simmer 4 minutes. Add flour, whisking until blended. Add heavy cream, whisking constantly, and cook until sauce is bubbly and has thickened.

Gray Sole Stuffed with Shrimp in Red Pepper-Cilantro Sauce

SERVES 6-8

Ellen Brisch devised this recipe to meet the growing demand at The Fishmonger for take-out dinners. Because fish has such a short shelf life, it makes sense to prepare and freeze the dish until ready to use. Cream and butter sauces work very well without separating or drying out, and they protect the fish from freezer burn.

3 pounds gray sole filets (4 to 6 ounces each)
3 tablespoons unsalted butter
2 tablespoons chopped shallots
¾ pound raw shrimp, shelled, deveined, and chopped (see p. 221)
2 tablespoons flour
Juice and grated rind of 1 lemon

6 ounces cream cheese, cut into pieces
Salt and cayenne pepper to taste
1 small onion, sliced
½ cup dry white wine
Juice of 1 lemon
Red Pepper-Cilantro Sauce (recipe follows)
Chopped scallion greens for garnish

RED PEPPER-CILANTRO SAUCE

3 tablespoons unsalted butter
1 red bell pepper, minced
2 shallots, minced
3 tablespoons flour
2 cups fish stock (see p. 180) or bottled clam juice

½ cup heavy cream
1 tablespoon chopped fresh cilantro
¼ cup freshly grated Parmesan cheese
Salt and pepper to taste

Check sole for bones. Begin shrimp stuffing by melting butter over medium heat. Add shallots and cook until soft. Add shrimp and cook, stirring often, about 2 minutes, or until pink. Stir in flour to blend. Add juice and rind of 1 lemon and cream cheese, cooking over low heat until cheese melts and mixture is well blended. Season with salt and cayenne. Cool mixture slightly before rolling up in filets.

Place 1 to 2 tablespoons of stuffing in center of each filet and roll up securely. With overlapped end on bottom, place side by side in buttered baking dish. Lay onion slices on top of filets, pour wine and juice of second lemon over top, and cover dish with foil. Bake in preheated 350° oven for 20 minutes.

Meanwhile, begin sauce by melting butter in saucepan over medium heat. Add red bell pepper and shallots, and cook until soft, about 3 minutes. Add flour and stir to blend, then whisk in fish stock. Bring to simmer and cook until sauce thickens. Add cream, cilantro, and Parmesan cheese. Season with salt and pepper, and keep warm until filets are done.

Remove baked filets from oven and place on warm platter. Spoon on sauce and garnish with chopped scallion greens.

Flounder with Almonds, Pine Nuts, and Raisins

SERVES 4

As a child I would beg my parents to let me go fishing off the docks at the Manchester Yacht Club. They couldn't stand putting the worm on the hook, and God forbid I catch anything, for who was going to get the hook out? I, of course, thought I was going to catch a swordfish or a tuna, but one day when I reeled in a floppy flat flounder, I grinned with pleasure.

1 ½ pounds flounder filets	¼ cup dry sherry
Juice of 1 lemon	3 tablespoons apricot jelly or
Salt and pepper to taste	glaze
6 tablespoons unsalted	½ cup raisins or currants
butter	Chopped fresh parsley for
¼ cup pine nuts	garnish
¼ cup sliced almonds	

Lay filets on dish and pour lemon juice over them. Dust with salt and pepper.

Melt 4 tablespoons of the butter over medium heat in skillet and add filets. Sauté 3 minutes per side, transfer to platter, and keep warm in low oven.

In clean skillet over medium heat melt remaining 2 tablespoons butter. Add pine nuts and almonds, and cook until nuts are browned and toasted. Add sherry, apricot jelly, and raisins. Mix well and simmer 3-5 minutes, or until sauce has reduced a bit. Pour over fish, garnish with chopped parsley, and serve.

Gray Sole Stuffed with Crabmeat in Lobster Sauce

SERVES 8-10

This hearty yet elegant dish is perfect for a special dinner party. It requires some work, but stuffing the fish the night before makes preparation easier. Always put the stuffing on the skin side of the filet because it will roll up tighter and hold together better when cooked.

3 pounds gray sole filets
(about 8 to 10 filets)
1 pound fresh, canned, or
frozen crabmeat (or
½ pound crabmeat and
½ pound cooked shrimp)
3 tablespoons unsalted
butter
2 large shallots, minced

2 tablespoons flour
¾ cup heavy cream
3 tablespoons minced fresh
parsley
Salt and cayenne pepper to
taste
½ cup water
¾ cup dry white wine

LOBSTER SAUCE

6 tablespoons unsalted
butter
⅓ cup minced shallots
Grated rind and juice
of 1 lemon
6 tablespoons flour
3 cups Lobster Cream (recipe
follows)

¼ cup dry sherry
2 tablespoons tomato paste
Salt and pepper to taste
½ pound lobster meat, diced
2 tablespoons minced fresh
parsley

Check filets for bones and set aside. Check crabmeat for shell particles and cartilage. Begin stuffing by melting butter in saucepan and sautéing shallots until soft. Add flour to make a roux and cook 2 minutes. Whisk in cream and cook until sauce thickens. Add parsley and season with salt and cayenne. Transfer to bowl and cool, then add crabmeat and chill in refrigerator until cool enough to handle.

Place 1 to 2 tablespoons of crab mixture on each filet and roll up so overlapped end is on bottom. Put side by side in buttered oven-proof baking dish. Combine water and wine, pour over filets, and cover dish with foil. Bake in preheated oven at 350° for 15-20 minutes. Drain off juices and reserve.

Meanwhile, make Lobster Sauce. Melt butter in saucepan, add shallots, and cook until soft. Stir in lemon rind and flour, and cook 2 minutes. Whisk in Lobster Cream and cook until sauce has thickened. Add sherry, tomato paste, and lemon juice, and season with salt and pepper. To this sauce, add juices from dish in which filets were baked. Add lobster meat and parsley. Serve stuffed filets on platter with sauce spooned over top.

LOBSTER CREAM

4 cooked lobster bodies   3 cups light cream

Break apart lobster bodies and legs. Discard sand sack behind eyes. Place bodies and legs in saucepan, add cream, and bring to simmer. Remove from heat and let sit 15 minutes. Strain cream through sieve and use as directed for sauce.

Fried Flounder with Sesame Seed Coating SERVES 4

Be sure the filets are completely dry before dredging in the flour; too much flour will make them gummy and pasty. The sesame seeds will be toasted as they cook in the skillet.

1 ½ pounds flounder filets
¾ cup flour
2 eggs
2 tablespoons fresh lemon
   juice
1 cup white cornmeal
Salt and pepper to taste
½ teaspoon paprika

1 tablespoon sesame seeds
4 tablespoons olive oil
4 tablespoons unsalted
   butter
Lemon wedges and chopped
   scallions for garnish

Pat filets dry with paper towel. Roll in flour, shaking to remove excess. Whisk eggs with lemon juice in shallow bowl. Combine cornmeal, salt and pepper, paprika, and sesame seeds on plate. Dip floured flounder into egg mixture, then coat with cornmeal mixture.

Heat oil and butter in skillet over medium-high heat and add filets in one layer. (You might need two skillets.) Cook 2 minutes per side until browned and crispy. Add more oil and butter as needed to keep filets from sticking. Serve with lemon wedges and chopped scallions.

Pan-Fried Flounder with Parsley and Lemon

SERVES 2

The tricks to pan-frying flounder are having a well-seasoned pan so the filets don't stick and not frying too many at a time. You might have to use two pans so all the fish will be ready at the same time.

¾ pound flounder filets
(about 4 equal pieces)
½ cup finely ground
cornmeal
Salt and pepper to taste
1 tablespoon olive oil

4 tablespoons unsalted
butter
1 tablespoon chopped fresh
parsley for garnish
Lemon wedges for garnish
Capers for garnish (optional)

Pat filets dry with paper towel, coat with cornmeal, and dust with salt and pepper. In skillet heat oil and butter until hot and bubbly. Add filets and cook 2 minutes.

With wide spatula, carefully turn over filets and cook 2 minutes on other side. Transfer to warm plate and garnish with chopped parsley, lemon wedges, and capers if desired.

Gray Sole with Green Grapes

SERVES 4

Customers who want something light for dinner always ask for gray sole. Combining it with a mild fruit makes it easy to digest. Although grapes are the most traditional, try substituting cantaloupe, honeydew melon, or kiwifruit.

1½ pounds gray sole filets
2 tablespoons dry white wine
2 tablespoons unsalted
butter

Salt and pepper to taste

CREAM SAUCE

4 cups fish stock (see p. 180)
2 tablespoons unsalted
butter
2 tablespoons flour

½ cup dry white wine
1 cup heavy cream
1 cup white grapes, halved

Lay filets, folded in half, in buttered baking dish. Sprinkle with wine and dot with butter. Dust with salt and pepper. Cover dish with foil and bake in preheated oven at 350° for 10-12 minutes.

Meanwhile, make sauce. In saucepan boil fish stock until reduced to ½ cup. Set aside. In another saucepan melt butter over medium heat, add flour to make a roux, and cook 2 minutes, stirring constantly. Combine fish stock reduction with white wine and cream, and whisk into roux. Simmer until sauce thickens. Add grapes to sauce and stir. Remove fish to platter, spoon on sauce, and serve.

Gray Sole with Bananas in Chutney Sauce

SERVES 4-6

This recipe was inspired by the Caribbean. I usually make it in the winter and imagine being at one of those romantic restaurants right on the beach, with steel drums playing in the background.

2 pounds gray sole filets	3 tablespoons fresh lemon
½ cup dry white wine	juice
4 bananas	½ cup dry sherry
½ cup superfine sugar	8 tablespoons unsalted
1 teaspoon ground cloves	butter, melted
1 teaspoon cinnamon	2 tablespoons unsalted
4 tablespoons unsalted	butter, softened
butter	2 tablespoons flour
½ cup chutney, finely	
chopped	

Roll filets so overlapped ends are on bottom. Place in baking dish side by side and pour on wine. Cover and bake in preheated oven at 350° for 20 minutes.

Peel bananas and slice in half lengthwise. Combine superfine sugar with cloves and cinnamon, and sprinkle over bananas. Melt 4 tablespoons butter in sauté pan and cook bananas briefly on both sides until browned. (Don't cook too long, or bananas will get mushy.) Remove to dish to keep warm.

Add chopped chutney, lemon juice, sherry, and melted butter to sauté pan. Bring to simmer and cook for a couple of minutes, scraping bottom of pan as you stir. Combine softened butter and flour. Add 1 tablespoon at a time to thicken sauce, whisking to remove lumps, until light glaze is obtained. (You might not use all of this.)

Transfer baked fish to plates, place bananas alongside, and spoon sauce over top. Serve immediately.

Flounder with Mushrooms

SERVES 4

Flounder filets are thin and uniform and cook very quickly. Their taste is mild and nonoily, and it blends well with many vegetables.

1 ½ pounds flounder filets
Salt and pepper to taste
3 tablespoons unsalted
  butter
1 bunch scallions, sliced
½ pound mushrooms, thinly
  sliced

½ teaspoon nutmeg
1 cup sour cream
¼ cup chopped fresh dill
Juice of 1 lemon
1 tablespoon grated onion

Lightly salt and pepper flounder filets and set aside. Melt butter in sauté pan over medium heat and cook scallions 4 minutes, or until soft. Add mushrooms and cook until soft and browned. Add nutmeg and mix well.

Spread mushroom-scallion mixture in ovenproof baking dish. Lay flounder filets on top. Combine sour cream, dill, lemon juice, and onion. Pour over fish, bake in preheated oven at 350° for 20 minutes, and serve.

Gray Sole with Orange Sauce

SERVES 4

Any orange-flavored liqueur can be used here or omitted altogether.

1 ½ pounds gray sole filets
Salt and pepper to taste
4 tablespoons unsalted
  butter
½ pound mushrooms, sliced
½ cup dry white wine
¼ cup fresh orange juice

1 teaspoon grated orange
  rind
2 tablespoons Grand
  Marnier
2 tablespoons chopped fresh
  parsley for garnish

Lightly salt and pepper filets and set aside. Melt 2 tablespoons of the butter in shallow baking dish, spreading it over bottom. Lay filets, folded in half, on top. Dot with remaining 2 tablespoons butter and arrange mushrooms evenly over filets.

In bowl combine wine, orange juice and rind, and liqueur. Pour over fish and mushrooms, and bake in preheated oven at 400° for 15 minutes. Garnish with chopped parsley and serve.

Haddock

Melanogrammus aeglefinus

Haddock is the overfished seafood of the 1980s. The supply is dwindling daily, and the price keeps going up. A member of the cod family, it is found from Newfoundland to New Jersey in the deeper waters of the continental shelf.

Haddock is almost always sold fileted with the skin left on to distinguish it from cod. There is a unique dark splotch on its side near the head called the "devil's thumbprint" or "St. Peter's mark," which allows for easy identification.

"Finnan haddie" are haddock filets that have been brined and smoked. ("Haddie" is the Scottish word for haddock.) They are best poached in milk. Serve finnan haddie with eggs for breakfast or add a piece to fish chowder for a lovely smoky flavor.

Haddock can be poached, baked, broiled, or sautéed. It has a larger flake than cod and a sweet, mild flavor. If it is not fresh, haddock will smell and taste "fishy" and have an iodine or metallic flavor. Cod, pollock, and hake are good substitutes.

Finnan Haddie Pâté

MAKES ABOUT 2½ CUPS

A great hors d'oeuvre for a party. Smoked cod can be substituted if haddock is not available.

1 pound finnan haddie
1 cup fish stock (see page 180)
½ cup dry white wine
1 tablespoon unsalted butter
1½ pounds cream cheese, cut into bits
¼ cup fresh lemon juice

2 tablespoons Dijon mustard
1 tablespoon grated onion
2 tablespoons Worcestershire sauce
Cayenne pepper to taste (optional)

Skin finnan haddie, cut into chunks, and check for bones. Combine fish stock, wine, and butter in saucepan and bring to simmer. Add finnan haddie and poach about 15 minutes, or until fish flakes easily. Remove fish with slotted spoon, chill, and flake into bits.

In food processor fitted with metal blade, blend finnan haddie and cream cheese. In separate bowl combine lemon juice, mustard, onion, and Worcestershire sauce. Add to food processor and blend. Taste for seasoning and add cayenne if desired. Transfer to bowl or crock and refrigerate until thoroughly chilled. Serve with crackers or toast.

Haddock Seviche

SERVES 4 AS APPETIZER

This is one of my favorite summer dishes. It is light and refreshing, yet aromatic and spicy.

1-pound haddock filet, skinned
½ cup fresh lemon juice
½ cup fresh lime juice
1 medium-size red onion, sliced into thin rings
1 small hot jalapeño pepper, seeded and chopped
3 small mild green chilies, seeded and chopped
1 medium-size red bell pepper, diced

2 medium tomatoes, peeled, seeded, and chopped
2 tablespoons chopped fresh cilantro
2 tablespoons fresh lemon juice
¼ cup tomato juice
Lettuce leaves
1 avocado, peeled, seeded, and sliced

Slice haddock into thin strips and marinate in ½ cup lemon juice and lime juice for 12-18 hours. Haddock will be solid white color when done.

In separate bowl mix together drained haddock pieces, onion, jalapeño, chilies, bell pepper, tomatoes, and cilantro. Mix in 2 tablespoons lemon juice and tomato juice until moist. Serve on bed of lettuce, garnished with sliced avocado.

Finnan Haddie Salad   SERVES 4

This hearty salad can be made with any combination of vegetables.

1 pound finnan haddie
1½ cups milk
1½ cups fish stock (see p. 180)
1 pound small red-skinned potatoes
½ pound fresh green beans
2 small red onions, sliced
4 scallions, sliced

¾ cup pitted black olives, sliced
1 cup cherry tomatoes
6 strips bacon, cooked crisp and crumbled
Mustard Dressing (recipe follows)
3 tablespoons chopped fresh dill

Remove any skin and bones from finnan haddie, then cut into 2 inch pieces and set aside. Bring milk and fish stock to simmer in sauté pan. Add finnan haddie and poach 15 minutes, or until flaky. Transfer fish to strainer and drain.

Cook potatoes in boiling water for about 15 minutes, or until done but still firm. Drain, cool, and slice, but do not remove skins. Cook beans 3-4 minutes in boiling water, then cut into thirds.

In bowl flake fish into chunks and add sliced potatoes, beans, onions, scallions, black olives, cherry tomatoes, and bacon. Combine thoroughly. Toss salad with enough Mustard Dressing to coat. Stir in 2 tablespoons dill and garnish with remaining dill.

MUSTARD DRESSING

¼ cup red wine vinegar
2 tablespoons Dijon mustard
2 anchovy filets, mashed

½ teaspoon minced garlic
¾ cup olive oil

In food processor fitted with metal blade, blend vinegar, mustard, mashed anchovies, and garlic for 10 seconds. Add oil in steady stream, blending until dressing thickens to creamy consistency.

Finnan Haddie, Mussels, and Potato Salad

SERVES 4-6

Finnan haddie adds a delightful flavor to potato salad, as do other smoked seafoods, such as mussels, tuna, or shrimp.

2 pounds raw mussels or ½ pound smoked mussels*
1 cup dry white wine
½ cup water
2 sprigs parsley
1 pound finnan haddie
1 cup milk
1 cup fish stock (see p. 180)
1 pound small red-skinned potatoes
½ cup mayonnaise (see p. 283)

½ cup sour cream
¼ cup olive oil
2 tablespoons prepared horseradish
Cayenne pepper to taste
1 small red onion, thinly sliced
Chopped fresh parsley for garnish

Wash and debeard mussels (see p. 141). In saucepan bring wine, water, and 2 sprigs parsley to simmer. Add mussels, cover, and steam 5-6 minutes, or until shells open. (Stir mussels after first 3 minutes for even cooking.) Drain mussels and reserve broth. Remove mussels from shells and refrigerate. Reduce broth over high heat to ¼ cup.

Poach finnan haddie in milk and fish stock for about 15 minutes. With slotted spoon, transfer fish to bowl and let cool, then flake into medium-size pieces. In saucepan boil potatoes until just done, about 15 minutes; drain and cut into quarters.

In small bowl make dressing by whisking together mayonnaise, sour cream, oil, horseradish, reserved mussel broth, and cayenne. Combine mussels, finnan haddie, potatoes, and sliced onion. Toss with dressing and refrigerate until chilled. Serve cold, garnished with chopped parsley.

* If smoked mussels are used, substitute ¼ cup fish stock for mussel broth when making dressing.

The Fishmonger Fish Chowder

SERVES 10-12

One Sunday in June, I was invited for cocktails to Julia Child's house here in Cambridge to honor a new cookbook author. It was a large party, and I brought a customer along with me: rock star Peter Wolf. Peter, who turns just as many heads as Julia, ended up signing more cookbooks than the author. We were asked to stay for supper, and Peter wanted to help Julia in the kitchen. To his chagrin, however, he was quickly whisked out. Among the dishes we were served was The Fishmonger Fish Chowder à la Julia Child.

3 pounds haddock filets (or a combination of skinned haddock, cod, hake, and pollock)	4 tablespoons flour
	1 teaspoon white pepper
	1 teaspoon salt
	8 cups fish stock (see p. 180)
4 Idaho potatoes, peeled and diced	¾ cup sour cream
	4 cups milk
8 tablespoons unsalted butter	2 cups evaporated milk
	4 cups light cream
3 cups finely chopped onions	Chopped fresh parsley for garnish
2 tablespoons dried dill	

Check fish for bones, then cut into large chunks. Set aside in refrigerator. Cook potatoes until just done; they should be firm, not mushy. Drain and set aside.

Meanwhile, melt butter in large soup pot. Add onions and cook until soft and translucent. Stir in dill, flour, white pepper, and salt, and cook about 2 minutes, stirring constantly.

In separate pot heat fish stock to simmer and, cup by cup, add 5 cups to onion mixture, whisking after each addition. Leave 3 cups fish stock in pot and add sour cream to it, whisking until lumps disappear. Add this to onion mixture and bring to simmer. This is the base to which the fish and cream will be added just before serving. You can make this ahead of time up to this point, but be sure you do not leave it in an aluminum pot, for that will affect the taste.

When ready to serve, heat base to simmer, add fish chunks, and cook until fish flakes. Add milk, evaporated milk, cream, and cooked potatoes. Heat until warmed through, but do not boil. *Be careful not to burn the bottom.* With slotted spoon, evenly dole out solid ingredients into chowder bowls and ladle liquid on top to fill. Garnish each bowl with chopped parsley and serve with chowder crackers.

Steamed Haddock and Vegetables   SERVES 4

This method of cooking without oil is ideal for dieters. Choose fish and vegetables of the highest quality and freshness.

1 ½ pounds haddock filets, skinned	½ green bell pepper, sliced into thin strips
Salt to taste	½ red bell pepper, sliced into thin strips
4 teaspoons sake or dry white wine	1 medium onion, thinly sliced
4 dried shiitake mushrooms	1 lemon, thinly sliced
2 carrots, peeled and sliced into thin ovals	

Check filets for bones, then salt lightly. Sprinkle 2 teaspoons of the sake over filets and let stand 10 minutes. Remove stems from mushrooms and discard. Soak caps in water to cover until limp, about 10 minutes.

Cut a piece of foil large enough to cover all the fish when folded up. Moisten center of foil with remaining 2 teaspoons sake so fish will not stick. Arrange fish, vegetables, and lemon slices in center and fold up sides of foil. Crimp edges to seal so steam does not escape. Bake in preheated 425° oven for 15 minutes. Remove fish and vegetables from foil and serve on warm platter.

Broiled Haddock with Bananas   SERVES 4

When my daughter Rebecca started crew training for the "Head of the Charles" one fall, I stuffed her with good healthy food, including lots of fresh fish and bananas, the latter being a good source of potassium, which helps prevent leg cramps.

1 ½ pounds haddock filets	⅛ teaspoon paprika
4 tablespoons unsalted butter	¼ teaspoon dry mustard
¼ cup fresh lemon juice	¼ teaspoon salt
¼ teaspoon dried tarragon	2 bananas, sliced crosswise

Check filets for bones. Melt butter in saucepan and add lemon juice, tarragon, paprika, mustard, and salt. Brush over haddock filets and broil 5-7 minutes. Top fish with banana slices and baste with remaining butter mixture. Return to broiler for 2 minutes, or until bananas are browned.

Grandmother's Finnan Haddie Casserole SERVES 4-6

I never knew my paternal grandmother, but her legend lives on in my family. Eleanor Crocker, her daughter and my aunt, has my grandmother's cookbook, from which I chose this recipe.

1½ pounds finnan haddie
1½ cups milk
1½ cups fish stock (see p. 180)
2 bay leaves, crumbled
1 small onion, sliced
6 whole black peppercorns
1 green bell pepper, diced
1 red bell pepper, diced
6 tablespoons unsalted butter

3 tablespoons flour
2 teaspoons fresh lemon juice
4 hard-boiled eggs (optional)
½ pound mushrooms, sliced
½ pound shell macaroni (or any shape pasta you like)
Bread crumbs

Cut finnan haddie into large chunks. In sauté pan heat milk, fish stock, bay leaves, onion, and peppercorns to simmer. Add finnan haddie and poach 15 minutes, or until fish flakes easily. Remove fish with slotted spoon and reserve poaching liquid.

Sauté bell peppers in 3 tablespoons of the butter until soft. Stir in flour and cook 1 minute over low heat. Slowly add 3 cups poaching liquid (using more milk if needed to reach 3 cups), whisking until sauce is creamy and smooth. Stir in lemon juice, flaked finnan haddie, and 2 hard-boiled eggs cut into wedges if desired. Remove from heat.

Sauté mushrooms in remaining 3 tablespoons butter for 3 minutes, then fold into sauce. Cook pasta al dente, combine with sauce, and pour into ovenproof casserole dish. Sprinkle with bread crumbs and bake in preheated oven at 350° for 15-20 minutes. Serve garnished with remaining 2 hard-boiled eggs cut into wedges.

Kedgeree

The English took this dish home with them from India. Serve it for a light supper or brunch. Traditionally, any leftover fish could be used, but I prefer the taste of finnan haddie.

1½ pounds finnan haddie, skinned	1 cup fish stock (see p. 180)
9 tablespoons unsalted butter	1 bay leaf
1 cup chopped onion	1 small onion, quartered
1 tablespoon curry powder	1 teaspoon whole peppercorns
1½ cups white rice, uncooked	3 tablespoons flour
3 cups hot water	1 teaspoon curry powder
2 cups milk	Salt and cayenne pepper to taste
	3 hard-boiled eggs (optional)

Cut finnan haddie into chunks and set aside. Melt 6 tablespoons of the butter in saucepan and sauté chopped onion until soft. Mix in 1 tablespoon curry powder and cook until blended. Add rice and stir until coated. Add hot water and simmer rice, covered, until water is absorbed and rice is tender, about 15 minutes. Set aside.

In sauté pan heat milk and fish stock to simmer, then add bay leaf, quartered onion, and peppercorns. Stir in finnan haddie pieces and poach 15 minutes, or until fish flakes apart. With slotted spoon, remove fish to plate. Strain and reserve poaching liquid.

Make white sauce by melting remaining 3 tablespoons butter in saucepan. Stir in flour and cook about 3 minutes. Slowly add 2 cups strained poaching liquid from finnan haddie, whisking continuously. Add 1 teaspoon curry powder and season with salt and cayenne.

Cover bottom of buttered casserole dish with half the rice mixture. Drizzle ½ cup of sauce over rice. Break up poached finnan haddie and evenly distribute over rice. If desired, cut hard-boiled eggs into eighths and place on top of fish. Drizzle 1 cup of sauce over this, add remaining rice, and top with remaining sauce. Cover with foil and bake in preheated oven at 350° for 20-30 minutes.

Haddock Baked in Sour Cream and Dill   SERVES 4

In 1900 whole haddock cost about 6 to 8 cents a pound at the Boston Fish Pier. Now, 88 years later, haddock rings in at $1.50 to $3 a pound, and it probably will go higher unless consumers mount some resistance.

1½ pounds haddock filets, skinned	¼ teaspoon dried thyme
2 cups sour cream	½ teaspoon paprika
Juice and grated rind of 1 lemon	2 teaspoons dried dill
½ cup mayonnaise (see p. 283)	¼ teaspoon pepper
	¼ teaspoon salt
	Chopped fresh parsley for garnish

Place haddock filets in buttered shallow baking dish. Combine sour cream, lemon juice and rind, mayonnaise, thyme, paprika, dill, pepper, and salt. Pour over fish and bake in preheated 350° oven for 20 minutes. Serve garnished with chopped parsley.

Steamed Haddock with Tofu   SERVES 4

Tofu is a firm, custardlike soybean cake. It has very little taste of its own but works as a blotter to pick up other flavors.

1½ pounds haddock filets, skinned	Salt to taste
4 or 8 dried shiitake mushrooms	4 tablespoons sake
½ pound fresh spinach	4 scallions, chopped
½ pound tofu	Soy-Ginger Dipping Sauce (see p. 228)

Check filets for bones. Remove and discard stems from mushrooms and soak caps in water until limp, about 10 minutes. Cut haddock into 4 equal pieces and arrange on 4 pieces of foil. Place 1 or 2 mushrooms in each packet.

Wash spinach, remove and discard tough stems, and blanch 10 seconds in boiling water. Drain, squeezing out excess water, and divide among fish packets. Cut tofu into 1-inch cubes and divide among packets. Season each with salt. Drizzle 1 tablespoon sake over ingredients in each and fold up foil to make airtight package. Bake in preheated 425° oven for 15 minutes. Garnish with chopped scallions and serve with dipping sauce.

Haddock Baked with Thyme

SERVES 4

Frank Vorenberg was my oldest customer. Over the years, I convinced him to try other kinds of fish, but every Friday, he would come to get his haddock.

1 ½ pounds haddock filets	½ pound mushrooms, sliced
¾ cup crushed Ritz crackers	Chopped fresh parsley for
1 teaspoon dried thyme	garnish
8 tablespoons unsalted	1 lemon, quartered, for
butter	garnish

Check filets for bones. Combine cracker crumbs and thyme on plate. Melt 6 tablespoons of the butter and dip filets in it, turning to coat both sides. Coat filets with crumbs, then place, skin side down, in buttered baking dish. Bake in preheated 400° oven for 15 minutes. Melt remaining 2 tablespoons butter in skillet, add mushrooms, and sauté until browned.

When fish is done, place on warm plates, spoon mushrooms on top, and garnish with chopped parsley and lemon quarters.

Haddock with Creamy Green Peppercorn Sauce

SERVES 4

Green peppercorns are the fresh, undried fruit of the pepper tree. They come canned or bottled in pickling juice and have the flavor of pepper without the fiery bite.

1 ½ pounds haddock filets,	8 tablespoons unsalted
skinned	butter, melted
1 large egg yolk	¼ cup crème fraîche (see p.
⅛ teaspoon salt	16) or heavy cream
2 teaspoons fresh lemon	1 tablespoon green
juice	peppercorns, minced

Place haddock in buttered baking dish. Cover with foil and bake in preheated 400° oven for 15 minutes.

Meanwhile, in top of double boiler placed over warm water, whisk egg yolk, salt, and lemon juice until light lemon color. Add melted butter, 1 tablespoon at a time, whisking constantly until all is incorporated. Increase heat and, over boiling water, whisk until mixture thickens. Whisk in crème fraîche until incorporated. Add peppercorns and blend. If sauce breaks, add a little boiling water, 1 teaspoon at a time, to pull sauce back together.

Place haddock on platter and spoon on sauce just before serving.

Haddock Neapolitan

SERVES 6

This low-calorie dish is a favorite at The Fishmonger. Any extra sauce can be frozen for later use.

2 pounds haddock filets,
   skinned

NEAPOLITAN SAUCE

35-ounce can tomatoes	3 ribs celery, finely chopped
4 slices lean bacon	½ cup raisins or currants
1 large Spanish onion,	½ cup pine nuts, roasted
chopped	½ cup pitted black olives,
3 cloves garlic, minced	thinly sliced

Cut haddock into 6 equal pieces, place in buttered ovenproof dish, and set aside while making sauce. Drain tomatoes and put liquid in large sauté pan. Over high heat reduce to paste, being careful not to burn toward the end. Purée tomatoes in food processor fitted with metal blade. Set aside.

Fry bacon until crispy and drain on paper towels. Leave just enough bacon fat in pan to cover bottom, add onion and garlic, and cook until soft. Stir in puréed tomatoes, celery, raisins, pine nuts, and black olives. Crumble bacon and add. Simmer for 30 minutes.

Meanwhile, bake haddock in preheated oven at 350° for 15-20 minutes. After sauce has cooked specified amount of time, add reduced tomato paste and stir to combine.

When haddock is done, place on platter, pour on sauce, and serve.

Hake (or Whiting)

Silver *(Merluccius bilinearis)*

Hake is a member of the cod family and sometimes is marketed as "whiting," or "poor man's cod." Found from Newfoundland to the Carolinas, hake has a silvery iridescent sheen when alive but turns brownish or gray when killed.

Hake has a coarser flake than cod or haddock and a slightly higher oil content. Its flesh is creamy tan in color, similar to that of pollock. Sold fileted, hake can be fried, baked, or broiled and holds up nicely when added to soups and casseroles. Because of its bland taste, it is complemented by a flavorful sauce. Hake can be used instead of pollock and the more costly cod and haddock.

Broiled Sesame Hake   SERVES 2

Sesame seeds add a sweet, nutty flavor to the hake. Be sure to toast raw seeds in a clean, nonstick pan until they are golden and aromatic.

1-pound hake filet	2 tablespoons soy sauce
¼ cup sesame seeds	Grated rind of 1 lemon
2 tablespoons sesame oil	1 tablespoon fresh lemon
3 tablespoons unsalted	juice
butter	Pepper to taste
1 small onion, finely	Chopped scallion greens for
chopped	garnish

Put hake in buttered ovenproof dish. Toast sesame seeds in nonstick frying pan, stirring until golden brown, then set aside. In saucepan heat oil and butter. Add onion and cook 3 minutes over medium heat, or until soft. Add soy sauce, lemon rind, lemon juice, and toasted sesame seeds. Season with pepper. Pour over filet and broil 8-10 minutes. Garnish with chopped scallion greens.

Baked Hake with Potatoes and Cheese   SERVES 4

Serve this hearty dish with a garden salad or steamed vegetable for a complete meal.

1 ½ pounds hake filets	2 teaspoons dry mustard
3 Idaho or red-skinned potatoes	2 cups milk, scalded
5 tablespoons unsalted butter	Salt and pepper to taste
3 tablespoons flour	1 ½ cups grated sharp Cheddar cheese

Cut filets into 4 equal pieces and place in liberally buttered baking dish. Peel potatoes and slice in thin rounds. Stack slices three deep and cut crosswise into thin julienned matchsticks. Put in saucepan, cover with cold water, and bring to boil. Cook 2 minutes after they have reached the boil. Drain in colander. In the same saucepan melt 2 tablespoons of the butter and add potatoes, stirring to coat.

Melt remaining 3 tablespoons butter in another saucepan, add flour, and stir to blend. Stir in mustard and gradually add scalded milk, whisking as you add. Simmer 2 minutes and season with salt and pepper.

Ladle sauce over fish and spread potatoes on top. Sprinkle with grated cheese and bake in preheated oven at 400° for 15 minutes, or until potatoes are crisp and golden.

Hake with Ground Pecan Coating

SERVES 4

Make sure fish pieces are thoroughly dry before dusting with flour.

1 ½ pounds hake filets
¾ cup flour
¼ teaspoon salt
¼ teaspoon pepper
2 eggs
1 cup bread crumbs
1 cup whole pecans, ground
1 teaspoon grated lemon
  rind

½ teaspoon dried thyme
4 tablespoons unsalted
  butter
4 tablespoons olive oil
Chopped fresh parsley and
  lemon wedges for garnish

Cut hake into 4 equal pieces and pat dry with paper towel. Mix flour with salt and pepper, and dust hake. Beat eggs until light. Mix together bread crumbs, ground pecans, lemon rind, and thyme. Dip floured hake in beaten egg, then in bread crumb mixture.

Heat butter and oil in skillet over medium heat. Add hake pieces and fry 4-5 minutes per side, or until browned and crispy. Garnish with chopped parsley and lemon wedges.

Hake Baked with Mushrooms

SERVES 4

Given its firm texture, hake is especially well suited for baking.

1 ½ pounds hake filets
2 tablespoons unsalted
  butter
6 large mushrooms, thinly
  sliced
1 medium onion, sliced in
  thin rings

½ cup dry white wine
1 bay leaf, broken in half
1 cup heavy cream
Chopped fresh parsley for
  garnish

Lay hake filets in buttered baking dish. Dot with butter and bake in preheated 400° oven for 7 minutes.

Combine mushrooms, onion, wine, and bay leaf, then pour over top of fish. Cover dish with foil, decrease temperature to 350°, and bake another 7 minutes. Remove from oven and pour juices from dish into saucepan, discarding bay leaf. Heat to simmer and add heavy cream, cooking until sauce thickens. Pour over fish, garnish with chopped parsley, and serve.

Hake with Blue Cheese Sauce

SERVES 6

This strong cheese sauce might not be for everyone, but I find it just right with any mild-tasting fish. Instead of artichoke hearts, you can use broccoli, brussels sprouts, or any other colorful vegetable.

2½ pounds hake filets, cut into 6 equal pieces
7 tablespoons unsalted butter
¼ cup dry white wine
12 canned artichoke hearts, quartered
4 tablespoons flour

2 cups light cream
½ pound blue cheese, crumbled
Cayenne pepper to taste
½ cup chopped toasted pecans or walnuts for garnish

Place hake in buttered ovenproof dish. Dot with 3 tablespoons of the butter and pour wine over top. Arrange artichokes around fish and bake in preheated oven at 350° for 15-20 minutes depending on thickness.

Meanwhile, in saucepan over medium-low heat melt remaining 4 tablespoons butter, stir in flour, and cook 1 minute. Add cream, whisking to blend. Stir in blue cheese and add more cream if needed to achieve sauce consistency. Dust with cayenne and blend.

When fish is done, transfer to platter, top with sauce, and garnish with chopped nuts.

Halibut (Atlantic)

Hippoglossus hippoglossus

The Atlantic halibut is the largest member of the flat flounder family, reaching weights of more than 200 pounds, although 300- to 400-pound halibut are rare. These "hippos of the sea," as they've been called, take ten years to mature and reproduce and can have the life span of a human being. The halibut's back is dark olive green; its belly, white. It is found in the cold, deep waters of the North Atlantic.

Small halibut (between 3 and 12 pounds) are sold fileted like flounder or sole. The larger ones are trimmed of their petticoat fins and cut into steaks, which include part of the backbone. When buying steaks, you should allow slightly more than half a pound per person because of the bone and skin waste.

Halibut is firm, lean, and white. It has a sweet, delicate taste and is suitable for a variety of preparations, including grilling, baking, and poaching, and any number of sauces, from a mild herb butter or a rich cream to a hot and spicy marinade. Cook the steaks with the bones left in. They are large and easily re-moved after cooking, and, along with the skin, they tend to add flavor and moisture to the flesh, as well as hold the fish together while it cooks. The filets are best when baked in a hot oven or sautéed quickly in a pan on top of the stove.

Fresh halibut is becoming scarce, but it comes to market more often in the spring and summer than in the fall and winter. To tell the difference between fresh and frozen, check the color of the flesh. Frozen halibut will look *too* white, whereas fresh will have an iridescent pink tinge to it.

Halibut with Cracked Peppercorns   SERVES 2

This is a variation of steak au poivre. It is important that the pepper-corns be cracked rather than ground.

1-pound halibut steak, ½ inch thick	3 tablespoons unsalted butter
1 tablespoon whole black peppercorns	Lemon-Chive Butter (recipe follows)
Olive oil	

Cut halibut into 2 equal pieces. Put peppercorns in plastic bag and pound with mallet or hammer until cracked thoroughly. Rub oil over halibut steaks and coat with cracked peppercorns, pressing them into the flesh with the palm of your hand.

Melt butter in skillet over medium-high heat and add steaks. Cook 2 minutes, then turn and cook 3 minutes more. Dot with Lemon-Chive Butter and serve.

LEMON-CHIVE BUTTER

4 tablespoons unsalted butter, softened	2 teaspoons snipped fresh chives
2 teaspoons fresh lemon juice	

Combine ingredients in bowl, mixing with fork until well blend-ed. Freeze any leftover butter, sealed in plastic wrap.

Grilled Halibut with Barbecue Sauce   SERVES 4

This spicy barbecue sauce adds flavor to the outside of the fish without changing its internal texture and white color.

2 pounds halibut steaks,
   1 inch thick

BARBECUE SAUCE

3 tablespoons olive oil
½ cup minced onion
3 tablespoons minced red
   bell pepper
2 tablespoons minced green
   bell pepper
1 clove garlic, minced

8-ounce can tomato sauce
2 tablespoons fresh lemon
   juice
1 tablespoon Worcestershire
   sauce
1 tablespoon molasses

Cut halibut into 4 equal pieces and place in flat-bottom glass dish. Heat oil in saucepan. When hot, add onion, bell peppers, and garlic, and sauté until soft. Stir in tomato sauce, lemon juice, Worcestershire sauce, and molasses, and cook 5 minutes, or until flavors have blended. Cool, then pour over fish. Marinate in refrigerator for 1 hour.

Grill over charcoal fire, about 5 minutes per side, basting with sauce. Serve immediately.

Halibut with Spinach   SERVES 4

Martha Lawrence is a favorite customer and a pleasure to wait on because she is always open to fresh ideas and experimentation. She loves fish and enjoys creating new dishes, such as this one.

1 ½-pound halibut filet
½ cup flour
Salt and pepper to taste
4 tablespoons unsalted
   butter

¾ cup dry white wine
10-ounce bag fresh spinach
½ cup crème fraîche (see
   p. 16)
Nutmeg

Cut halibut into 4 equal pieces. On plate mix flour seasoned with salt and pepper, and dip fish pieces in mixture, coating lightly. Melt butter in large sauté pan over medium-high heat and add halibut, browning on both sides for about 2 minutes total. Turn heat down to medium, add wine, cover pan, and cook until done, about 10 minutes.

Meanwhile, wash and spin-dry spinach, then remove stems. Lay 2 or 3 leaves on top of each other, roll up like a cigar, and thinly slice crosswise into little strips.

When fish is done, remove it to platter and keep warm. Add spinach strips to sauté pan with liquid and simmer 2 minutes, or until wilted. Whisk in crème fraîche and season with salt and pepper. Spoon over fish, sprinkle with nutmeg, and serve.

Grilled Halibut with Rosemary-Garlic Marinade

SERVES 2

Halibut steaks have the bone and skin intact, which helps hold the flesh together when grilling. Once the fish is cooked, the bone and skin can easily be removed.

1-pound halibut steak, 1
    inch thick

ROSEMARY-GARLIC MARINADE

1 teaspoon minced garlic	¼ teaspoon salt
2 tablespoons fresh lemon juice	4 tablespoons olive oil
1 teaspoon dried rosemary, crumbled	

Place halibut in plastic bag. In bowl combine marinade ingredients and whisk together well. Pour into bag, making sure marinade coats fish. Close tightly, place in flat-bottom dish, and marinate 1-2 hours in refrigerator.

When ready to cook, remove fish and marinade from bag. Grill steaks about 2 inches from coals for 5 minutes per side, basting with marinade to keep flesh moist.

Broiled Halibut with Red Pepper Sauce   SERVES 4

When I ask my customers who always buy halibut why they prefer it over other fish, they generally say, "Because it's white." So I try to introduce them to other white fish, such as tilefish, which has a subtle flavor like halibut but a different texture.

2 pounds halibut steaks, 1 inch thick
2 tablespoons unsalted butter
2 teaspoons fresh lemon juice

Red Pepper Sauce (recipe follows)
Chopped fresh parsley for garnish

Place steaks on broiler pan. Melt butter, add lemon juice, and brush over both sides of fish. Put under preheated broiler for 4-5 minutes per side, basting frequently. Place fish on platter, spoon sauce over top, and garnish with chopped parsley.

RED PEPPER SAUCE

1 red bell pepper
2 tablespoons water

4 tablespoons heavy cream
½ teaspoon sugar

Roast pepper in 500° oven for 10 minutes, or until skin is black. (If you have a gas stove, roast it right over the burner flame, holding it with a long-handled fork and turning the pepper to scorch all the skin.) Enclose pepper in paper bag to cool so it is easier to handle. Tear in half, remove stem and seeds, and peel off and discard skin. Put in food processor fitted with metal blade, add water, and purée. Transfer to small saucepan, add cream and sugar, and heat.

Herring (Atlantic)

Clupea harengus

Herring are among the most valuable food fish. They are eaten not only by people but also by many other fish, birds, and mammals. Atlantic herring travel in large schools from Greenland to North Carolina and grow to lengths of up to 18 inches, with 10 inches being average. The best herring have a high fat content, which occurs when they are spawning. When fresh, herring are best broiled, grilled, or fried.

"Sardine" is a name given to a number of young 3- to 6-inch fish in the herring family. Fresh sardines are delicious and taste completely different from canned. If you are lucky enough to find them fresh in the market, the best way to cook them is over a charcoal grill, leaving the heads and tails on but removing the innards. Rub them with olive oil, place them on the grill, and brown both sides. Eat whole, pulling the flesh off the backbone with your teeth.

"Kippers" are a large whole herring that has been split, brined, air-dried, and smoked over hardwood. They make a fine breakfast served

with scrambled eggs. Broil or fry them in butter for 3-4 minutes, then remove the center
backbone and eat the strong smoky flesh off
the skin.

"Pickled herring" is a delicatessen term applied to pieces or whole filets of herring that
have been brined and then marinated in vinegar and spices. When buying commercially
prepared herring, look for those labeled "herring in white wine." You can add sour cream or
a mustard sauce of your choice.

Pickled Herring in Mustard Sauce

SERVES 6 AS FIRST COURSE

Mrs. Melville Chapin, a customer of The Fishmonger, buys a lot of herring. One day when I asked her why, she gave me this recipe, which speaks for itself.

8 herring filets, marinated in
   wine
4 tablespoons Dijon mustard
4 tablespoons sugar
4 tablespoons balsamic
   vinegar

2 tablespoons fresh lemon
   juice
½ cup chopped fresh dill
¼ teaspoon freshly ground
   black pepper
1 cup peanut oil or corn oil

Drain herring filets of excess juice and discard onions and spices. Trim off bones, if present. In bowl whisk together mustard, sugar, vinegar, and lemon juice. Add dill, pepper, and oil. Whisk until well blended. Add herring and marinate 6 hours. Serve with black bread.

The Fishmonger Herring in Sour Cream with Dill

MAKES ABOUT 2 PINTS

When grating the lemon rind, be sure to remove only the zest and none of the bitter white pulp.

2 pounds herring marinated
   in wine
Juice and grated rind
   of 1 lemon
2 cups sour cream

1 small red onion, thinly
   sliced
3 tablespoons chopped fresh
   dill (3 teaspoons dried)

Drain marinated herring of excess juice and discard onions and spices. Cut herring into bite-size pieces and put into mixing bowl. Add lemon juice and rind, sour cream, onion, and dill, and mix to combine. Serve as an hors d'oeuvre with crackers or rye bread.

Red Herring Salad

SERVES 6-8

My version of this Russian dish omits the veal or ham usually included.

2 pounds herring marinated
   in wine
1 large potato
3 fresh beets
¾ cup mayonnaise (see
p. 283)
¾ cup sour cream
2 tablespoons capers,
   squeeze-drained

1 tablespoon prepared
   horseradish
1 Granny Smith apple, cored
   and diced
1 dill pickle, seeded and
   diced
2 hard-boiled eggs, coarsely
   chopped

Drain herring, discarding onions and spices. Dice and set aside. Peel and dice potato, and cook in boiling water until done but still firm. Plunge in ice water to stop cooking, cool, and drain. Peel and dice beets, and cook in boiling water until just done, as with potatoes. Plunge in ice water, cool, and drain.

While potatoes and beets cool, combine mayonnaise and sour cream. Add capers and horseradish, and mix thoroughly.

In bowl combine cooked potatoes and beets, apple, pickle, and hard-boiled eggs. Toss to mix. Add herring and stir in dressing, a little at a time, until coated but not runny. Serve as part of a buffet or brunch.

Lobster

Homarus americanus

The American lobster is abundant in the waters around Maine, Massachusetts, Newfoundland, and Nova Scotia and can be found as far south as North Carolina. Yet it is New England's and Canada's cold waters, rocky coastlines, and shallow harbors that are especially suited to this large marine crustacean.

Lobsters are caught in baited traps that rest on the ocean bottom, but of those trapped, only a small portion are of legal salable size: 81 millimeters (or 3.19 inches) in length, measured from the rear of the eye socket to the beginning of the tail. It can take five to seven years for a lobster to reach this size, and those that are smaller, plus any egg-bearing females, are tossed back into the sea to be caught another time.

During June and July lobsters might have soft shells, which indicates that they recently shed their shells, or "molted." (A lobster can molt four or five times over its lifetime.) Because they are defenseless at this point, they are easily caught and readily available in markets, at a reduced price. Although there won't be as much meat in them as during their hard-shell stage, the meat is usually much sweeter.

Lobsters are scavengers of the ocean floor and eat just about anything — the ranker the bait, the better. Their powerful digestive system rids them of wastes and turns their flesh into a firm, sweet-tasting delicacy.

When buying lobsters, be sure to select those that are most active, with claws snapping and tails arching. The shells are a dark greenish blue with a mottling of brown throughout, but once cooked, they turn bright vermilion.

Lobsters are sold according to their weight. The smallest whole size you can buy is a 1-pound, or "chicken," lobster. (A "cull" is a lobster that has lost a claw and usually weighs less than a pound.) The meat yield of a 1-pound lobster is a little less than ¼ pound, yet this size has the highest flesh-to-shell ratio and is usually lowest in price. You will get more edible lobster meat from two 1-pound lobsters than from one 2-pound lobster.

The next larger size lobsters are called "selects," weighing from 1¼ to 1½ pounds each. "Large" lobsters weigh 1½ to 2 pounds each, and "jumbos" weigh 2 pounds or more. It has been said that these larger lobsters are tougher and less tasty than the smaller ones, but I disagree. The texture is determined by how they are cooked, and the taste is affected by the lobster's diet. If a lobster had a plentiful supply of seaweed, it will have an iodine or metallic taste.

The coral (roe), a red egglike mass in female lobsters, and the tomalley (liver), a pea-green substance in all lobster bodies, are both edible. Some people consider these delicacies, while others choose to leave them untouched. It's a matter of personal preference.

When baking lobster, I allow 12 minutes per pound; when broiling, 8 minutes; and when boiling, the following:

1 pound	10 minutes
1¼ pounds	12 minutes
1½ pounds	15 minutes
2 pounds	18 minutes
2½ pounds	20 minutes
3-5 pounds	21-25 minutes

How to Boil and Eat a Lobster

Put a couple inches of water in a large pot and bring to a boil. (A lobster does not have to be submerged in water to cook properly. The steam from the boiling water cooks it faster than the water itself and prevents it from becoming waterlogged.) Grab the lobster firmly in the middle of the back and put into the pot headfirst. Cover the pot and cook according to the lobster's weight, timing from when the lobster is put in the pot (see chart on p. 107). (If the lobster has just molted and the shell is soft, allow 7 minutes per pound.) When cooking time is up, remove the lobster to a platter, serve with drawn butter, and dig in.

Eating a boiled lobster requires an open mind and a willing spirit. First, I break off the tail from the body and let the liquid drain out. Because I like the tail best, I usually save that for when I'm halfway through. Next, I sever a claw from the body and separate it from the knuckles. I pull the "thumb" part back until it breaks off, sometimes leaving its little morsel of flesh intact. Then, with a large nutcracker, I crack the shell of the claw in the middle and extract the large chunk of meat. I also crack the knuckles and use the tine of a fork to extract the flesh — sweet, tender bites.

Now I turn my attention to the tail. I break off the tail ends, sucking out the meat and juices in each section. Then I push the meat back out of its shell. The green at the top end is the tomalley, and any red eggs that appear are the coral; both have a nice, sweet taste. I tear down the back flesh, or "shin," that goes across the back of the tail, exposing and discarding the intestine, which looks like a gray or white tube . Now I eat the tail — savoring each bite.

I break off the little feeler claws close to the

body shell and suck out the essence, one section at a time. Then I move on to the last claw and knuckles. I pick apart the body by lifting off the back shell and breaking the body cavity into pieces. Little morsels of meat can be found where the feeler claws attach to the body, and on bigger lobsters, the pickin's are real good.

Break the tail section from the body.

Sever the claws from the body and separate them from the knuckles.

Pull the "thumb" back until it breaks off.

Crack both claws in the middle using a nutcracker.

Break off each tail end or "flipper."

Using a fork, pry out the meat from the tail section.

Break off individual feeler claws.

Lift off the back shell and break the body cavity into pieces.

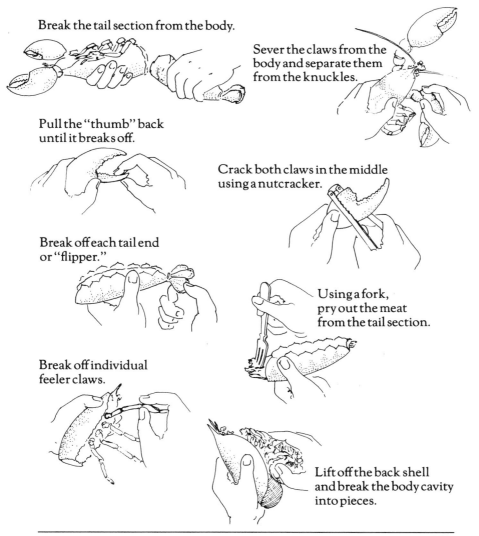

Lobster Bisque   SERVES 6

Thalia Large worked for me at The Fishmonger for five years. She was a graduate of the Rhode Island School of Design, and her artistry was apparent even in the food she prepared.

3 live 1-pound lobsters or
  two 1½-pound lobsters
6 tablespoons unsalted
  butter
⅓ cup diced carrot
1 medium onion, diced
2 bay leaves, crumbled
½ teaspoon dried thyme
4 tablespoons cognac

½ cup dry white wine
¾ cup bottled clam juice
1 tablespoon dry sherry or
  Madeira
3 tablespoons flour
1 tablespoon tomato paste
3 cups light cream, scalded
1½ cups heavy cream
Watercress sprigs for garnish

Split each live lobster in half, removing intestine and stomach. Cut entire lobster crosswise into 2-inch pieces and crack claws and knuckles in half. Set aside.

In large sauté pan melt 3 tablespoons of the butter and add carrot and onion. Cook until onion is soft, about 4 minutes. Add bay leaves, thyme, and cut-up lobster. Sauté until lobster turns red, about 5 minutes, making sure all sides are cooked.

Add 2 tablespoons of the cognac and ignite. When flame goes out, add white wine, clam juice, and sherry. Simmer 15 minutes. Remove lobster with slotted spoon, reserving liquid in pan, and cool. Remove meat from shells and cut meat into bite-size pieces. Set aside. Put shells (except for claws) and reserved broth and vegetables from sauté pan in food processor fitted with metal blade and purée.

In sauté pan melt remaining 3 tablespoons butter and add flour to make a roux. Cook 2 minutes, then add tomato paste. Pour in scalded cream, whisking until sauce thickens. Combine puréed shell mixture and cream sauce in large nonreactive soup kettle. Cover and simmer 45 minutes.

Strain through fine double-mesh sieve to remove any shell particles. Return to kettle, add remaining 2 tablespoons cognac and heavy cream, and stir. Add lobster meat last to heat up in soup. Ladle into bowls and garnish each with sprig of watercress.

Lobster Salad
with Caper-Tarragon Mayonnaise

SERVES 6

For my daughter Rebecca's graduation from Buckingham, Browne &
Nichols, we had a garden party at home with this as the centerpiece.

2 pounds lobster meat, cut
   into ½-inch pieces
1½ cups diced celery
6 scallions, thinly sliced

½ cup watercress leaves,
   washed and spun dry
2 tablespoons chopped red
   bell pepper

CAPER-TARRAGON MAYONNAISE

1 cup mayonnaise (see
   p. 283)
½ cup sour cream
1 tablespoon chopped fresh
   tarragon (1 teaspoon
   dried)
2 tablespoons fresh lemon
   juice

1 tablespoon grated red
   onion
2 tablespoons capers,
   squeeze-drained and
   chopped

Combine lobster meat, celery, scallions, watercress leaves, and
bell pepper, tossing to mix.

In small bowl whisk together all ingredients for dressing. Pour
over lobster mixture just before serving and garnish as desired.

Lobster and Fresh Basil with Linguine   SERVES 4-6

The ease and elegance of this dish makes it ideal for entertaining.

1 pound lobster meat
2 tablespoons unsalted
 butter
2 tablespoons minced
 shallots
2 cups peeled, seeded, and
 chopped tomatoes
4 sun-dried tomatoes,
 chopped
1 cup fresh basil leaves,
 packed, then chopped

2 tablespoons Pernod
3 cups crème fraîche (see
 p. 16)
Salt and freshly ground
 white pepper to taste
1½ pounds fresh tomato
 linguine
6 fresh basil leaves for
 garnish

Cut lobster into 1-inch pieces and set aside. In sauté pan melt butter and add shallots. Cook 3 minutes, or until soft. Add chopped tomatoes, sun-dried tomatoes, and chopped basil, and cook 5 minutes. Add Pernod and cook 2 minutes more. Stir in crème fraîche and cook until bubbly, about 3 minutes. Season with salt and white pepper. Add lobster meat and cook 3 minutes more. Remove from heat.

Cook pasta al dente, about 3-4 minutes. Drain and put on serving platter. Spoon sauce over top and serve garnished with basil leaves.

Lobster Newburg   SERVES 3-4

To make this a seafood Newburg, simply add other cooked shellfish, such as scallops or shrimp. Allow ⅓ pound of meat per person.

5 live 1-pound lobsters or 1
 pound meat (about 3 cups)
4 tablespoons unsalted
 butter
½ teaspoon salt
¼ teaspoon cayenne pepper
3 tablespoons cognac

3 tablespoons dry sherry
1½ cups heavy cream
4 egg yolks
1 tablespoon fresh lemon
 juice
Paprika

Boil lobsters for 6 minutes and remove all meat. Cut into 2-inch pieces. In nonreactive skillet melt butter over medium heat, add lobster meat, and stir to coat. Sprinkle salt and cayenne over meat and stir. Add cognac, sherry, and 1 cup of the cream. Bring to boil and cook 2 minutes. Reduce heat to low. When bubbling stops, whisk together egg yolks and remaining ½ cup cream, and add to skillet. Cook over low heat until sauce thickens, but do not let boil. Stir in lemon juice. Serve over rice, fresh pasta, or toast points, and dust with paprika.

Baked Stuffed Lobster

SERVES 2

I realize that killing lobsters is not for everyone (luckily, they do not have vocal cords), but it is important to have them as fresh as possible before cooking. If you live close enough to your local fish market, ask to have the lobsters killed just before you arrive.

2 live 1¼- to 1½-pound lobsters	1 tablespoon chopped fresh tarragon
8 tablespoons unsalted butter	2 tablespoons finely chopped fresh parsley
1 clove garlic, minced	2 tablespoons dry sherry
¼ cup chopped onion	2 cups fresh bread crumbs
¼ cup diced red bell pepper	Salt and pepper to taste
2 tablespoons finely chopped scallion greens	

Lay live lobster on its back and place large knife down the center of its body. Give knife a whack with mallet so lobster is opened from head to tail, but not severed through back shell. Discard "craw," or stomach, located in top of body and long, gray intestine running down center of tail meat. Repeat with other lobster.

In skillet melt 6 tablespoons of the butter over medium heat. Add garlic, onion, and bell pepper, and sauté until soft, about 5 minutes. Stir in scallion greens, tarragon, parsley, and sherry. Cook 2 minutes. Add fresh bread crumbs, remove from heat, and mix thoroughly. Season with salt and pepper.

Stuff body cavity of each lobster and place in shallow baking dish. Dot each with remaining 2 tablespoons butter and bake in preheated oven at 400° for 20 minutes.

Lobster Thermidor

SERVES 4

This requires a lot of time, but you are well rewarded for your effort.

4 live 1¼- to 1½-pound
  lobsters
8 tablespoons unsalted
  butter
½ pound mushrooms, thinly
  sliced (about 1 cup)
2 tablespoons chopped
  shallots
2 tablespoons diced red bell
  pepper

¼ cup cognac
2 cups heavy cream
4 egg yolks
1 tablespoon Worcestershire
  sauce
½ teaspoon Tabasco
½ cup bread crumbs
½ cup freshly grated
  Parmesan cheese
Paprika

Boil lobsters 10 minutes, remove from pot, and set aside until cool to the touch. Break off claws and feeler feet, and slit body down the middle with large, sharp knife, making sure not to cut through back shell. Carefully remove tail meat, tomalley, and coral (if any), keeping back and tail shell intact, as this becomes the container for the thermidor mixture. Remove and discard long, gray intestine and sac behind head and eyes. Wipe body clean with paper towel and set aside.

Remove lobster meat from claws, knuckles, and tails, and cut into ½-inch cubes. Set aside. In large skillet melt 2 tablespoons of the butter, add mushrooms, and cook 5 minutes. Drain and set aside.

Melt 2 more tablespoons butter in skillet and add shallots and bell pepper. Cook until soft, about 3 minutes. Add lobster meat and stir to coat. Heat cognac in saucepan, pour over lobster, and ignite, swirling skillet until flames go out. Transfer lobster meat to bowl. Add 1½ cups heavy cream to skillet and simmer 5 minutes, or until cream is reduced and evenly coats metal spoon.

In bowl whisk remaining ½ cup heavy cream with egg yolks, Worcestershire sauce, and Tabasco. Turn down heat under reduced cream and add egg yolk mixture, stirring as you add. Cook until sauce thickens. Add lobster meat and stir to coat. Spoon mixture into lobster shells and spread with bread crumbs mixed with Parmesan cheese. Dot each lobster with remaining 4 tablespoons butter and sprinkle with paprika. Bake in preheated oven at 400° for 10-15 minutes, or until bubbly.

Tomalley Sauce and Tomalley Butter

MAKES ABOUT 1½ CUPS SAUCE;
½ CUP BUTTER

Lobster tomalley is the green liver found in the body of the lobster. Its distinctive, rich flavor perks up sauces and butters.

TOMALLEY SAUCE

4 tablespoons tomalley
3 tablespoons unsalted butter
3 tablespoons flour

1 cup milk, scalded
2 tablespoons sherry
⅛ teaspoon cayenne pepper
Salt to taste

Force tomalley through fine sieve into bowl. Set aside. Melt butter in saucepan, add flour to make a roux, and cook 3 minutes. Add scalded milk in steady stream, whisking as you pour. Add sherry, cayenne, and tomalley, and season with salt. Serve over pasta garnished with bits of lobster.

TOMALLEY BUTTER

8 tablespoons unsalted butter, softened
2 teaspoons fresh lemon juice

1 tablespoon tomalley from cooked lobster
Salt and pepper to taste

Put butter in bowl. Add lemon juice, tomalley that has been forced through sieve, and salt and pepper to taste. Mix with fork until blended and use on swordfish or bluefish. Shape leftover butter into log, seal in plastic wrap, and freeze until needed.

Mackerel (Atlantic)

Scomber scombrus

Atlantic mackerel are small, streamlined fish with dark steely blue or green wavy stripes on their upper backs and silvery gray-blue bellies. Like other dark-flesh fish, they are fast swimmers and travel in large, closely packed schools along the surface of the water as they feed on squid, shrimp, and other small seafood. As a result, they become prey for larger fish and mammals. They are an oily fish, high in omega-3, which breaks down cholesterol in our blood. Because of their oily, dark flesh, they are well suited for smoking.

Atlantic mackerel are found from Labrador to Cape Hatteras. Their average length is about 14 inches and their average weight between 1 and 3 pounds. The young mackerel, called "tinkers," are 6 to 10 inches long and are sweet and delicious.

Mackerel are sold whole or in filets; allow ¾ pound per person of the former, ½ pound of the latter. Mackerel can be baked, broiled, sautéed, or grilled over charcoal. You can use bluefish or tuna in place of mackerel in the following recipes.

Mackerel Gravlax   SERVES 4-6

Gravlax is a Scandinavian way of curing fish with salt and sugar. Salmon is traditionally used, but mackerel is much less expensive and very tasty.

2 whole mackerel, fileted, with skin (about 1 pound each)	½ cup sugar
	½ cup chopped fresh dill
	Mustard-Dill Sauce (see
¼ cup salt	p. 179)

Place filets flesh side down on plate. Combine salt and sugar, and sprinkle half the mixture over skin side of filets. Turn over and sprinkle remaining mixture over flesh side of filets. Distribute dill over flesh and put 2 corresponding filets together, like a sandwich. Place fish in flat-bottom glass or ceramic dish and lay plastic wrap on fish. Place 1 pound bag of dried beans or rice on top of fish as a weight. Refrigerate 24 hours, pouring off liquid that leaches out. Fish is done when it is firm and does not give when pressed with finger. To serve, remove from dish, discard juices, and slice on the diagonal with sharp knife. Serve with Mustard-Dill Sauce and dark rye bread.

Mackerel Seviche SERVES 8 AS APPETIZER

Either lemons or limes can be used here, whichever are less expensive. Be sure to discard the juice after marinating and use fresh juice when assembling the dish.

2 pounds mackerel filets, with skin
1 cup fresh lemon or lime juice
2 tomatoes, peeled, seeded, and coarsely chopped
1 or 2 fresh or canned hot green chilies (jalapeño or serrano)
¼ cup olive oil

2 tablespoons chopped fresh cilantro
Juice and grated rind of 1 lemon or lime
1 ripe avocado, peeled, seeded, and sliced
1 small Bermuda onion, sliced
Chopped fresh parsley and citrus slices for garnish

Check mackerel for bones and cut into ½-inch-thick pieces. Place in flat-bottom glass dish and toss with 1 cup lemon or lime juice. Cover with plastic wrap and marinate in refrigerator 12 hours, stirring occasionally. Drain off juice and discard. Transfer mackerel pieces to clean bowl, add tomatoes, and stir. Seed chilies, slice into rings, and add.

Whisk oil with cilantro and lemon or lime juice and rind. Pour over mackerel mixture and stir to coat. Divide among 8 salad plates, arrange avocado and onion slices around each serving, and garnish with fresh parsley and thin lemon or lime slices.

Mackerel with Gooseberry Sauce SERVES 4

The tartness of gooseberries blends nicely with the assertive flavor of mackerel.

4 mackerel filets (about ½ pound each)	2 tablespoons sugar
	Pinch of nutmeg
5 tablespoons unsalted butter	1 teaspoon fresh lemon juice
	Snipped scallion greens for garnish
½ pound fresh gooseberries*	

Check filets for bones and set aside while making sauce. Melt 2 tablespoons of the butter in saucepan. Add gooseberries and sauté, stirring constantly, for 10 minutes, or until they become a soft pulp. Rub fruit through fine sieve to remove seeds and skin. Put juice into clean saucepan. Add sugar, nutmeg, and lemon juice, and cook 2 minutes. Taste for sweetness and add more sugar if too tart. Keep warm while cooking mackerel.

Melt remaining 3 tablespoons butter in heavy skillet. Sauté filets, skin side up, for 2 minutes. Turn over and cook 2-3 minutes, or until flesh flakes when tested with fork. Transfer mackerel to warm platter, pour sauce over top, and garnish with snipped scallion greens.

* Rhubarb can be used instead of gooseberries as follows:

RHUBARB SAUCE

½ pound rhubarb, sliced	1 tablespoon sour cream for garnish
4 tablespoons water	
2 tablespoons sugar	
1 teaspoon grated lemon rind	

Stir rhubarb into water and sugar, and simmer 20 minutes, or until soft. Cool and process in food processor fitted with metal blade. Put purée through fine mesh sieve and discard pulp. Reheat rhubarb juice in saucepan, add lemon rind, and taste for sweetness, adding more sugar if too tart. Pour over cooked mackerel filets and garnish with sour cream.

Broiled or Grilled Mackerel SERVES 2

Mackerel, like bluefish, has a high oil content and will broil nicely without becoming dry. Its distinctive taste will prevail even with the addition of sharp condiments.

2 whole mackerel, split (about ¾ pound each)	Mint Butter or Mustard Butter (recipes follow)

Lay mackerel skin side down and dot each with 1 tablespoon Mint Butter or Mustard Butter. If broiling, place on foil-lined broiler pan; if grilling, place directly on grill. Cook 6-8 minutes. When done, transfer to serving platter, remove backbone and discard, and dot flesh with more butter right before serving.

MINT BUTTER

4 tablespoons unsalted butter, softened	2 teaspoons tarragon vinegar
2 teaspoons chopped fresh mint	

Using fork, combine all ingredients until thoroughly blended. Store unused butter, sealed in plastic wrap, in freezer.

MUSTARD BUTTER

4 tablespoons unsalted butter, softened	2 teaspoons Dijon mustard
2 teaspoons fresh lemon juice	

Using fork, combine all ingredients until thoroughly blended. Wrap leftover butter in plastic wrap and freeze.

Mackerel with Dill and Cucumber   SERVES 6

This sauce can be made less fattening by using yogurt instead of sour cream.

6 mackerel filets (about ½ pound each)
2 medium cucumbers
6 tablespoons unsalted butter
¼ cup sliced scallions
2 tablespoons chopped fresh parsley
2 tablespoons chopped fresh dill

1 tablespoon fresh lemon juice
½ cup sour cream or yogurt
Salt and pepper to taste
Flour seasoned with salt and pepper
Lemon wedges and chopped fresh dill for garnish

Check filets for bones and set aside. Peel cucumbers and cut in half lengthwise. Scrape out seeds and cut each half into thin slices. In skillet melt 2 tablespoons of the butter over medium heat and sauté cucumbers, scallions, parsley, and dill until cucumber is limp and wilted. Add lemon juice and sour cream, and season with salt and pepper. Keep warm while cooking filets.

Melt remaining 4 tablespoons butter in large sauté pan. Dredge filets in seasoned flour and cook over medium-high heat for 3 minutes per side. Transfer to warm platter, pour cucumber sauce over top, and garnish with lemon wedges and sprinkling of fresh dill.

Baked Stuffed Mackerel   SERVES 4-6

Mackerel, like small bluefish, is an impressive fish to bake whole. Stuffing it adds more texture and flavor and makes a nicer presentation.

2 whole mackerel (about 1½ pounds each)
5 tablespoons unsalted butter
1 cup chopped onion
¾ cup diced green bell pepper

2 cloves garlic, minced
1 cup peeled, seeded, and diced tomato
2 teaspoons dried basil
2 teaspoons dried oregano
½ teaspoon salt
¼ teaspoon black pepper

Remove head and intestines from mackerel and split in half, making sure to leave back skin intact (try to leave tail on). Discard backbone and small rib bones. Rinse thoroughly under cold running water to remove excess blood and innards. Pat dry with paper towel.

In skillet melt 3 tablespoons of the butter and sauté onion, bell pepper, and garlic until onion is soft and translucent. Add diced tomato, basil, oregano, salt, and black pepper. Cook 3 minutes.

Spoon vegetable mixture into cavity of mackerel and tie with twine to keep stuffing from seeping out while cooking. Place in buttered baking dish and dot top with remaining 2 tablespoons butter. Bake in preheated oven at 350° for 20 minutes, basting every 10 minutes with additional melted butter.

Mackerel with Mustard Hollandaise   SERVES 2

Mustard either without seeds (Dijon) or with them (Pommery) makes a delicious sauce for mackerel.

1 pound mackerel filets	1 tablespoon unsalted butter

MUSTARD HOLLANDAISE

8 tablespoons unsalted butter	1 tablespoon Dijon or Pommery mustard
2 egg yolks	
1 tablespoon fresh lemon juice	

Check filets for bones. Place on foil-lined broiler pan, dot with 1 tablespoon butter, and set aside while making hollandaise.

In saucepan melt 8 tablespoons butter to bubbling. Meanwhile, whisk egg yolks in top of double boiler until creamy dark yellow. Place over hot water and add melted butter in slow stream, whisking as you add. Cook over hot water until thickened. Add lemon juice and mustard, and whisk to blend. (If hollandaise separates, add a dash of boiling water and whisk until smooth.)

Broil mackerel, skin side down, for 5 minutes. Spoon hollandaise over top and serve.

Mahi-Mahi
(Dolphin Fish)

Coryphaena hippurus

In native Hawaiian, mahi-mahi means "strong-strong," and for marketing reasons, we at The Fishmonger prefer to use the Hawaiian name. Let me assure you that this dolphin fish is *not* related to the mammal of the same name. That dolphin is of the porpoise family; mahi-mahi is not.

Mahi-mahi is a delicious meaty fish comparable in taste to swordfish. It lives in warm, tropical waters and is found off Florida and Hawaii all year long. In the summer months, some follow the Gulf Stream and can be found feeding as far north as Cape Cod.

These fish put up a good fight when caught and rank next to marlin and sailfish in popularity with sport fishermen. Mahi-mahi are beautiful, with a brilliant blue and silver coloring dappled with yellow and green, which unfortunately fades when the fish dies. They range in size from 5 to 40 pounds, with 10 to 20 pounds being average.

Mahi-mahi is usually sold fileted and is about half the price of swordfish. It is excellent grilled, baked, pan-fried, or smoked, but be sure to leave the skin on while cooking to keep the thick flesh intact. You can use mahi-mahi in most recipes calling for swordfish or marlin.

Mahi-Mahi Seviche SERVES 4

As with any fish used in making seviche, be sure to use only the freshest.

1 pound mahi-mahi filets
¾ cup fresh lime juice (about
   6 limes)
3 medium tomatoes, peeled,
   seeded, and chopped
1 small Bermuda onion,
   sliced
1 jalapeño pepper, seeded
   and sliced
1 tablespoon chopped fresh
   cilantro

3 tablespoons olive oil
2 tablespoons fresh lemon
   juice
½ teaspoon salt
¼ teaspoon freshly ground
   black pepper
Bibb lettuce leaves
1 avocado, peeled, seeded,
   and sliced, for garnish

Remove skin from fish and discard. Cut mahi-mahi into 1-inch cubes and place in flat-bottom nonreactive dish. Cover with lime juice, stirring to coat all sides, and refrigerate 6-12 hours, or until fish is opaque throughout.

In medium-size bowl mix together tomatoes, onion, jalapeño, and cilantro. In separate bowl combine oil, lemon juice, salt, and pepper, and pour over vegetables, stirring to blend. Drain fish of lime juice and mix mahi-mahi with vegetables. Place lettuce leaf on each of 4 small plates, mound a serving of seviche on each leaf, and garnish with avocado slices.

Grilled Mahi-Mahi SERVES 2

This firm-textured fish is ideal for grilling.

1 pound mahi-mahi filets,
   with skin
Juice of 2 limes
½ cup bottled chili sauce
2 tablespoons olive oil

1 tablespoon chopped fresh
   cilantro
1 tablespoon chopped
   scallions for garnish

Cut mahi-mahi into 2 equal pieces and place in flat-bottom non-reactive dish. Combine lime juice, chili sauce, oil, and cilantro, and pour over fish, stirring to coat. Marinate in refrigerator 1-2 hours.

Heat charcoal briquettes to just past red-coal stage and grill fish 3-5 minutes per side depending on thickness, basting with extra marinade. Serve garnished with chopped scallions.

Fried Mahi-Mahi
with Sesame Seed Coating

SERVES 4

Abby, Sally, Serita, Rosie, and I all played together in the summer when we were young. Now in our forties, we have been reunited, and our "playing" comes in the form of dinner parties. This is a recipe that I have fixed for them when we've gathered at my house.

2 pounds mahi-mahi filets	2 tablespoons fresh lemon
¼ cup peanut oil	juice
2 tablespoons rice wine	½ cup sesame seeds
2 tablespoons rice vinegar	3 tablespoons unsalted
2 tablespoons soy sauce	butter
1 clove garlic, minced	Chopped scallion greens for
1 tablespoon minced	garnish
gingerroot	

Remove skin from fish and discard. Cut mahi-mahi into 4 equal pieces and place in flat-bottom glass dish. In small bowl combine oil, wine, vinegar, soy sauce, garlic, gingerroot, and lemon juice. Pour over fish and let marinate in refrigerator 1 hour.

In nonstick skillet toast sesame seeds over medium-high heat, stirring constantly, until evenly browned. Set aside.

Remove fish pieces from marinade and coat with sesame seeds. Melt butter in skillet and cook fish over medium-high heat for 3-5 minutes per side. Serve garnished with chopped scallion greens.

Marlin (Atlantic)

Blue *(Makaira nigricans)*
White *(Tetrapturus albidus)*

The blue marlin is the larger of the two Atlantic marlin, averaging around 200 to 300 pounds. Abundant off the Florida coast, it is a solitary swimmer and feeds near the ocean's surface, dining on squid and other small fish. It is equipped for rapid bursts of speed and has a dark, reddish flesh similar to that of tuna.

The white marlin is a much smaller fish, averaging around 80 to 100 pounds, and can be found as far north as New England in the summer. Its flesh is a lighter pinkish tan color.

Marlin has a sweet taste and a firm, solid texture similar to that of turkey breast. Marlin can be baked, broiled, or grilled, but be careful not to overcook it — better to err on the side of undercooking. It is leaner than swordfish, tuna, and shark, and should be marinated before grilling or broiling and basted while cooking so it can absorb more oil. Marlin is about half the price of swordfish and has a heartier flavor. It can be used in most recipes calling for swordfish, tuna, or mako shark.

Broiled Marlin with Chutney Butter SERVES 4

Compound butters taste wonderful with many foods, so it's always a good idea to have some extra on hand in the freezer.

2 pounds marlin steaks,
   1 inch thick
2 tablespoons unsalted
   butter

2 tablespoons fresh lemon
   juice

CHUTNEY BUTTER

6 tablespoons unsalted
   butter, softened
1 tablespoon chopped
   chutney

1 teaspoon Worcestershire
   sauce
1 tablespoon chili sauce

Place marlin steaks on broiler pan. Dot tops with butter and sprinkle with lemon juice. Broil 3 inches from heat for 4-5 minutes per side. Meanwhile, thoroughly combine all ingredients for Chutney Butter. When steaks are done, transfer to serving platter, dot with Chutney Butter, and serve immediately.

Grilled Marlin with Hot Chili Sauce SERVES 6

An ancho chili is a dried red chili about 2 to 3 inches long. Its flavor is full yet milder than its green chili cousin.

3 pounds marlin steaks, 1
   inch thick
2 tablespoons olive oil
1 cup chopped onion
1 clove garlic, minced
⅛ teaspoon ground cloves
¼ teaspoon cinnamon
¼ teaspoon dried oregano
¼ teaspoon ground cumin
½ teaspoon dried thyme

1 teaspoon sugar
3 tomatoes, peeled, seeded,
   and chopped
6 ancho chilies, stemmed,
   seeded, torn into pieces,
   and soaked 1 hour in
   1 cup water
3 tablespoons fresh lemon
   juice

Brush steaks with oil and set aside while making sauce. Heat 2 tablespoons oil in skillet and add onion and garlic. Sauté until translucent, about 3-5 minutes. Add cloves, cinnamon, oregano, cumin, thyme, and sugar, stirring to blend. Add tomatoes and chilies, along with soaking water, and cook 5 minutes over medium heat. Let mixture cool slightly. Pour into food processor fitted with metal blade and purée 15-20 seconds. Return to skillet and cook 5 minutes more over medium heat, or until sauce thickens. Stir in lemon juice.

Grill marlin steaks over charcoal fire 4-5 minutes per side, brushing from time to time with additional oil. When done, transfer steaks to platter, spoon on sauce, and serve immediately.

Grilled Marlin Kebabs SERVES 4

Marlin has a unique backbone structure. At The Fishmonger, Howard Richardson cleaned a section of one and displayed it on top of the fish case, along with a set of red snapper jawbones and wolffish teeth. My customers were intrigued by the "exhibit" and still ask for more lessons in fish anatomy and identification.

2 pounds marlin steaks, 1 inch thick	3 cloves garlic, minced
½ cup olive oil	¼ teaspoon cayenne pepper
⅓ cup fresh lemon juice	½ teaspoon salt
½ cup chopped onion	½ cup chopped fresh basil

Cut marlin into 1-inch chunks and put in flat-bottom glass dish. In food processor fitted with metal blade combine oil, lemon juice, onion, garlic, cayenne, salt, and basil. Blend 20 seconds, or until well mixed. Pour over fish chunks and stir to coat evenly. Marinate in refrigerator 1 hour.

Place fish chunks on skewers and grill 7-10 minutes, turning and basting frequently with marinade. Brush with marinade again right before serving.

Monkfish

Lophius piscatorius

The monkfish sits on the bottom of the ocean waiting for unsuspecting prey to be enticed by its intricate "lure," which dangles from its head. Because this appendage looks a bit like a rod and line, monkfish are sometimes called "anglers." Other names, such as "goose," "frog," "belly," and "sea devil," also have been given to this bizarre-looking creature, which the French call "lotte."

In Europe during the Middle Ages fishermen in search of cod frequently found this odd fish in their nets. They considered it to be more head and teeth than anything else and routinely discarded it to die on the beach as they sorted their catch. What the local townspeople didn't want, the poor, hungry monks did, and thus the name "monkfish" came to be.

Monkfish are covered with a slippery, brown, scaleless skin, which acts as a camouflage. They will eat almost anything they encounter, from sharks to diving ducks and gulls. They range from Newfoundland to North Carolina and can grow to 4 feet long and weigh up to 50 pounds.

The freshness and trimming of monkfish are very important. When buying cleaned monkfish filets, make sure the flesh has a pink tinge; if it is too white or gray, the fish was probably frozen or is not fresh. In preparing the filets for cooking, it is essential to trim all the excess red fleshy membrane from the loins; otherwise, this shrinks and becomes tough, distorting the clean, pure texture of the flesh.

Monkfish has a sweet, mild flavor and a firm texture that lends itself to a variety of cooking methods. It can be pounded flat into cutlets and sautéed, breaded and fried, or stir-fried with vegetables. It can be marinated, broiled, grilled, poached, or steamed.

When cooked, monkfish is similar to lobster and thus is sometimes called "poor man's lobster." Traditionally, it has been one of the main fish in bouillabaisse and will hold its shape indefinitely in any soup, stew, or casserole. It is this versatility that has made monkfish a favorite of many cooks.

This is the fish Julia Child made "famous" when she brought it to the public's attention on her television program. Because of its growing popularity, monkfish is becoming scarce and its price is rising.

Cusk and wolffish work well as substitutes for monkfish.

Roasted Monkfish with Mustard Coating   SERVES 4

A whole loin of monkfish can be roasted just as you would a leg of lamb or rolled beef. There is no fat on monkfish, so adding butter will help it brown. When it is ready to serve, carve into large, thick slices.

2 pounds loin of monkfish

3 tablespoons unsalted
  butter, melted

MUSTARD COATING

3 tablespoons Pommery
  mustard
1 tablespoon Dijon mustard
2 cloves garlic, minced
1 tablespoon fresh rosemary
  (1 teaspoon dried)

Freshly ground black pepper
  to taste
2 tablespoons unsalted
  butter, melted
½ cup bread crumbs

Trim monkfish of its red membrane and liberally brush loin with melted butter. Chill, and prepare Mustard Coating.

In bowl combine mustards, garlic, rosemary, and black pepper. Add butter and bread crumbs, and combine thoroughly. Press coating over top of monkfish, put in roasting pan, and bake in preheated oven at 350° for 20-30 minutes.

Monkfish in Fresh Tomato Sauce SERVES 4

New Yorker *cartoonist Roz Chast is my favorite, and we frequently post her cartoons on the back of the cash register for everyone to read. I'm waiting for her to do something about monkfish, for I think it's Roz's kind of fish.*

1½ pounds monkfish	¼ cup dry red wine
¼ cup olive oil	1 tablespoon tomato paste
1 cup chopped onion	Salt and pepper to taste
1 tablespoon minced garlic	Chopped fresh parsley or
4 tomatoes, peeled, seeded, and chopped (about 2 cups)	basil for garnish

Trim red fleshy membrane from monkfish and discard. Cut into 8 pieces and set aside. In skillet heat oil over medium heat, add onion and garlic, and sauté until soft, about 3 minutes. Add tomatoes and stir, cooking 4 minutes more. Stir in red wine and tomato paste, and simmer 10 minutes.

Lay monkfish pieces on top of tomato mixture. Cover and cook 5 minutes. Turn over fish and cook another 5 minutes, or until done. Season with salt and pepper. Serve over cooked buttered pasta and garnish with chopped parsley or basil.

Cold Poached Monkfish with Herb Dressing SERVES 6

Poaching keeps fish from drying out and becoming rubbery, plus it is a low-calorie cooking method.

2 pounds monkfish	4 whole peppercorns
2 cups water	Boston lettuce
1 cup dry white wine	Tarragon Mayonnaise or
1 rib celery, chopped	Yogurt-Dill Dressing
1 onion, peeled and coarsely chopped	(recipes follow)
1 carrot, peeled and chopped	Tomato wedges, cucumber slices, and watercress
2 bay leaves	sprigs for garnish
½ teaspoon salt	

Trim monkfish of red membrane and cut fish into 1½-inch chunks. In enamel or stainless steel saucepan combine water, wine, celery, onion, carrot, bay leaves, salt, and peppercorns. Simmer 10 minutes. Add monkfish chunks, simmer 2 minutes, then turn off heat and let stand in liquid 5 minutes. Remove monkfish to covered container and fill three quarters full with poaching liquid. Refrigerate until cold.

When ready to serve, drain monkfish thoroughly. Line serving platter with Boston lettuce and mound monkfish in middle. Drizzle dressing over fish and serve extra dressing on the side. Garnish platter with tomato wedges, cucumber slices, and watercress sprigs.

TARRAGON MAYONNAISE

2 shallots, minced
2 tablespoons tarragon
  vinegar
2 tablespoons dry white wine
1 tablespoon chopped fresh
  tarragon (1 teaspoon
  dried)

1 cup mayonnaise (see p. 283)
1 cup sour cream
2 tablespoons capers,
  squeeze-drained

In small saucepan over medium heat cook shallots with vinegar, wine, and tarragon until liquid evaporates and glaze forms, about 5 minutes. Cool, then combine with mayonnaise, sour cream, and capers.

YOGURT-DILL DRESSING

1½ cups plain yogurt
1 tablespoon minced onion
2 tablespoons chopped fresh
  dill

2 tablespoons capers,
  squeeze-drained
1 tablespoon fresh lemon
  juice

Drain yogurt in fine-mesh sieve for 1 hour to remove excess liquid. Combine with onion, dill, capers, and lemon juice, and blend.

Monkfish in Muscadet Wine SERVES 4

I received this recipe from Maison Robert years ago, when I first started selling monkfish at The Fishmonger. Maison Robert was one of the first restaurants in Boston to put monkfish on its menu — back in 1978.

1½ pounds monkfish	1 medium carrot, finely
4 tablespoons unsalted	diced
butter	2 cups Muscadet wine
2 shallots, finely chopped	⅓ cup heavy cream
1 leek, rinsed and sliced	⅓ pound white seedless
(white part only)	grapes, halved (optional)

Trim monkfish of red membrane, cut into 1-inch chunks, and set aside. Melt 3 tablespoons of the butter over medium heat in enamel or stainless steel saucepan. Add shallots and leek, and sauté 2 minutes. Add carrot and cook 5 minutes. Add monkfish chunks and stir well to combine. Pour in wine, bring to a simmer, and cook 3 minutes. Cover, remove from heat, and let sit 6 minutes.

With slotted spoon, remove fish and vegetables from liquid and keep warm on serving platter. Return liquid to heat and reduce to one quarter of the volume. Remove from heat and add remaining 1 tablespoon butter and heavy cream, whisking together. Return to low heat and warm, making sure not to let boil. Add seedless grapes if desired, pour over fish and vegetables, and serve immediately.

Monkfish with Dried Fruit SERVES 4

The tartness of dried fruit combines beautifully with monkfish. This makes a fine entrée for a special dinner.

1½ pounds monkfish	Salt and freshly ground black
8 tablespoons unsalted	pepper to taste
butter	½ cup crème fraîche (see
¼ cup cognac	p. 16), sour cream, or
½ pound dried fruit, cut into	yogurt
pieces and soaked in water	2 tablespoons Dijon mustard
to cover for 1 hour (any	Chopped fresh parsley for
combination of apricots,	garnish
pears, prunes, etc.)	

Trim monkfish and cut into 4 thick serving chunks. Melt 4 tablespoons of the butter in saucepan over medium heat and sear monkfish briefly on all sides until lightly browned. Add cognac, let it warm, then ignite. Shake pan back and forth until flames are extinguished. Add dried fruit and season with salt and pepper. Cover and simmer over low heat for 6 minutes. Turn over monkfish and cook 6 minutes more.

With slotted spoon, transfer monkfish and fruit to warm serving platter. Add crème fraîche and mustard to juices in pan, whisking until blended. Heat to simmer and cook 3 minutes, then whisk in remaining 4 tablespoons butter, 1 tablespoon at a time, until blended. Pour over monkfish and fruit, and garnish with chopped fresh parsley.

Sautéed Monkfish and Fresh Vegetables   SERVES 2

We make this recipe often at The Fishmonger for our lunch. It's easy, nutritious, and low in calories.

1 pound monkfish
4 tablespoons peanut oil
2 cloves garlic, minced
2 leeks, rinsed and sliced
  (white part only)
½ cup dry white wine or
  water
1 carrot, julienned
6 broccoli florets

4 stalks asparagus, cut up
1 cup sliced mushrooms
12 snow peas
1 tablespoon minced
  gingerroot
Zest of ½ orange, sliced into
  tiny strips*
2 scallions, sliced, for
  garnish

Trim monkfish, cut into 1-inch chunks, and set aside. In skillet heat oil over high heat until hot and bubbly. Add garlic and leeks, and cook 2 minutes, stirring constantly so they won't burn. Add monkfish chunks and sauté 3 minutes, or until browned. Pour in wine and bring to simmer. Add carrot, broccoli, and asparagus, and cook, stirring often, for 3 minutes. Stir in mushrooms and snow peas, and cook 2 minutes, or until vegetables are done but still crisp. Add gingerroot and orange zest, and cook 1 minute more. Transfer to warm dish and garnish with scallions.

* To obtain the zest of the orange, use a sharp vegetable peeler and remove a thin layer of skin. Then cut these pieces into very thin strips with a sharp knife.

Monkfish in Tarragon Cream Sauce SERVES 4-6

A rich and creamy entrée. Serve with boiled new potatoes and fresh broccoli or green beans.

2 pounds monkfish
3 tablespoons unsalted
   butter
2 tablespoons chopped
   shallots
1 tablespoon chopped fresh
   tarragon (1 teaspoon
   dried)
¼ cup brandy

½ cup fish stock (see p. 180)
½ cup dry white wine
2 sprigs parsley
2 egg yolks
¾ cup heavy cream
1 tablespoon dry sherry
Chopped fresh parsley for
   garnish

Trim monkfish and cut into 1½-inch chunks. Melt butter in skillet, add shallots, and cook 3 minutes, or until soft but not brown. Stir in tarragon, add monkfish, and combine. Warm brandy in small pan. Pour over monkfish and ignite. When flames die down, add fish stock, wine, and parsley sprigs. Cover and cook over low heat 10 minutes.

With slotted spoon, remove monkfish to serving dish and keep warm. Discard parsley sprigs. Boil liquid in skillet briskly until reduced to about ½ cup. Remove from heat. Whisk egg yolks together with ½ cup of the heavy cream and slowly add to hot reduced liquid, whisking vigorously so yolks will not curdle. Return to medium heat and stir constantly until sauce thickens. Whisk in sherry and remaining ¼ cup cream, and spoon over monkfish. Garnish with chopped parsley.

Sweet-and-Sour Monkfish

SERVES 4

Here a traditional sweet-and-sour chicken recipe is adapted to accommodate monkfish.

1½ pounds monkfish
4 tablespoons rice wine
Peanut oil for frying
2 egg yolks, beaten
6 tablespoons cornstarch
Sweet-and-Sour Sauce
 (recipe follows)

2 carrots, peeled and thinly
 sliced on diagonal
1 green bell pepper, seeded
 and cut into large pieces
1 cup canned unsweetened
 pineapple chunks

Trim monkfish of red membrane and discard. Cut fish into 2-inch chunks, place in glass bowl, and add rice wine. Toss to coat and let sit 10 minutes.

Heat oil in wok over high heat. Meanwhile, dip each fish chunk in beaten egg yolk, then in cornstarch. Fry fish in small batches until browned and crispy, about 5 minutes. Remove to drain on paper towels and keep warm in oven (200°) while making sauce.

In saucepan steam carrots and bell pepper for 3 minutes. Add to sauce along with pineapple chunks, then add fish pieces. Stir to coat well with sauce and serve with boiled rice.

SWEET-AND-SOUR SAUCE

5 tablespoons sugar
3 tablespoons water
3 tablespoons pineapple
 juice
4 tablespoons rice vinegar
3 tablespoons ketchup

2 tablespoons dry sherry
1 tablespoon sesame oil
1 tablespoon cornstarch
 mixed with 2 tablespoons
 water

In bowl whisk together sugar, water, pineapple juice, vinegar, ketchup, sherry, and oil. Place in clean wok and heat to simmer. Cook 3 minutes, or until flavors are blended. Add combined cornstarch and water, stirring until thickened.

Poached Monkfish
with Garlic and Rosemary

SERVES 4

The garlic-rosemary combination creates an aromatic sauce. Instead of using it with the traditional leg of lamb, substitute monkfish escalopes.

1½ pounds monkfish
Salt and pepper to taste
2 tablespoons olive oil
3 tablespoons unsalted
  butter
2 cloves garlic, minced
½ cup chopped onion
1 tablespoon chopped
  shallots

½ cup chopped carrot
2 teaspoons dried rosemary
½ cup dry white wine
½ cup fish stock (see p. 180)
½ cup heavy cream
Chopped fresh parsley for
  garnish

Cut monkfish into 8 thin escalopes. Season with salt and pepper, and set aside. Place oil and butter in skillet over medium heat. Sauté garlic, onion, and shallots for 3 minutes. Add carrot and cook 3 minutes more. Stir in rosemary, wine, and fish stock, and simmer 3 minutes more. Lay seasoned monkfish slices on top of this mixture and poach 8 minutes, turning once. Remove fish and solids from skillet with slotted spoon and keep warm on serving platter. Reduce juices in skillet to one half the volume by boiling vigorously. Reduce heat, add heavy cream, and bring to simmer. Pour over monkfish, garnish with chopped parsley, and serve with rice.

Breaded and Sautéed Monkfish

SERVES 4

Monkfish holds together well and does not flake apart the way many other fish do. It can be treated like chicken breasts or veal, offering countless ways of preparation — from simple to elaborate.

1½ pounds monkfish
½ cup milk
1 egg
1 cup bread crumbs
2 tablespoons freshly grated
  Parmesan cheese
½ cup flour

¼ cup olive or safflower oil
4 tablespoons unsalted
  butter
Juice of 1 lemon
Lemon wedges and chopped
  fresh parsley for garnish

Trim monkfish and cut into 8 thin slices crosswise. Pat dry with paper towel. Whisk together milk and egg in shallow dish. Combine bread crumbs and Parmesan cheese in another shallow dish. Dredge fish slices in flour and shake to remove excess. Dip into egg mixture and then dredge in bread crumbs.

In the meantime, heat oil in large sauté pan over medium-high heat. Add monkfish slices as they are coated and cook until golden brown, about 3-4 minutes per side. Transfer to warm platter.

Melt butter until bubbly, and just as it starts to brown, remove from heat and add lemon juice. Pour over fish pieces and serve hot. Garnish with lemon wedges and chopped parsley.

Curried Monkfish   SERVES 4

This lovely curry can be made spicier by adding more cayenne. Be sure to presoak the dried fruit before using.

1 ½ pounds monkfish	1 teaspoon cayenne pepper
½ cup chopped pitted prunes	2 tablespoons flour
½ cup raisins	2 tablespoons red wine
½ cup chopped apricots	vinegar
1 ½ cups water	1 tablespoon fresh lemon
5 tablespoons peanut oil	juice
1 large onion, thinly sliced	¼ cup chopped peanuts for
2 tablespoons curry powder	garnish
1 tablespoon turmeric	1 banana, sliced, for garnish
2 tablespoons ground cumin	

Trim monkfish of red membrane. Cut into 1½-inch chunks and refrigerate. Soak prunes, raisins, and apricots in water for 1 hour.

In skillet heat 3 tablespoons of the oil and brown monkfish on all sides, about 3 minutes. Remove to dish and set aside. In same skillet, heat remaining 2 tablespoons oil, add onion, and cook 4 minutes, or until soft and light brown. Reduce heat to low and stir in curry powder, turmeric, cumin, cayenne, and flour. Cook 2 minutes. Add soaked fruit pieces and their liquid, vinegar, and lemon juice. Increase heat and bring to a boil, stirring constantly. Reduce heat to low, cover, and simmer 30 minutes. Add browned monkfish pieces and simmer 15 minutes, adding more water if needed. Garnish with chopped peanuts and banana slices. Serve over white rice with chutney on the side.

Poached Monkfish and Vegetables with Saffron-Thyme Sauce

SERVES 4-6

Any colorful combination of fresh vegetables can be used. The saffron gives the sauce a pale yellow hue, but be careful not to use too much, or it will overwhelm the other ingredients.

2 pounds monkfish
6 new potatoes
3 carrots, sliced diagonally
3 stalks broccoli (use only florets trimmed from stalks)

1 bulb fennel, quartered
½ pound green beans
2 small zucchini, cut into strips
10 sugar snap peas
4 cups fish stock (see p. 180)

SAFFRON-THYME SAUCE

¼ cup olive oil
2 shallots, finely chopped
1 teaspoon chopped fresh thyme (½ teaspoon dried)
Pinch of saffron
½ cup dry white wine

2 tablespoons heavy cream
4 tablespoons unsalted butter, cut into bits
1 tablespoon chopped scallion greens for garnish

Trim red membrane from fish and discard. Cut fish into ½-inch-thick escalopes and set aside. In large skillet heat enough water to simmer vegetables, adding them according to how long each needs to cook: start with potatoes, end with peas. Cook each until just tender.

Meanwhile, in another skillet heat fish stock to simmer and poach monkfish 5 minutes. At the same time, make sauce.

Heat oil in small skillet, add shallots, and cook 3-4 minutes, or until soft. Add thyme and saffron, and stir. Add wine and simmer until reduced to one third of volume. Whisk in cream, then add butter, a bit at a time, whisking constantly.

Arrange vegetables and fish on serving platter, top with sauce, and garnish with chopped scallion greens.

Monkfish in Red Wine

SERVES 6

A fruity red wine is the best kind to use in this recipe, for a white wine tends to be too dry and bland.

2 pounds monkfish	1 cup fish stock (see p. 180)
4 tablespoons unsalted butter	4 sprigs fresh parsley
	1 bay leaf
½ cup finely chopped onion	3 whole cloves
4 shallots, minced	½ teaspoon dried thyme
½ cup finely chopped carrot	4 whole peppercorns
2 cloves garlic, finely minced	Salt to taste
4 tablespoons flour	1 tablespoon cognac
3 cups Burgundy	

Trim monkfish of red membrane and discard. Cut fish into 2-inch chunks and set aside.

Melt 2 tablespoons of the butter in large sauté pan and add onion, half the shallots, carrot, and half the garlic. Cook 5 minutes, stirring occasionally, until all are wilted. Sprinkle 2 tablespoons of the flour over vegetables, stirring to combine. Add wine and fish stock, and stir rapidly. Add parsley, bay leaf, cloves, thyme, peppercorns, and salt. Bring to simmer and cook, uncovered, 30 minutes.

In large enamel saucepan melt remaining 2 tablespoons butter. Add remaining shallots and garlic, and cook about 2 minutes, stirring often. Add monkfish chunks and sauté 3 minutes. Sprinkle with remaining 2 tablespoons flour, stirring to coat. Pour onion and carrot mixture through sieve into fish mixture and stir. Discard solids in sieve. Cover pot and simmer over low heat about 10 minutes, or until monkfish is done. Add cognac, stir, and serve piping hot.

Mussels (Blue)

Mytilus edulis

Blue mussels are abundant along the rocks and beaches of New England. They have a dark blue, almost purple, shell with orange- to peach-colored flesh inside.

The mussel is a highly nutritious bivalve mollusk that feeds by filtering 10 to 15 gallons of water a day through its body, consuming virtually everything that passes through. For this reason, mussels are particularly susceptible to pollution. Gathering wild mussels can be risky unless you are familiar with the area where you are collecting them. Commercial mussel farming has been a boon to the market, as it provides consistently safe, uniform mussels of good flavor.

The warning not to use a mussel if it is open must be revised to say don't use a mussel if it does not close. Mussels that are farmed have thinner shells and tend to need to breathe more once they are harvested from the sea. To check their freshness, squeeze their shells together with your thumb and forefinger. This will activate their closure muscle, and if they are alive, they should stay closed.

Farmed or cultivated mussels are washed and sorted according to size. They are separated from their web or beard and usually are free of grit and barnacles, so extensive scrubbing when you get them home is not necessary.

Mussels are delicious steamed in water and wine and served similarly to clams, with broth and butter. They can be added to soup, smoked as an appetizer, prepared in a sauce for pasta, or stuffed and baked. Allow 1 pound of mussels per person as a main course, ½ pound for soups or appetizers.

How to Debeard a Mussel

Rinse the mussels. Then, with your
fingers, pull off and discard the little tuft
of black hair, known as the beard, that is
attached to each mussel.

Steamed Mussels
with Herbed Curry Sauce

SERVES 10-12 AS APPETIZER

Betsy Jones served these on board the Silver Heels *during an outing of
the Cruising Club of America, which my father and I (on* Serene*)
attended. We were just off New Meadows River in Maine, overlooking
Batchelder Hill.*

4 pounds mussels
1 cup dry white wine

1 cup water

HERBED CURRY SAUCE

1 cup sour cream
½ cup mayonnaise (see
   p. 283)
3 tablespoons fresh lemon
   juice
2 tablespoons grated red
   onion
2 tablespoons minced fresh
   parsley

1 tablespoon curry powder
1 tablespoon snipped chives
   or sliced scallion greens
1 teaspoon Dijon mustard
½ teaspoon paprika
¼ teaspoon cayenne pepper
1 tablespoon chopped fresh
   cilantro for garnish

Clean and debeard mussels (see above). In large pot heat wine and
water to boil. Add cleaned mussels, cover, and simmer 5 minutes, or
until shells open. Drain, reserving broth for another use, and refrigerate mussels until chilled.

Make sauce by combining all ingredients except cilantro in bowl,
mixing well. Discard top shell of each mussel and loosen meat from
bottom shell, but do not remove. Put dollop of sauce on top of each
mussel and garnish with chopped cilantro. Serve with toothpicks.

Mrs. Kaloosdian's Stuffed Mussels

SERVES 6 AS APPETIZER

My landlady Grace Kaloosdian grew up in Watertown, Massachusetts. She is a petite lady who has been in the food business all her life. At Christmas she used to bring us her favorite stuffed mussel dish, which we devoured with relish. Traditionally, the mussels are stuffed raw and then cooked, but they can be steamed slightly to open, stuffed, and cooked further.

3 pounds mussels
½ cup rice, uncooked
2 cups water
¼ cup olive oil
1 cup chopped onion
½ teaspoon salt
1 tablespoon chopped fresh parsley

½ teaspoon nutmeg
¼ teaspoon allspice
½ teaspoon cinnamon
¼ cup currants
¼ cup roasted pine nuts
¼ cup fresh lemon juice
Lemon wedges for garnish

Clean and debeard mussels (see p. 141). In saucepan cook rice in 1 cup of the water until done, about 15 minutes. Let sit off heat 5 minutes.

In sauté pan heat oil and sauté onion 3 minutes, or until soft. Add cooked rice and mix well. Stir in salt, parsley, nutmeg, allspice, cinnamon, currants, and pine nuts. Combine well and let cool slightly.

Open each mussel with sharp knife, cutting through muscle on top shell. Put heaping teaspoon of rice mixture on top of mussel meat and close shell. Fill all mussels and place, bottom shell down, in heavy enamel pot, stacking them on top of each other. Combine remaining 1 cup water and lemon juice, and pour over mussels. Put heavy plate on top of mussels to keep them closed. Cover and simmer 15 minutes, or until mussels are cooked. Transfer mussels to platter and chill, covered, 3 hours. Serve with lemon wedges.

Chilled Mussels
with Horseradish Cream Sauce

SERVES 4

Anytime I have mussels, I think of Freddy Richardson, an old family friend who went to both Milton Academy and Harvard with my father. He used to have an annual lobster and mussel feed on the beach by his home in Ipswich, Massachusetts. A fire would be made in the rocks, and the mussels, hauled right out of the ocean, would be laid on the hot coals and covered with seaweed. The mussels were divine — but their fresh-from-the-sea flavor is hard to duplicate at the store.

4 pounds mussels	1 teaspoon prepared
½ cup dry white wine	mustard
1 cup water	1 teaspoon Worcestershire
½ cup heavy cream	sauce
1 tablespoon fresh	1 tablespoon tomato paste
horseradish, grated, or	¼ teaspoon cayenne pepper
2 tablespoons prepared	Dash of nutmeg

Clean and debeard mussels (see p. 141). In large saucepan bring wine and water to simmer. Add mussels, cover, and steam over medium heat until mussels open, about 5 minutes. Strain mussels, reserving broth and discarding any unopened shells. Freeze broth for another use and chill mussels until cool. Remove and discard top shells and loosen mussels from bottom shells. Place mussels in shells on platter, then make sauce.

Whisk cream until thick, then whisk in horseradish, mustard, Worcestershire sauce, tomato paste, cayenne, and nutmeg. Place sauce in small bowl and serve with chilled mussels, accompanied by toothpicks.

Blue Mussels

SERVES 2

A strong cheese does not detract from the essence of mussels, so let your taste be your guide.

2 pounds mussels	2 tablespoons unsalted
½ cup water	butter
¼ cup dry white wine	1 tablespoon chopped fresh
⅛ pound blue cheese,	parsley
Stilton, Gorgonzola, or	Freshly ground black pepper
Saga blue	to taste

Clean and debeard mussels (see p. 141) and set aside. In saucepan heat water and wine over high heat and add mussels. Cover, lower heat to simmer, and steam 5 minutes, or until shells open. Drain mussels, reserving broth and discarding any unopened shells. Freeze broth for later use. Remove top shell from each mussel and discard. With knife, loosen mussels from shells, and place in a baking dish.

Put blue cheese, butter, parsley, and pepper in blender and combine. Dab mixture on each mussel, using it all, and broil until tops are bubbly.

Mussel-Saffron Soup

SERVES 6

Saffron is a strong, expensive spice, and there are different grades on the market at various prices. Make sure you are buying pure saffron, which is the stamen of a fall crocus, not the whole bud or flower. This elegant dish is the most sought after soup in our display case.

2 pounds mussels	¼ teaspoon freshly ground
4 tablespoons unsalted	white pepper
butter	1½ pounds tomatoes,
1 cup finely minced onion	peeled, seeded, and
2 cloves garlic, pressed	chopped
½ cup finely minced carrot	¼ teaspoon saffron
¼ teaspoon dried thyme	4 cups fish stock (see p. 180)
½ teaspoon salt	½ cup heavy cream

Clean and debeard mussels (see p. 141) and set aside. Melt butter over low heat in large saucepan and add onion, garlic, and carrot. Cook until soft, about 5 minutes. Stir in thyme, salt, and pepper. Cover and cook slowly, stirring occasionally, for 20 minutes, or until vegetables are quite soft. Add tomatoes and saffron, cover, and cook 20 minutes more at same low heat, stirring occasionally.

Meanwhile, in separate saucepan over high heat bring ½ inch water to boil, add mussels, cover, reduce heat, and steam 5 minutes, or until mussels open. Drain, reserving broth, and discard any unopened mussels. Remove meats from shells and discard shells. Add fish stock and 2 cups mussel broth to vegetables, increase heat, bring mixture to simmer, and cook about 10 minutes. Stir in cream and shelled mussels, and cook until mussels are heated through. Ladle into soup bowls, dividing mussels evenly.

Mussels and Shrimp Soup with Cilantro   SERVES 6

Like most mothers, mine used to come up with very good reasons why I should eat foods I didn't particularly like. If I ate lots of carrots, she told me, I would be able to see in the dark; if I ate lots of mussels, I would become very strong. To this day, I eat lots of carrots and mussels.

2 pounds mussels	8-ounce bottle clam juice
¼ cup olive oil	½ cup dry white wine
2 medium onions, finely chopped	½ pound medium shrimp, peeled and deveined (see p. 221), tail intact
1 small can (4 ounces) green chilies or 2 fresh serrano chilies, chopped	½ cup unsweetened coconut milk (see p. 165)
½ cup minced red bell pepper	Salt and pepper to taste
2 teaspoons minced fresh cilantro	

Wash and debeard mussels (see p. 141) and set aside. Heat oil in large saucepan and sauté onions, chilies, bell pepper, and cilantro over medium heat until onions are soft, about 3 minutes. Add clam juice and wine, and bring to boil. Reduce heat, add mussels, and simmer, covered, about 4 minutes, or until mussels just begin to open. Add shrimp and simmer 2½ minutes, or until pink and firm. Discard any unopened mussels, stir in coconut milk, season with salt and pepper, and serve immediately.

Mussels and Dill Soup

SERVES 6-8

This is a variation of Billie-Bi Soup, which was "invented" at Maxim's. The original recipe used just the broth, but I've included mussels, too — some puréed, others left whole.

6 pounds mussels
4 tablespoons unsalted
  butter
2 onions, chopped
4 cloves garlic, minced
2 cups dry white wine
1 cup water
2 tablespoons chopped fresh
  dill

1 tablespoon chopped fresh
  parsley
Salt and pepper to taste
4 egg yolks
1 cup heavy cream
Chopped fresh dill for
  garnish

Clean and debeard mussels (see p. 141) and set aside. Melt butter in large saucepan, add onions and garlic, and cook over medium heat until onions are soft, about 3 minutes. Add wine and water, and bring to simmer. Add mussels, cover, and steam 5 minutes, or until shells open. Strain, reserving broth and discarding any unopened mussels. Remove meats from shells and discard shells. In blender or food processor fitted with metal blade purée half the mussels with reserved broth in batches. Return to saucepan, add dill and parsley, season with salt and pepper, and heat. In bowl beat egg yolks and cream together. Whisk in 1 cup of the hot broth, then slowly add to saucepan and heat slowly. Do not boil. Serve garnished with remaining shucked mussels and chopped dill.

Mussel Risotto

Arborio is a short-grain Italian rice used in risotto. Unlike other rice dishes, risotto requires that the liquid be stirred into the rice at intervals, creating a moist, creamy mixture.

3 pounds mussels	1 large tomato, peeled,
4 cups dry white wine	seeded, and chopped
6 tablespoons unsalted	2 cups Arborio rice,
butter	uncooked
4 scallions, chopped	½ cup freshly grated
2 cloves garlic, minced	Parmesan cheese
½ cup chopped onion	2 tablespoons chopped fresh
1 tablespoon chopped fresh	parsley for garnish
basil (1 teaspoon dried)	

Clean and debeard mussels (see p. 141). In large saucepan heat wine to simmer and add mussels. Cover and cook 5 minutes, or until shells open. Place colander in large bowl and drain mussels, reserving broth. Remove mussels from shells, discarding shells and unopened mussels.

In large enamel pot melt butter over medium-low heat. Add scallions, garlic, and onion, and sauté 3-4 minutes, or until soft. Add basil and tomato, and sauté 2 minutes. Add rice and stir to coat.

Meanwhile, pour strained mussel broth into measuring cup. Add enough water to equal 5 cups. Transfer to saucepan and bring to simmer. Add 1 cup of liquid to rice mixture, bring to boil, and cook, stirring, until liquid is absorbed. Repeat, pouring in 1 cup liquid at a time and stirring until absorbed. Continue until rice is tender, adding mussels with remaining liquid. (The rice should take 20-30 minutes to cook.)

Stir in Parmesan cheese and serve garnished with parsley.

Smoked Mussels and Pasta Salad
SERVES 6

We make this colorful salad at The Fishmonger, obtaining the ingredients we don't have from two other food stores on our block. From Formaggio we buy the turkey and pasta; from Le Jardin, the fresh vegetables.

1 pound smoked mussels	1 cup olive oil
1 pound pasta shells	¼ cup red wine vinegar
1 red bell pepper	1 tablespoon prepared
1 green bell pepper	horseradish
1 yellow bell pepper	1 tablespoon Dijon mustard
1 cup pine nuts	Juice of 2 lemons
1 cup fresh or frozen peas	Salt and pepper to taste
½ pound smoked turkey	

Cut mussels in half if large; otherwise keep whole. Cook pasta al dente, about 6 minutes. Drain and cool. (The pasta absorbs some of the oil from the dressing, and if overcooked, it can become soggy, so keep it on the firm side.)

Trim peppers of inside pulp and seeds. Cut into thin slices lengthwise and cut slices in half. Roast pine nuts in nonstick sauté pan until browned. Cook fresh peas until just done; if frozen, thaw out under hot tap water and drain. Slice turkey into strips and then cut into cubes.

Make dressing by whisking together oil, vinegar, horseradish, mustard, lemon juice, and salt and pepper. In large bowl combine mussels, pasta, vegetables, nuts, and turkey. Toss with dressing to coat.

Mussel Stew

To vary the flavor of this dish, try it with other vegetables, and toward the end of cooking, add some hot sausage that has been fried and drained.

3½ pounds mussels	1 tablespoon dry sherry
3 tablespoons unsalted butter	1½ cups water
	1 bay leaf
2 ribs celery, diced	Salt and pepper to taste
1 onion, finely chopped	1 tablespoon flour
4 scallions, thinly sliced	2 egg yolks
1 carrot, diced	½ cup heavy cream
2 cloves garlic, minced	2 tablespoons chopped fresh
1½ cups dry white wine	parsley for garnish

Clean and debeard mussels (see p. 141) and set aside. In large saucepan melt 2 tablespoons of the butter over low heat. Add celery, onion, scallions, carrot, and garlic, and cook until soft, about 5 minutes. Add mussels, wine, sherry, water, and bay leaf. Season with salt and pepper. Raise heat, cover, and steam until mussels open, about 5 minutes. Remove mussels and vegetables with slotted spoon and place in large serving tureen. Discard any unopened mussels. Boil broth in saucepan to reduce by one third.

In separate saucepan melt remaining 1 tablespoon butter and add flour to make a roux. Stir over low heat for 1 minute. Add 1 cup of reduced broth to roux, whisking until thickened. Keep adding broth until all is used. Remove from heat.

Beat egg yolks and cream together, and slowly add to broth mixture, whisking continuously. Place over medium-low heat until thickened, making sure not to boil. Pour over steamed mussels, garnish with chopped parsley, and serve with garlic bread and garden salad.

Baked Mussels with Garlic

SERVES 4

This Italian recipe comes from our gregarious mailman, Bobby, who suggested I try mussels his way.

4 pounds mussels
¼ cup olive oil
2 tablespoons unsalted
    butter, melted
3 cloves garlic, minced
¼ cup chopped fresh parsley
2 tablespoons chopped fresh
    basil (2 teaspoons dried)

1 tablespoon chopped fresh
    oregano (1 teaspoon dried)
½ teaspoon black pepper
½ teaspoon crushed red
    pepper flakes
1 cup bread crumbs

Clean and debeard mussels (see p. 141) and transfer to shallow baking pan. Combine oil and melted butter, and spoon over mussels. Mix together garlic, parsley, basil, and oregano, and sprinkle over mussels. Combine black pepper and red pepper flakes with bread crumbs and distribute evenly over mussels. Cover pan with foil and bake in preheated oven at 375° for 20 minutes. Transfer to warm plates, spoon on pan juices, and serve with garlic bread.

Mussel Sauce for Pasta

SERVES 3-4

Mussels are one of the best bargains going and can be cooked as simply or elaborately as you wish.

4 pounds mussels
¾ cup dry white wine
½ cup water
½ teaspoon dried thyme
1 bay leaf
2 sprigs parsley
¼ cup olive oil
2 cloves garlic, minced
½ cup chopped onion
2 tablespoons capers,
    squeeze-drained

1 tablespoon chopped
    pimiento
½ cup imported black olives,
    pitted and quartered
2 tablespoons flour
¼ cup chopped fresh parsley
½ teaspoon crushed red
    pepper flakes
1½ pounds pasta
¼ pound feta cheese,
    crumbled

Clean and debeard mussels (see p. 141). In large pot over high heat bring wine, water, thyme, bay leaf, and parsley sprigs to boil. Add mussels, cover, reduce heat to medium, and cook 5 minutes, or until shells open. Place colander in large bowl and drain mussels.

Discard any unopened shells and reserve liquid. When cool enough to handle, remove mussels from shells, leaving 15 to 20 intact for garnish at the end.

Meanwhile, in skillet heat oil, add garlic and onion, and cook until soft, about 3 minutes. Add capers, pimiento, and olives, and combine. Dust mixture with flour, stirring to blend. Add 2 cups reserved mussel broth, heated, and stir until thickened. Bring to simmer and add chopped parsley, pepper flakes, and mussel meats. Cook 1 minute.

Cook pasta al dente, drain, and put on serving platter. Pour sauce over top and garnish with feta cheese and whole steamed mussels.

Linguine with Smoked Mussels in Wine and Mushroom Sauce

SERVES 4

Ducktrap River Fish Farm in Lincolnville, Maine, is owned by Des Fitzgerald, who runs an excellent smokehouse and ships his products all over the country. This recipe is one of his.

½ pound smoked mussels
  and oil
4 tablespoons unsalted
  butter
½ cup sliced scallions
2 cloves garlic, crushed
1½ cups sliced mushrooms
1 tablespoon fresh tarragon
  (1 teaspoon dried)

3 tablespoons flour
1¼ cups dry white wine
1½ cups heavy cream
¼ cup minced fresh parsley
1½ pounds linguine
2 tablespoons olive oil
Chopped fresh parsley for
  garnish

Cut mussels in half if large; otherwise leave whole. Melt butter in sauté pan over medium heat. Add scallions and garlic, and sauté 2 minutes. Add mushrooms and tarragon, and sauté 4 minutes more. Sprinkle flour over mixture and stir until blended. Slowly add wine and cook until sauce thickens. Stir in cream and parsley, and heat to simmer. Add smoked mussels and cook 2 minutes, or until mussels are warmed through.

Meanwhile, cook linguine al dente. Drain and toss with olive oil. Top with sauce and garnish with chopped parsley.

Ocean Perch
(Atlantic)

Sebastes marinus

Ocean perch are found across much of the North Atlantic, where these slow-growing fish live long lives in cold, deep water. They are small fish, requiring nearly ten years to mature, at which time they are only about ten inches long. Originally marketed as "rosefish" or "redfish" because of their brilliant red and orange color, ocean perch grew in popularity as a substitute for the disappearing freshwater perch of the Great Lakes. Some dealers try to sell redfish as red snapper, but the two are not alike in taste, texture, or price. Perch has small scales, and its red color is bright along the back, then fades toward the belly. If you see a red snapper filet in the market without the skin, it's probably ocean perch, since snapper is always sold with the skin on. Also, don't confuse this redfish with the Gulf species popular in Cajun cooking.

Ocean perch is sold fileted. If fresh, it has a firm, meaty flesh that is somewhat reddish in color; when cooked, it turns snow white and has a light, delicate flavor. Perch can be baked, poached, pan-fried, or barbecued.

Sautéed Ocean Perch with Mango Sauce   SERVES 2

This tart, creamy sauce enhances the delicate flavor of ocean perch.

1 pound ocean perch filets
¼ cup flour
Salt and freshly ground black
    pepper to taste

2 tablespoons unsalted
    butter
Mango Sauce (recipe follows)

Remove skin from filets and dust fish with flour seasoned with salt and pepper. Melt butter in sauté pan and add filets, cooking over medium heat 3 minutes per side, or until golden brown.

Place filets on warm platter and dress with Mango Sauce.

MANGO SAUCE

1 ripe mango
2 tablespoons unsalted
   butter
2 teaspoons grated lemon
   rind

1 tablespoon fresh lemon
   juice
½ cup heavy cream

Peel mango, separate pulp from seed, and purée pulp in food processor fitted with metal blade. Melt butter in saucepan and add mango purée. Cook 3 minutes over medium heat. Add lemon rind and juice, whisk in heavy cream, and heat to simmer.

Steamed Ocean Perch with Tomato-Basil Butter

SERVES 4-6

Steaming fish cooks it quickly yet keeps it moist. Leave the skin on the filets to hold the flesh together while it cooks.

2 pounds ocean perch filets
1 tablespoon minced shallots
2 tablespoons white wine
   vinegar
¼ cup dry white wine
8 tablespoons cold unsalted
   butter, cut into pieces

1 medium tomato, peeled,
   seeded, and chopped
2 tablespoons chopped fresh
   basil
¼ teaspoon salt
¼ teaspoon freshly ground
   black pepper

Place perch on rack over boiling water. Cover tightly with lid or foil. Steam 6-10 minutes depending on thickness of filets.

Meanwhile, in saucepan combine shallots, vinegar, and white wine. Boil gently until reduced to 2 tablespoons. Remove pan from heat and whisk in butter piece by piece until sauce becomes thick and creamy. (You might have to put the pan back on the heat occasionally to warm, but the key to this sauce is not to let the butter melt and to keep whisking it.) Add tomato, basil, salt, and pepper.

When done, place filets on platter. Spoon on sauce and serve with steamed vegetables.

Oysters (Atlantic)

Crassostrea virginica

The Atlantic oyster can be found from Nova Scotia to Mexico and is a wild, not farmed, oyster. The Atlantics are named according to the location where they are harvested: Blue Points (New York), Chincoteague (Maryland), Cape Cod (Massachusetts), and so on. Oyster lovers generally have a favorite kind because the flavor does vary.

These bivalve mollusks thrive in estuaries, where they find just the right amount of salinity. Oysters are filter feeders and siphon through their bodies up to 25 gallons of water a day to get food. Their flavor differs depending on the trace minerals found in the water of their habitat. Oysters are high in iron. They vary in color from pale tan to green-gray but usually are creamy white with black around the edges.

The time to buy oysters is in the late fall and winter; thus the old adage of eating them only in those months that have an "r" in their name is a reliable guide. During the summer, when oysters spawn, their flesh is depleted and they're not as tasty.

You can buy oysters in the shell by the bushel (from 40 to 60 pounds), by the dozen, or by the pound. When buying oysters in the shell, make sure they are alive. You can tell whether they are alive by tapping together the shells of two oysters. They should sound solid and compact, like two rocks. If there is a hollow, dull sound, the oyster is dead. Oysters that have turned bad have a sulfurous smell; fresh oysters are plump and smell like the ocean.

Raw oysters will keep for up to a week if refrigerated and unopened. Once opened, they should be eaten within an hour if they are to be served raw. Do not wash oysters once they are opened, for their liquid, or "liquor," helps keep them moist and succulent.

Oysters of the Chesapeake Bay are harvested in great quantities and arrive on the market as fresh-shucked oysters. They are sold in half-pint, pint, or gallon containers, depending on their count per gallon. Extra-large oysters, or "counts," are the largest oysters; there are about 160 counts per gallon (remember, there are 16 cups to a gallon). Each gallon of large oysters, or "extra selects," has 161 to 200 oysters; each gallon of medium oysters, or "selects," which are good for frying, has 201 to 300 oysters; and each gallon of small oysters, or "standards," has 301 to 400 oysters.

Chesapeake Bay oysters are best used in oyster stew, for frying, and for baking. I don't recommend eating them raw, as they usually have been open too long to be very tasty. Shucked oysters should have a creamy color, and the liquor should be clear with a viscous consistency. Slightly pink liquor is a sign of aging and spoilage.

When cooking oysters, do not heat them too quickly or for too long a period of time. Pay close attention, for as soon as the mantle around the oyster starts to curl, the oyster is done, regardless of the cooking method. Once cooked, serve them immediately.

Opening oysters requires a certain amount of strength and finesse. A pair of heavy leather gardening gloves is essential, for oyster shells are sharp and jagged and carry bacteria, which, if they get into the bloodstream, can cause an infection. To start, hold the oyster bottom (the deeper bowled shell) in one hand and an oyster knife in the other. (An oyster knife should not be pointed on the end but sharp on both edges.) Using the knife, break through the sealed shell on the right side. Once in, turn the knife sideways to open the shell a bit, then slip the knife along the top and cut the one adductor muscle that holds the two shells together. Remove the top shell and free the oyster from the bottom half of the shell. Eat the first oyster you open and enjoy your labor before tackling the rest. If a shell won't open for some reason, set it aside and try it later once you're feeling comfortable with the procedure.

How to Open an Oyster*

Cupping a well-scrubbed oyster (deep shell down) in the palm of one hand, break through the sealed shell by inserting the blade of an oyster knife near the hinged end. (Hold the oyster over a sieve and bowl in order to catch the oyster liquor.)

Rotate the blade of the knife to pry apart the top and bottom shells, and cut the hinge muscle that holds the shells together.

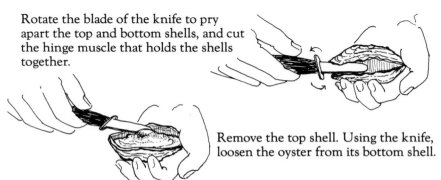

Remove the top shell. Using the knife, loosen the oyster from its bottom shell.

*To protect your hands from the jagged oyster shells, you should wear a pair of heavy gardening gloves.

Oysters Rockefeller

Elegant and sumptuous. Serve with champagne or chilled mineral water.

24 oysters in shells
Rock salt
8 tablespoons unsalted
  butter
½ cup finely chopped celery
½ cup finely chopped fresh
  parsley
½ cup finely chopped
  scallions
1 bunch watercress, washed
  and dried (leaves only)

½ pound fresh spinach,
  washed, stems removed,
  and coarsely chopped
1 tablespoon anchovy paste
Cayenne pepper to taste
2 tablespoons Pernod
½ cup unseasoned bread
  crumbs

Open oysters (see p. 156) and leave on half shell. Put rock salt in 4 individual ovenproof dishes large enough to hold 6 oysters each. Place oysters on top of salt.

Melt butter in skillet until bubbly, add celery, and cook until softened, stirring constantly. Stir in parsley and scallions, and cook 30 seconds. Add watercress and spinach, mixing to coat with butter. Cook until wilted, about 2 minutes, then add anchovy paste, cayenne, and Pernod. Stir to combine. Add bread crumbs and stir until liquid is absorbed.

Place spoonful of spinach mixture on each oyster. Place under preheated broiler for 3-5 minutes, or until tops are bubbly and oysters begin to curl.

Sherry Mignonette Sauce for Raw Oysters

SERVES 2-4

When I was young, my brother Bobby used to coax me into trying raw oysters. I was "dared to eat one" to become a sister in good standing and was told to "just swallow it, don't chew." I think I was about eight years old before I could complete the task, after many failed attempts, and now I can easily down a dozen at a time.

12 to 18 oysters in shells

SHERRY MIGNONETTE SAUCE

½ cup sherry wine vinegar
1 tablespoon dry sherry
3 tablespoons minced
   shallots

1 tablespoon freshly ground
   black pepper
1 teaspoon chopped fresh
   cilantro (optional)

Check oysters for freshness (see p. 155), scrub shells to clean, and refrigerate while making sauce.

Combine vinegar, sherry, shallots, black pepper, and cilantro if desired. Blend well and refrigerate 1 hour.

Open oysters (see p. 156), leaving them in the half shell. Arrange on platter and accompany with sauce.

Baked Oysters with Crabmeat SERVES 2-3 AS APPETIZER

This recipe combines the richness of crabmeat with the fruitiness of oysters.

12 oysters in shells
Rock salt
4 ounces cream cheese,
   softened
2 tablespoons mayonnaise
   (see p. 283)

2 tablespoons minced onion
1 tablespoon plus 1 teaspoon
   dry sherry
2 teaspoons dry mustard
¼ pound crabmeat, checked
   for shells

Open oysters (see p. 156) and leave on half shell. Place in oven-proof dish containing bed of rock salt to steady shells. Combine cream cheese, mayonnaise, onion, sherry, and mustard, beating with fork until smooth and well blended. Fold in crabmeat. Put spoonful of mixture on top of each oyster. Place under preheated broiler for 3 minutes, or until tops are bubbly and browned and oysters' edges begin to curl. Serve immediately.

The Fishmonger Oyster Stew SERVES 4

My nephew Jack Batchelder lives in Washington State on the Olympic Peninsula and works for an oyster farming operation. When he and I get together, we always "talk shop."

1 pint shucked oysters, with liquor
6 tablespoons unsalted butter
1 bay leaf, crumbled
2 shallots, finely chopped
½ cup finely chopped celery
1 teaspoon grated lemon rind

2 tablespoons flour
4½ cups light cream or half-and-half
¼ teaspoon salt
½ teaspoon Tabasco
2 teaspoons Worcestershire sauce
¼ teaspoon paprika

Use hands to check oysters for pieces of shell, then set aside. In 2-quart saucepan melt 3 tablespoons of the butter until bubbly. Add bay leaf and shallots, and sauté until soft. Add celery and lemon rind, and cook 3 minutes. Add flour and stir until well blended. Gradually pour in cream, 1 cup at a time, whisking as you go. Add salt and cook until cream is scalded. Stir in oysters and cook about 3 minutes, or until edges begin to curl. Combine Tabasco, Worcestershire sauce, and paprika, and add to stew, stirring until blended.

With slotted spoon, divide oysters among individual bowls and ladle liquid over them. Garnish each with pat of remaining butter and dash of paprika, and serve with oyster crackers and green salad.

Fried Oysters

SERVES 2-4

These are great added warm to a Caesar salad or as a hot hors d'oeuvre. Fry them in hot oil very quickly so they stay moist and do not become greasy.

1 pint shucked oysters (about 20), with liquor	¾ cup flour
2 cloves garlic, minced	1½ cups bread crumbs
½ cup milk	Vegetable or olive oil for frying
1 egg	Lemon wedges for garnish
1 tablespoon Worcestershire sauce	Tartar Sauce (see p. 40)

Use hands to check oysters for pieces of shell. Drain oysters in sieve over bowl, reserving liquor. Mix garlic, milk, egg, and Worcestershire sauce together in bowl. Dust oysters with flour and remove to sieve, shaking off excess. Dip oysters in egg mixture and roll in bread crumbs, coating well. In deep skillet heat 1 inch oil until hot. Add oysters in small batches, frying 40-50 seconds per side. Remove with slotted spoon and drain on paper towels. Serve with lemon wedges and Tartar Sauce.

Oyster-Cornbread Stuffing

ENOUGH FOR 10-POUND TURKEY

At Thanksgiving, my customers always want lots of oysters for stuffing, stews, or baking. When they ask for recipes, this is one I recommend.

1½ pints shucked oysters, with liquor	5 cups stale bread crumbs
5 tablespoons unsalted butter	5 cups stale corn bread crumbs
1 cup chopped onion	1 teaspoon dried thyme
¾ cup chopped celery	⅓ cup chopped fresh parsley
½ cup chopped carrot	¼ cup dry white wine
1 Granny Smith apple, peeled, cored, quartered, and sliced	Boiling water (about 2 cups)

Use hands to check oysters for pieces of shell and set aside. In skillet melt 4 tablespoons of the butter, add onion, and sauté 3 minutes. Add celery, carrot, and apple, and cook 3 minutes more. In large bowl combine bread crumbs, corn bread crumbs, thyme, and parsley. Add sautéed mixture to crumb mixture and toss well with hands.

In saucepan melt remaining 1 tablespoon butter and add wine. Stir in oysters and poach until edges begin to curl. Add to stuffing and mix gently with hands. Gradually pour in boiling water until you achieve texture you desire, being careful not to add too much, as stuffing will absorb juices from bird as it cooks. Stuff loosely in body cavity of turkey right before cooking. Never stuff the night before because the oysters could turn bad. Bake turkey according to your favorite recipe.

The Read Family Oyster Sauce

ENOUGH FOR 15- TO 20-POUND TURKEY

On Thanksgiving Day the descendants of John Read gather to eat turkey and be of good cheer. Years ago, my mother, Peggy Read, would have the whole family to our house for Thanksgiving dinner. Now that there are 65 of us, we rent space in a church for the occasion. This recipe is my Grandmother Read's, and it is served, instead of gravy, over the sliced turkey.

2 pints shucked oysters, with liquor	½ cup dry white wine
5 tablespoons unsalted butter	3 tablespoons flour
2 tablespoons finely chopped shallots	2 cups light cream or half-and-half
	1 teaspoon Tabasco
	Paprika and salt to taste

Use hands to check oysters for pieces of shell and set aside. In nonreactive skillet melt 2 tablespoons of the butter and add shallots. Sauté 3 minutes over medium heat until softened. Add wine and bring to simmer, then add oysters and liquor, and simmer 3-4 minutes, or until oysters' edges begin to curl. With slotted spoon, remove oysters to bowl, reserving poaching liquid.

In saucepan melt remaining 3 tablespoons butter over medium heat until bubbly. Add flour and cook 2 minutes. Whisk in cream until combined. Heat to simmer and cook until sauce thickens. Add Tabasco and oyster poaching liquid. Just before serving add oysters and heat through. Season with paprika and salt. Put in gravy boat and ladle over turkey. Any leftover sauce can be thinned with milk and used later for oyster stew.

Oysters in Champagne

SERVES 2-4

Stephanie Ablondi was a long-standing customer. She lived alone with her two cats, who ate everything she did and naturally liked fish the best. She would come by often and get them various treats, such as shrimp, scallops, or salmon (nothing but the best for her cats). This recipe came from Stephanie.

1 pint shucked oysters, with liquor	1 cup champagne
6 tablespoons unsalted butter	1 pound fresh spinach, washed and stems removed
4 tablespoons olive oil	2 tablespoons flour
2 tablespoons chopped shallots	Salt and cayenne pepper to taste

Use hands to check oysters for pieces of shell and set aside. In skillet melt 4 tablespoons of the butter, add oil, and heat until bubbly. Add shallots and sauté over medium heat. Add champagne, bring to simmer, and add oysters and liquor. Lay spinach leaves on top of oysters, cover, and simmer 3-5 minutes, or until edges of oysters just begin to curl. Remove spinach to platter. Spoon oysters on top.

In saucepan heat remaining 2 tablespoons butter until bubbly. Add flour and stir to combine. Whisk in hot oyster-champagne liquid and cook until thickened. Season with salt and cayenne, and pour over oysters and spinach. Serve with toasted French bread.

Oyster Pie

SERVES 4 AS SIDE DISH

This is one of my mother's favorite dishes, yet I would never eat it as a child. Now I like to make it for her because we can enjoy it together without any squabbling — except, perhaps, over who gets the last piece.

1 pint shucked oysters, with liquor	2 tablespoons flour
2 cups heavy cream (approximately)	2 egg yolks
4 tablespoons unsalted butter	2 tablespoons dry sherry
	1 teaspoon Tabasco
	2 cups Ritz cracker crumbs

Use hands to check oysters for pieces of shell. Drain oysters of their liquor by putting them in sieve over bowl. To liquor add enough heavy cream to make 1½ cups, then pour into saucepan and scald. In another saucepan melt 2 tablespoons of the butter, stir in flour, and cook roux over low heat, stirring, for 1 minute. Whisking continuously, add scalded cream in stream and simmer until smooth and thickened, about 5 minutes. Mix ½ cup of the heavy cream with egg yolks and add to cream sauce. Stir in sherry and Tabasco, and cook until hot but not boiling, about 2 minutes. Add drained oysters and remove pan from heat.

Butter 12-inch gratiné dish, add 1 cup of the cracker crumbs, and spread evenly over bottom. Pour in oyster mixture. Sprinkle remaining 1 cup cracker crumbs over top and dot with remaining 2 tablespoons butter. Bake in preheated oven at 350° for 15-20 minutes, or until bubbly and oysters curl.

Oyster and Anchovy Sauce for Pasta   SERVES 2-4

This is a colorful, sensuous dish — the basil provides aroma, the anchovies saltiness, the oysters a soft texture, and the tomato color.

1 pint shucked oysters (about 20), with liquor
3 tablespoons olive oil
1 cup chopped onion
3 cloves garlic, minced
6 anchovy filets, chopped
1 cup peeled, seeded, and chopped tomato

¼ cup dry white wine
¼ cup chopped fresh basil
Salt and cayenne pepper to taste
¾ to 1 pound pasta

Use hands to check oysters for pieces of shell. Drain oysters in sieve over bowl, reserving liquor. Heat oil in skillet over moderate heat. Add onion and garlic, and sauté until onion is translucent, about 3 minutes. Add anchovies and cook, stirring, 2 minutes more. Add tomato, oyster liquor, and wine, and cook until sauce thickens, about 10 minutes. Reduce heat to low, add oysters and basil, and cook 2-3 minutes, or until edges of oysters curl slightly. Season with salt and cayenne. Cook pasta al dente and serve with warm sauce.

Pollock (Atlantic)

Pollachius virens

Atlantic pollock goes by a number of names, including "blue cod" and "Boston bluefish." A member of the cod family, it is a cold water fish found from Newfoundland to New Jersey. Pollock can grow to as long as 4 feet and weigh 35 pounds, but 4 to 12 pounds is the average.

Pollock filets can be recognized by their tan or cream-colored flesh, which whitens when cooked. The skin side of the filet has a dark maroon layer of flesh down its center, similar to that of bluefish. Check this layer to determine freshness. If it is more brown or green than red, the fish is not particularly fresh.

Given the scarcity and high price of haddock and cod, pollock is becoming a popular alternative. It has a large flake and holds together well during cooking, which makes it well suited for soups and chowders. It also can be baked or broiled.

Fishyssoise

SERVES 8

This is a modification of the traditional French vichyssoise. It should have a smooth consistency, which can be attained by pouring the puréed liquid through a fine-mesh sieve. Serve the soup chilled or hot, whichever you prefer.

1-pound pollock filet
3 tablespoons unsalted
  butter
4 leeks, white part only,
  thinly sliced, then washed
1 large onion, thinly sliced
6 potatoes, peeled and thinly
  sliced

4 cups fish stock (see p. 180)
2 cups milk
1 cup light cream
1 cup heavy cream
Salt and pepper to taste
Snipped fresh chives or curry
  powder for garnish

Check pollock for any stray bones, cut into chunks, and set aside. Melt butter in large saucepan over medium heat. Add leeks and onion, and sauté 4 minutes, or until soft. Add potato slices and fish stock, and cook 20 minutes, or until potatoes are well done. Add pollock and cook 10 minutes more, or until fish flakes when tested with fork. Remove from heat and let cool, then purée in food processor fitted with metal blade in small batches. Strain through sieve, stir in milk and light cream, and chill. Stir in heavy cream just before serving and season with salt and pepper. Garnish with snipped chives or curry powder.

Pollock and Coconut Curry

SERVES 4

Homemade coconut milk calls for unsweetened coconut and will not be as thick as the canned variety.

1 ½-pound pollock filet	2 teaspoons grated
3 tablespoons olive oil	gingerroot
1 onion, thinly sliced	½ teaspoon cayenne pepper
1 teaspoon minced garlic	1 cup Coconut Milk (recipe
½ cup diced green bell	follows)
pepper	2 tablespoons fresh lime
2 teaspoons turmeric	juice

Cut pollock into 4 equal pieces and set aside. In deep skillet heat oil until hot. Add onion, garlic, and bell pepper, and sauté until browned and soft. Stir in turmeric, gingerroot, and cayenne, and cook 2 minutes. Add Coconut Milk and bring to simmer. Add pollock and cook in sauce 6 minutes, or until flaky. Remove fish to platter. Add lime juice to curry sauce and stir. Spoon over fish and serve with boiled potatoes.

COCONUT MILK

1 cup shredded unsweetened coconut	1 cup milk

Combine coconut and milk in saucepan and bring to boil. Remove from heat and let sit 1 hour. Strain through sieve, discarding solids.

Baked Pollock with Ginger   SERVES 2

Maggie Lettvin still looks as fit and healthy as she did 25 years ago when I used to watch her exercise show on WGBH-TV. Now she is a customer of mine, and we have frequent discussions about nutrition. This is a recipe she shared with me. By cooking the fish at such a low temperature, none of the natural juices escape, and the fish stays moist and tender.

¾-pound pollock filet   Grated rind of 1 lemon
2 teaspoons minced garlic
1 tablespoon grated
  gingerroot

Place pollock in buttered ovenproof dish. Sprinkle with garlic, gingerroot, and lemon rind. Bake in very low preheated oven (250°) for 15 minutes, then turn oven to 150° and cook until fish is flaky and moist, about 30 minutes.

Test for doneness by placing fork in thickest part and pulling to separate flakes. If there's any resistance, fish is not done and should cook a while longer.

Pollock with Tomatoes and Lime   SERVES 2

Pollock is an economical fish, but because it is not a white fish, customers shy away from it. Here its color is disguised with a tart tomato sauce with peppers and onions.

¾-pound pollock filet   1 clove garlic, minced
4 tablespoons unsalted   8-ounce can stewed tomatoes
  butter   2 tablespoons fresh lime
½ cup sliced onion   juice
½ cup sliced green bell   Chopped fresh cilantro or
  pepper   parsley for garnish

Cut pollock into 2 pieces and set aside. Melt 2 tablespoons of the butter in skillet. Add onion, bell pepper, and garlic, and cook 5 minutes. Remove vegetables from skillet and add remaining 2 tablespoons butter. Melt over medium-high heat and add pollock pieces, browning quickly on both sides, about 2 minutes total. Remove fish to plate. Add tomatoes and lime juice to skillet and bring to simmer. Place fish pieces in tomato sauce, spread sautéed onion and bell pepper over top, cover, and let simmer 10 minutes, or until fish flakes when tested with fork. Transfer fish to platter, spoon on sauce, and garnish with chopped cilantro or parsley.

Pollock with Avocado Sauce   SERVES 4

When I was little and learning to say all the big words my parents used, I would try and make rhymes out of the words I thought I heard. Avocado became "alligator pear." I was convinced that these were things alligators loved to eat, so I ate them, too, and would click my teeth together to make my brothers laugh.

1½-pound pollock filet	Juice of 1 lemon
2 tablespoons unsalted butter	Salt and pepper to taste

AVOCADO SAUCE

1 cup mashed avocado pulp	1 teaspoon chili powder
¼ cup boiling water	¼ teaspoon cayenne pepper
¼ cup heavy cream	Salt to taste
2 tablespoons fresh lime juice	1 small jalapeño pepper, seeded and chopped

Place pollock filet in buttered ovenproof dish and dot with butter. Sprinkle with lemon juice and dust with salt and pepper. Bake in preheated oven at 400° for 12-15 minutes.

Meanwhile, make sauce. Place all but last ingredient in food processor fitted with metal blade. Blend 10 seconds, or until mixture is puréed.

When fish is done, transfer to warm platter, ladle sauce over top, and garnish with jalapeño to taste.

Sweet-and-Sour Pollock

SERVES 4-6

Pollock has a subtle taste that gets a boost from this traditional Chinese sweet-and-sour sauce.

2-pound pollock filet
2 tablespoons unsalted
  butter
½ cup dry white wine
4 tablespoons olive oil
1 tablespoon minced garlic
1 green bell pepper, seeded
  and cut into 1½-inch
  chunks

1 red bell pepper, seeded and
  cut into 1½-inch chunks
6 scallions, sliced
Sweet-and-Sour Sauce
  (recipe follows)
2 tablespoons chopped fresh
  cilantro

Place pollock in buttered ovenproof dish. Dot with butter and pour wine over top. Cover dish with foil and bake in preheated oven at 350° for 15-20 minutes depending on thickness of filet.

In skillet heat oil until hot. Add garlic and sauté 2 minutes. Add bell pepper chunks and scallions. Sauté until softened, about 6 minutes. Remove from heat.

Arrange fish on platter. Lay vegetables over top and ladle sauce over all. Garnish with chopped cilantro.

SWEET-AND-SOUR SAUCE

3 tablespoons soy sauce
3 tablespoons cider vinegar
2 tablespoons dry sherry
2 tablespoons sugar
3 tablespoons pineapple
  juice
1 tablespoon minced
  gingerroot

2 tablespoons ketchup
1 tablespoon cornstarch
1 tablespoon fish cooking
  juices
½ cup pineapple chunks
½ cup mandarin orange
  sections
¼ cup sliced water chestnuts

In saucepan combine soy sauce, vinegar, sherry, sugar, pineapple juice, gingerroot, and ketchup. Bring to simmer and cook 5 minutes. In cup mix together cornstarch and fish cooking juices. Add 2 tablespoons hot ingredients to cup, mix well, and add all back to saucepan. Cook until sauce is thick and coats spoon. Fold in pineapple chunks, orange sections, and water chestnuts to add sweetness and texture.

Porgy (or Scup)

Stenotomus chrysops

Porgy is found from Cape Cod to the Carolinas. Also known as scup, it is a small fish with numerous sharp bones and thick scales. The Narragansett Indians called porgy *mishcuppauog*, and used it for fertilizer.

A porgy can grow up to 18 inches long and weigh 4 pounds, but smaller ones are more common. Generally sold whole, it is a lean fish with a firm, flaky flesh. Porgy can be grilled whole, with its flesh scored before cooking, or pan-fried or poached. The larger ones are good fileted.

Sautéed Porgy
SERVES 2

Make sure the fish is as dry as possible before coating with the cornmeal-flour mixture and frying.

2 whole porgy (¾ to 1 pound
  each)
¼ cup milk
¼ cup cornmeal
¼ cup flour
2 tablespoons unsalted
  butter

2 tablespoons olive oil
2 tablespoons peeled,
  seeded, and chopped
  tomato
2 tablespoons chopped
  scallions
Lemon wedges for garnish

Clean fish by removing innards, scales, and gills. Rinse and pat dry with paper towel. Dip fish in milk and then in combined cornmeal and flour. Place on plate and refrigerate 30 minutes. Heat butter and oil in skillet over medium heat. Add fish and sauté 4 minutes per side, or until crispy and golden brown. Serve topped with tomato and scallions and garnished with lemon wedges.

Grilled Porgy with Butter Sauce   SERVES 2

This fish is very bony, so eat it slowly and carefully.

2 whole porgy (¾ to 1 pound
  each)
4 tablespoons unsalted
  butter
1 clove garlic, minced

2 teaspoons fresh lemon
  juice
1 teaspoon dried thyme
1 tablespoon chopped fresh
  parsley for garnish

Clean fish by removing innards, scales, and gills. With sharp knife, make two shallow slashes — just enough to break through skin — on each side of fish. Put fish in glass dish.

Melt butter in saucepan over medium heat, add garlic, and cook 2 minutes, or until soft. Add lemon juice and thyme, and stir to blend. Brush fish thoroughly with butter sauce and refrigerate 1 hour.

Heat charcoal briquettes until past red-coal stage and white ashes begin to form. Place fish on grill and cook 3-4 minutes per side, basting frequently with remaining butter sauce. Serve garnished with chopped fresh parsley.

Red Snapper

Lutjanus campechanus

Red snapper is not indigenous to New England waters; it is found, instead, around Florida and in the Gulf of Mexico. I am including it because, thanks to air freight, it is becoming more readily available in New England fish markets and restaurants. Also, with the ban imposed on striped bass, red snapper has gained popularity. (It should not be confused with our local redfish, which is a perch.)

Red snapper is very easy to distinguish because of its rosy red color, light-colored fins, and bright red eyes. Some weigh up to 40 pounds, but the average market size is usually 2 to 6 pounds.

Red snapper is sold whole or as filets. Figure 1 pound per person when buying it whole, as the head and bones can account for 60 percent of its weight, and ⅓ to ½ pound per person when buying filets. It is a bony fish, so you might wish to have it fileted at the market. If so, be sure to ask for the head and bones, as they make delicious stock. Should you want to do the fileting yourself, be careful of the spines, which are hard, pointed, and very sharp. Trim these fins with kitchen shears to avoid puncturing your fingers. Small snappers around 1 to 2 pounds should be cooked whole.

The flesh of this fish turns white when cooked, yet a tinge of red will show if it was bought at its freshest. It is lean, moist, and firm, with a sweet, distinctive flavor. The smaller ones have a finer flake.

Red snapper is costly, but when it is stuffed and baked, few other fish can rival its impressive presentation.

Whole Poached Red Snapper SERVES 4-6

Red snapper is a beautiful fish to serve whole, as the red coloring of its skin remains even after cooking. Its flesh is firm with a large flake ideal for poaching.

1 whole red snapper (about 4 to 5 pounds), scaled	1 handful fresh parsley
¼ cup chopped shallots	Salt to taste
1 large rib celery without leaves, coarsely chopped	4 cups water
1 carrot, peeled and coarsely chopped	2½ cups rosé wine

Clean snapper, making sure all gills and entrails are removed. In 2-quart stainless steel saucepan, combine shallots, celery, carrot, parsley, salt, and water. Simmer, uncovered, 20 minutes. Strain through fine-mesh sieve, discarding vegetables.

Pour this and rosé in poacher, heat to simmer, and place fish on poaching rack in bath. Liquid should just reach top of fish at its thickest part. Add more water if needed. Cover and poach, with liquid just simmering, for 20-30 minutes, or until flesh gives some resistance when pressed with finger. Remember that fish will continue cooking once you take it out of poacher, so be careful not to overcook. (If you don't have fancy fish poacher, use roasting pan. Place fish on rack on bottom, cover pan with foil, and bake in preheated 350° oven for 30-40 minutes.) Carefully remove fish to serving platter and serve immediately.

Baked Stuffed Red Snapper

SERVES 6-8

Red snapper is easy to stuff because it has a large, stocky body. If you don't want to bother with a whole fish, you can use two equal-size filets. Place stuffing between them and tie together with twine. You can use all wild rice or all brown rice, depending on your taste.

1 whole red snapper (about 6 pounds), backbone removed but head and tail intact

Salt and pepper to taste
Juice of 1 lemon

WILD RICE STUFFING

1 cup cooked wild rice
1 cup cooked brown rice
7 tablespoons butter
½ pound mushrooms, sliced
1 cup chopped onion
1 cup chopped celery
3 scallions, chopped

½ cup julienned carrot
3 tablespoons chopped fresh parsley
½ teaspoon dried thyme
½ teaspoon dried rosemary
½ cup dry white wine

Rub inside of snapper with a little salt and pepper and squeeze lemon juice over flesh. Then make stuffing.

Put rice in bowl and set aside. Melt 2 tablespoons of the butter in skillet and sauté mushrooms about 5 minutes. Drain juices and toss mushrooms with rice. Melt 3 more tablespoons of the butter in clean skillet, add onion, and cook 3 minutes. Add celery, scallions, and carrot, and cook another 3 minutes. Remove from heat and stir in parsley, thyme, and rosemary, mixing thoroughly. Combine with rice and stuff into body cavity of snapper.

Place stuffed fish on foil in roasting pan. Fold up sides of foil to keep liquids from seeping out. Pour wine over top of fish and dot with remaining 2 tablespoons butter. Bake in preheated oven at 400° for approximately 30-40 minutes, or 10 minutes to the inch, measured at thickest part.

Grilled Red Snapper

SERVES 2

If fresh herbs aren't available, use dried, in reduced amounts.

1 whole red snapper (about 2
  pounds)
Juice of 1 lime
¼ cup olive oil

¼ teaspoon salt
¼ teaspoon freshly ground
  black pepper

HERB BUTTER

6 tablespoons unsalted
  butter, softened
1 teaspoon chopped fresh
  thyme (¼ teaspoon dried)
1 teaspoon chopped fresh
  basil (¼ teaspoon dried)

1 teaspoon chopped fresh
  tarragon (¼ teaspoon
  dried)
¼ teaspoon salt

Clean and scale snapper, making sure gills and innards are removed. Combine lime juice, oil, salt, and pepper, and brush fish thoroughly. Place on grill over hot coals and cook 4-5 minutes per side.

Combine all ingredients for herb butter and dab on top of fish. Serve immediately. (Wrap leftover butter in plastic wrap and freeze for another use.)

Red Snapper with Fresh Herbs

SERVES 2

The key to this recipe is having the fish thoroughly chilled before cooking it in the hot skillet.

¾ pound red snapper filets
2 tablespoons olive oil
2 tablespoons unsalted
  butter, melted
Juice of 1 lime
2 teaspoons chopped fresh
  thyme (½ teaspoon dried)

2 tablespoons chopped fresh
  basil (2 teaspoons dried)
1 tablespoon chopped fresh
  parsley
Salt and pepper to taste
Watercress sprigs and lime
  wedges for garnish

Check filets for bones. Combine oil, melted butter, lime juice, thyme, basil, and parsley in glass pie plate. Season with salt and pepper. Place filets in marinade, turning to coat thoroughly on both sides. Refrigerate 1 hour.

Heat until hot a nonstick skillet large enough to hold filets in one layer. Place filets, skin side up, in hot skillet, searing on one side for 1 minute. Turn over, brush with marinade, and cover. Reduce heat to medium-low and cook 6-8 minutes on other side. Brush tops with marinade and serve, garnished with watercress sprigs and lime wedges. Accompany with remaining marinade.

Red Snapper with Mangoes in Green Peppercorn Sauce

SERVES 4

Mangoes are a sweet, tangy fruit and a particular favorite of mine. Each time I make this dish, I am reminded of an Earthwatch expedition I went on to Costa Rica to study howler monkeys. At one point while taking a break, I sat eating a ripe, juicy mango and noticed a group of monkeys nearby doing the same thing. Who was mimicking whom?

2 pounds red snapper filets, skinned
1 tablespoon fresh lime juice
3 tablespoons flour
½ teaspoon salt
¼ teaspoon black pepper
7 tablespoons unsalted butter

2 large, ripe mangoes, peeled and sliced
2 tablespoons green peppercorns, drained
½ cup heavy cream
Watercress sprigs for garnish

Place filets in shallow glass dish and sprinkle with lime juice. Chill 1 hour. Combine flour, salt, and black pepper, and dust fish with mixture, shaking off excess. Melt 4 tablespoons of the butter in skillet and sauté fish 4-5 minutes per side depending on thickness. Transfer to warm oven.

In clean skillet melt 2 tablespoons of the butter and sauté mango slices 2 minutes; arrange around snapper in warm oven. Melt remaining tablespoon butter in skillet, add green peppercorns, and sauté 1 minute. Add heavy cream and boil 3 minutes, or until cream is reduced by one half. Pour over snapper and serve at once, garnished with sprigs of watercress.

Salmon (Atlantic)

Salmo salar

In New England, commercial fishing for Atlantic salmon is practically nonexistent. So at The Fishmonger we rely on the plentiful supply of farmed salmon from Canada and Europe. They are consistently of excellent quality, packed to perfection head to tail in insulated boxes, and available year-round.

Salmon is sold whole, in steaks, or as filets. When buying whole salmon, look at the gills, which should be a rosy red color if the fish is fresh, not brown or gray-red; the eyes should be bright and clear. Because salmon are gutted before shipping, fresh blood frequently appears in the body cavity — this is another sign of freshness. Silvery scales should cover the skin, and the fish should be firm and solid to the touch. If soft, there's a good chance the fish has been frozen and thawed.

Steaks are cut off the body at 1-inch intervals up to the last dorsal fin before the tail. I recommend buying whole fish that weigh between 6 and 8 pounds, as each steak will then be about ½ pound, a good serving size.

A whole filet of salmon has small pin bones embedded in the center of the flesh. You can feel them with your fingers as you stroke the flesh downward toward the tail. Tweezers or small needle-nosed pliers are handy in pulling these out.

Salmon can be prepared in a variety of ways: poached, baked, broiled, grilled, smoked, or cured when making Gravlax. A foolproof guideline for cooking salmon is the "Canadian method," which calls for cooking it 10 minutes per inch, measured at its thickest part.

When poaching a whole salmon, I cut off the head and tail and then remove all the center bones and pin bones, keeping the back intact and uncut. Using heavy cotton twine, I tie the fish together at 2-inch intervals before putting it in the poacher. This eliminates having to wrap the salmon in cheesecloth, which is difficult to remove without breaking the fish.

Salmon Tartare   SERVES 10 FOR HORS D'OEUVRES

Use only the freshest salmon, since the fish is not cooked, and make this at the last minute. It should be served immediately.

2-pound salmon filet, skinned and cut into 1-inch pieces
3 tablespoons fresh lime juice
½ cup chopped scallions
1 clove garlic, minced
3 tablespoons capers, squeeze-drained and chopped

2 tablespoons olive oil
3 tablespoons chopped fresh dill
Salt and freshly ground black pepper to taste

Put salmon pieces in food processor fitted with metal blade. Pulse briefly a few times, being careful not to grind too finely. Transfer to bowl, add lime juice, scallions, garlic, capers, oil, and chopped dill, and mix together with your hands. Season with salt and pepper if needed. Serve on pumpernickel triangles or cucumber rounds.

Smoked Salmon Mousse SERVES 10 FOR HORS D'OEUVRES

At the store, when we have trimmings left over from smoked salmon, we use them to make a spread or this tangy mousse.

½ pound smoked salmon
    pieces
1 envelope unflavored gelatin
½ cup water
½ cup light cream, scalded
8 ounces cream cheese,
    softened
1 cup sour cream
2 teaspoons Worcestershire
    sauce
½ teaspoon Tabasco
1 clove garlic, minced

2 tablespoons chopped fresh
    chives or scallion greens
1 tablespoon fresh lemon
    juice
¼ cup chopped fresh dill
1 tablespoon prepared
    horseradish
½ cup chopped black olives
¼ pound red salmon caviar
    (optional)
Dill sprigs and lemon slices
    for garnish

Chop salmon pieces and set aside. Dissolve gelatin in water, add hot cream, and stir. Let cool.

In bowl combine cream cheese, sour cream, Worcestershire sauce, Tabasco, garlic, chives, lemon juice, dill, and horseradish. Whisk or beat until blended. Add cooled gelatin mixture and whisk well. Fold in smoked salmon, black olives, and caviar if desired.

Pour into well-greased 3-cup fish mold. Refrigerate until firm (about 6 hours) and unmold onto platter. Decorate with fresh dill sprigs and lemon slices. Serve with thin rye bread.

Gravlaks/Gravlax SERVES 8-12

Gravlaks, or Gravlax, originated in Sweden and is served there as part of a smorgasbord. The sugar-to-salt ratio should be 2 to 1, and the more dill you use, the more aroma and taste will penetrate the flesh. Cognac and white peppercorns are usually added, but I find they discolor the salmon and choose to omit them. This is very easy to make for a crowd, and every bit gets eaten.

2 equal-size salmon filets
    (about 1 pound each)
½ cup sugar

¼ cup salt
½ bunch fresh dill
Mustard-Dill Sauce (recipe
    follows)

Carefully check salmon for bones, especially pin bones in center of flesh. Use needle-nosed pliers or tweezers to remove.

Combine sugar and salt in bowl and visually divide into 4 parts. Using one quarter of the mixture, coat skin side of one filet, then place, skin side down, in glass or earthenware dish. Using one half the mixture, coat 2 middle flesh sides of filets. Break dill from stems and use to cover flesh sides of salmon. Now put 2 filets together like a sandwich and spread remaining sugar-salt mixture on top skin. Place a sheet of plastic wrap on top and sides to keep fish from drying out.

Weights must be applied evenly to cure salmon. I use bags of rice, sugar, or dried beans. Place bags in large plastic bag and lay on top of fish. A brick or plate makes large dents in fish and does not work as well. Cure fish in refrigerator 18-36 hours. Check for doneness by pressing center of filet with finger. Flesh should be firm and spring back.

Drain off juices that might have accumulated during curing. Take apart filets, place on wooden cutting board, and slice very thinly on an angle, cutting across the grain with long, sharp knife. Serve with Mustard-Dill Sauce and dark bread.

MUSTARD-DILL SAUCE — MAKES ABOUT 1 CUP

4 tablespoons Dijon mustard
1 teaspoon dry mustard
3 tablespoons sugar
2 tablespoons white vinegar
1 cup olive oil
4 tablespoons chopped fresh dill

Place all ingredients except dill in bowl and whisk until smooth and creamy. Add dill at end, mixing just until incorporated.

Poached Whole Salmon

SERVES 12-14

When I was growing up, my mother took great pleasure in poaching salmon for the Fourth of July, a great New England tradition. Fluted cucumbers for scales, a black olive for the eye, daisies all around the border — it is a wonderful childhood memory. Now it's my pleasure to arrive at her home and present her with a salmon of my doing. And at 79 years old, she is overjoyed.

1 whole salmon (6 to 8 pounds)	**Fish stock or court-bouillon (recipes follow)**

Bone entire salmon. Tie fish with cotton twine every 2 inches and place on rack of fish poacher. Add enough fish stock to cover top of fish. Turn heat to high, and when liquid starts to boil, lower heat to simmer and poach 20-25 minutes. (A good rule of thumb for poaching, whether it be a whole fish, steaks, or pieces, is to poach 10 minutes to the inch, measured at its thickest part. A ½-inch steak would need 5 minutes; a 2-inch piece, 20 minutes. Start timing once simmering begins.) Add more stock or water as liquid evaporates, always keeping the top covered. When done, remove fish from poacher and place in refrigerator 6-12 hours. Peel off skin, remove dark, fatty flesh along midsection, and serve on platter. Decorate to your pleasure.

Fish Stock

MAKES 3-4 QUARTS

Fish stock is the base for many soups and sauces and is equally good for poaching. It is very important to remove the gills from the fish carcass because they will make the stock bitter. Cooking time should be between 20 and 30 minutes, once the stock has reached a boil, for all the flavor will have been released into the broth by then. Use fish that have a lot of natural gelatin in their bones but are not oily or dark fleshed.* Ask your fish market for its leftover bones.

5 to 7 pounds fish carcasses or frames*	**2 bay leaves**
1 large onion, chopped	**1 tablespoon dried thyme**
5 carrots, peeled and sliced	**1 cup dry white wine**
5 ribs celery, chopped	**Cold water**
2 leeks, green part only, sliced and thoroughly rinsed	

Rinse fish carcasses or frames, removing gills and any entrails that might remain, and place in large kettle along with vegetables. (The smaller you chop the vegetables, the more flavor you will get from them.) Add bay leaves, thyme, and wine. Pour in enough cold water to just cover fish bones. Place over high heat and bring to boil, then reduce heat so stock just simmers. Cook 25 minutes.

Remove and discard bones and vegetables, then strain stock through sieve into bowl. Let cool and refrigerate. Some sediment will sink to the bottom, but do not use this sludge. Ladle extra stock into containers and freeze for future use.

* Fish to use: haddock, cod, flounder, wolffish, striped bass, red snapper, monkfish, tilefish.

Fish not to use: bluefish, mackerel, salmon, tuna, swordfish, herring, shad, pollock.

Court-Bouillon   MAKES 3 QUARTS

This is easier to make than fish stock but should be used only for poaching. There are many variations of ingredients, but you can use this as a basic guide. The vinegar and lemon juice acidify the water but should not leave any added flavor.

3 quarts water	10 black peppercorns
½ cup white wine vinegar	1 bay leaf
1 cup chopped onion	5 tablespoons fresh lemon
1 cup chopped carrot	juice
1 cup chopped celery	

Put all ingredients in large pot, bring to boil, and simmer 10 minutes. Strain before using.

The Fishmonger Salmon Salad SERVES 4

Salmon makes a colorful summer salad. The large chunks of fish will break apart when mixed together with the dressing.

1 pound poached salmon
  meat, skinned (see p. 180)
3 tomatoes, peeled, cored,
  seeded, and chopped
1 cucumber, peeled, seeded,
  and diced
¾ cup black olives, julienned
¼ cup capers, squeeze-
  drained
2 ribs celery, diced

1 red bell pepper, finely
  chopped
3 scallions, chopped
3 tablespoons chopped fresh
  dill
Watercress-Dill Sauce (see
  p. 190) or mayonnaise (see
  p. 283)
Lettuce leaves

Break up salmon into chunks, checking for bones, and set aside. In bowl toss together tomatoes, cucumber, black olives, capers, celery, bell pepper, scallions, and dill. Stir in dressing of your choice and mix to coat. Add salmon, mixing carefully with rubber spatula, and more dressing if needed. Serve on bed of lettuce.

Poached Salmon in Zinfandel Sauce SERVES 4

Zinfandel has a full, fruity flavor with an almost peppery taste. Combining it with salmon defies the rule of "no red wine with fish" and creates a beautiful claret-colored sauce. Try other red wines to find your favorite.

1½-pound salmon filet cut
  into 4 equal pieces
Fish stock (see p. 180)

Dry white wine

ZINFANDEL SAUCE

6 tablespoons unsalted
  butter
¼ cup chopped shallots
2 cups fish stock (see p. 180)

4 cups zinfandel
2 tablespoons flour
2 cups sliced mushrooms
  (about ½ pound)

In skillet poach salmon (see p. 180) for 10 minutes in fish stock and white wine to cover, using equal amounts of stock and wine.

Meanwhile, make sauce. Melt 2 tablespoons of the butter in saucepan over medium heat. Add shallots and sauté 4 minutes, or until soft. Add fish stock, bring to boil, and cook until reduced by one half. Add 2 cups of the zinfandel and reduce by one half again. Add remaining 2 cups zinfandel and reduce by one half once more. You should end up with about 1¾ to 2 cups of sauce, which should coat a spoon like thin syrup.

In small bowl combine 2 tablespoons butter, softened, and flour. Add 4 tablespoons sauce and mix well, whisking to remove lumps. Add to sauce, whisking continuously, and simmer until sauce thickens.

In skillet melt remaining 2 tablespoons butter and sauté mushrooms until soft. Remove with slotted spoon, discarding juices. Add half the mushrooms to the sauce.

When salmon is done, transfer to serving platter, ladle on sauce, and garnish with remaining mushrooms.

Poached Salmon Steaks with Dilled Cucumber Sauce

SERVES 6

This light, low-calorie sauce can accompany just about any cold poached fish.

6 salmon steaks, 1 inch thick	Fish stock (see p. 180) or court-bouillon (see p. 181)

DILLED CUCUMBER SAUCE

2 cups plain yogurt	2 tablespoons chopped fresh dill
1 cup peeled, seeded, and grated cucumber	2 cloves garlic, minced
4 tablespoons fresh lemon juice	Chopped fresh dill for garnish

Poach salmon (see p. 180) in fish stock or court-bouillon 6-10 minutes, then chill in refrigerator.

Put yogurt in fine sieve and let drain 2 hours, or until firm like cottage cheese but not lumpy. Do the same with cucumber so excess water is able to drain out and sauce does not become too runny. Combine yogurt, cucumber, lemon juice, 2 tablespoons chopped dill, and garlic in bowl. Mix well and garnish with more dill.

Remove and discard skin from chilled poached salmon. Place on platter and serve with sauce.

Poached Salmon with Mousseline Sauce SERVES 4

The vivid yellow sauce and pink salmon create an elegant dish for a dinner party. Garnish with snipped fresh dill and serve with steamed snow peas and boiled new potatoes.

1½-pound salmon filet, skinned	Fish stock (see p. 180) or court-bouillon (see p. 181)

MOUSSELINE SAUCE

12 tablespoons unsalted butter (1½ sticks)	½ teaspoon salt
3 egg yolks	Cayenne pepper to taste
3 tablespoons fresh lemon juice	½ cup heavy cream

Cut salmon into 4 equal pieces. In stainless steel pan poach pieces (see p. 180) in fish stock or court-bouillon 10 minutes.

Meanwhile, in small, heavy saucepan melt butter over low heat, being careful not to let it brown. In small metal bowl vigorously whisk egg yolks until foamy. Place bowl over pot of boiling water and pour in hot butter in slow, steady stream, whisking vigorously until all is incorporated. Continue cooking and whisking over hot water until sauce begins to thicken. Add lemon juice, salt, and cayenne. Let sauce cool to lukewarm.

Just before serving, beat heavy cream in clean, chilled bowl until stiff. With rubber spatula, fold cream into cooled sauce with easy up-and-down strokes. Pour into sauceboat and serve with salmon.

Baked Salmon in Foil

For extra flavor, add any variety of herbs or vegetables to the foil packets. Try a thin, peeled lemon or lime slice, chopped fresh tomato, julienned carrot, tarragon, basil, or cilantro.

⅓-pound salmon filet,
skinned, or ½-pound
salmon steak
2 tablespoons dry white wine

1 tablespoon fish stock (see
p. 180)
1 sprig dill

Using heavy-duty foil, cut a piece large enough to hold fish so that ends of foil can be folded together into sealed package without crowding fish. Butter center of foil and place fish on butter. Spoon wine and fish stock over top and lay dill on top. Close packet and bake in preheated 350° oven for 15-20 minutes.

Salmon Filet with Leeks

This simple recipe was inspired by a dish I had in the Caribbean a few years ago.

2½-pound salmon filet,
skinned
Salt and pepper to taste
1 pound leeks
4 tablespoons unsalted
butter

2 cups heavy cream
½ cup dry white wine
Lime slices for garnish

Cut salmon into 6 equal pieces and sprinkle both sides with salt and pepper. Prepare leeks by slicing white part of bulb into thin rings. Put into bowl of cold water, separating rings to clean thoroughly. Carefully scoop leeks from water, trying not to disturb sand that has fallen to bottom. Shake in sieve, then dry on paper towels.

Melt butter in skillet and sauté leeks until soft. Add heavy cream and simmer 5 minutes. Pour half the leek mixture into greased baking dish, place salmon on top, then pour rest of leeks on top of fish. Pour white wine over all and bake, covered with foil, in preheated 400° oven for 15 minutes. Serve garnished with lime slices.

Baked Salmon Steaks with Caper Sauce   SERVES 4

When I was a child, salmon was served only on the Fourth of July. Now, thanks to aquaculture, it is available all year round.

4 salmon steaks
4 tablespoons unsalted
  butter

¾ cup dry white wine

CAPER SAUCE

2 tablespoons unsalted
  butter
2 tablespoons flour
¼ teaspoon paprika
¾ cup bottled clam juice or
  fish stock (see p. 180)

¾ cup heavy cream
1 egg yolk
3 tablespoons capers,
  squeeze-drained

Place salmon steaks in baking dish, top each with 1 tablespoon butter, and pour wine over all. Bake in preheated 350° oven for 10-15 minutes.

Begin caper sauce by melting butter in saucepan over medium heat. Add flour and cook 2 minutes. Stir in paprika and clam juice, whisking until incorporated, and cook until thick. Blend heavy cream with egg yolk and whisk into sauce. Cook until hot, but not boiling. Add capers.

Place cooked salmon steaks on platter, spoon on sauce, and garnish as desired.

Salmon Escalopes with Crème Fraîche   SERVES 4

Escalopes are slices of meat or fish flattened slightly and cooked in butter or some other fat. These should be cooked very quickly over high heat just until browned.

1 ½-pound salmon filet, skinned and cut into eight ¼-inch-thick pieces	2 tablespoons minced shallots
½ cup flour	¼ cup dry white wine
½ teaspoon salt	2 tablespoons fresh lemon juice
Freshly ground black pepper to taste	1 cup crème fraîche* (see p. 16), sour cream, or yogurt
6 tablespoons olive oil	2 tablespoons chopped fresh dill or chives
6 tablespoons unsalted butter	

Lay salmon escalopes between pieces of waxed paper and flatten with rolling pin. Combine flour, salt, and pepper on plate. Lightly dredge salmon pieces in mixture.

In 2 large skillets heat equal parts oil and butter over medium-high heat. When bubbly add 4 salmon pieces to each pan. Cook 2 minutes per side and remove to warm platter.

Combine leftover fat in one skillet, including any browned bits in bottom of skillet. Add shallots and more butter if needed, then cook until soft, about 3 minutes. Add wine, bring to boil, and reduce to 3 tablespoons. Add lemon juice and whisk in crème fraîche and chopped dill. Bring to simmer, then pour over salmon and serve.

* Crème fraîche is wonderful for thickening sauces, for it will not separate or curdle upon cooking. Unfortunately, it contains a lot of calories and should be used sparingly.

Sautéed Salmon with Sorrel Sauce SERVES 4

Rebecca Olson has a passion for salmon. Her passion carries over into how she works at The Fishmonger. With independence and determination, she is fighting her way back upstream so she can go back to college. All I can do is cheer her on as I watch her grow and eventually leave.

1½-pound salmon filet
¼ cup flour mixed with salt
   and pepper to taste

4 tablespoons unsalted
   butter

SORREL SAUCE
½ pound sorrel
3 tablespoons unsalted
   butter
1 tablespoon fresh lemon
   juice

1 cup crème fraîche (see p.
   16), sour cream, or yogurt
½ teaspoon salt
¼ teaspoon freshly ground
   white pepper

Remove skin from salmon, cut into 4 equal pieces, and dust with seasoned flour. Melt butter in skillet over medium-high heat and sear salmon 2 minutes on each side. Put in ovenproof dish and bake in preheated 200° oven for 20 minutes.

Meanwhile, make Sorrel Sauce. Remove sorrel leaves from stems and rinse leaves thoroughly. Dry on paper towels. Roll 3 or 4 leaves together into a cigar shape and then, with large, sharp knife, cut leaves into thin strips. Melt butter in skillet and add sorrel. Sauté until wilted, about 3 minutes. Add lemon juice and crème fraîche, and bring to simmer. Stir in salt and white pepper.

Remove salmon from oven, spoon sauce over fish, and serve immediately.

Grilled Salmon Teriyaki SERVES 4

Salmon steaks hold together very well on the grill. Once they're cooked, you can easily peel off the skin and remove the center bone.

4 salmon steaks (about 2
   pounds)
¼ cup soy sauce
2 tablespoons honey or
   maple syrup
3 tablespoons dry sherry

3 tablespoons rice vinegar
1 clove garlic, mashed
1 teaspoon minced
   gingerroot
1 tablespoon olive oil

Place salmon in flat-bottom glass dish. Combine soy sauce, honey, sherry, vinegar, garlic, gingerroot, and oil in saucepan. Bring to boil, reduce heat to simmer, and cook 5 minutes.

Let marinade cool to room temperature, then pour over salmon steaks. Let marinate in refrigerator 1 hour. Grill over hot charcoal 5 minutes per side, brushing with marinade while cooking. Serve immediately along with extra marinade.

Grilled Salmon Steaks with Green Mayonnaise

SERVES 6

Sometimes I feel like a female Rodney Dangerfield as I go about my day. Selecting the freshest and best has a way of irritating some of my suppliers. I try not to take their comments personally, but on cold, rainy days, I, too, sometimes feel as though "I get no respect."

6 salmon steaks, 1 inch thick
(about 3 pounds)
3 tablespoons unsalted
butter

2 tablespoons olive oil

GREEN MAYONNAISE

½ cup spinach leaves
½ cup watercress leaves
½ cup fresh parsley sprigs
2 tablespoons fresh tarragon
2 teaspoons Worcestershire
sauce
5 tablespoons fresh lemon
juice

1 cup crème fraîche (see
p. 16), sour cream, or
yogurt
2 cups mayonnaise (see
p. 283)
Cayenne pepper to taste

Pat salmon dry with paper towel. Melt butter, add oil, and heat until hot. Brush on both sides of steaks and grill over hot coals 4-5 minutes per side.

Rinse and spin-dry spinach, watercress, and parsley. Place in food processor fitted with metal blade and add tarragon, Worcestershire sauce, lemon juice, and crème fraîche. Blend well, about 15 seconds, then pour into bowl and whisk in mayonnaise. Season with cayenne.

When steaks are done, remove to warm platter and serve with Green Mayonnaise.

189

Broiled Salmon
with Watercress-Dill Sauce

SERVES 6

My children consider this sauce their birthright and insist on it whenever I make broiled salmon. At the store, it is also in demand as an accompaniment to the cold poached salmon we sell.

6 salmon steaks or 2½-
  pound filet
4 tablespoons unsalted
  butter

1 tablespoon fresh lemon
  juice
1 tablespoon chopped fresh
  dill

WATERCRESS-DILL SAUCE

1 cup watercress leaves (no
  stems)
½ cup fresh dill weed
1 small Bermuda onion,
  grated

Juice of 1 lemon
Dash of cayenne pepper
½ cup sour cream
3 cups mayonnaise (see
  p. 283)

Place salmon in pan lined with foil. Melt butter in saucepan and stir in lemon juice and dill. Pour evenly over salmon and broil 7-10 minutes. (If cooking steaks, turn over after 5 minutes; if filets, do not turn.)

Meanwhile, make sauce. Put watercress, dill weed, onion, lemon juice, cayenne, and sour cream in food processor fitted with metal blade. Blend thoroughly. Transfer to bowl and whisk in mayonnaise until blended and smooth. Transfer broiled salmon to serving tray and serve with sauce.

Scallops

Sea scallops *(Placopecten magellanicus)*
Bay scallops *(Aequipecten irradians)*
Calico scallops *(Argopecten gibbus)*

In the eastern United States three types of scallops enter our markets: the sea scallop, the bay or cape scallop, and the calico scallop. The sea scallop averages about forty meats to a pound, but can range from the size of a dime to that of a hockey puck. The smaller ones are found from Digby Bay, Nova Scotia, to off the coast of Maine. New Bedford, Massachusetts, controls a large portion of the deep sea scallop industry and supplies most of Boston and New York. Large sea scallops are no less tasty or tender than small ones, but are best cut into uniform sizes for even cooking. Sea scallops are available year-round.

The seasonal bay or cape scallops of Massachusetts Bay are the sweetest tasting of all scallops. Their season is limited to a few months, from around the first of November through the end of March. The height of the season is usually at Christmastime, unless the area has subzero temperatures and the bays freeze, making the scallops difficult to harvest.

The calico scallop from Florida is also a very small scallop. These scallops are often sold by supermarkets at a low price and labeled as cape scallops. They are not the same scallop at all. Calicos have a long shelf life of up to two weeks, as they are partially cooked and mechanically shucked by processors on shore. They lack the distinctive sweet scallop flavor, yet the untrained palate might not detect any difference.

The scallop has a tough muscle, or "foot," that holds it to its shell. Although not essential, it's generally best to remove this by pulling it off with your fingers and discarding. If left on, this can give part of the scallop a chewy texture when cooked.

Scallops have a way of becoming "gassy." They don't give you gas, but they have a distinct odor if kept in a closed bag or container for more than a day. Consequently, they should be placed in a bowl to breathe with a wet paper towel laid over the top so air can pass through.

I am a purist and love the sweet taste of scallops, so I prefer them sautéed briefly in butter and served immediately with a bit of fresh lemon juice. But they also are delicious broiled, grilled, poached, or baked. Whichever way you choose, just remember that it's better to undercook than overcook them.

How to Remove the Foot from a Scallop

Locate the small muscle hinge, or foot, attached to one side of the scallop. Peel this off with your fingers and discard.

Marinated Scallops

When cooking scallops, the simpler and quicker the recipe is, the better.

1 pound sea or bay scallops
¼ cup dry vermouth
¼ cup olive oil

2 tablespoons chopped fresh
   parsley
1 clove garlic, minced

Remove feet from scallops (see p. 192). Mix vermouth, oil, parsley, and garlic in bowl and add scallops. Let marinate 2 hours in refrigerator. Remove scallops with slotted spoon to ovenproof dish, broil 3-5 minutes, and serve immediately.

Scallop Seviche

When making seviche, the shellfish or fish is actually "cooked" by marinating it in citric acid, which is present in all citrus fruits.

1¼ pounds sea or bay
   scallops
Juice of 6 lemons or 3
   lemons and 3 limes
1½ pounds tomatoes,
   peeled, cored, seeded, and
   finely chopped
1 Bermuda onion, chopped
½ cup pitted green olives,
   sliced into eighths
1 clove garlic, minced
¼ cup chopped fresh parsley
2 tablespoons chopped fresh
   cilantro

3 cups tomato juice
2 tablespoons olive oil
1 tablespoon chopped fresh
   oregano (1 teaspoon dried)
¼ teaspoon salt
¼ teaspoon black pepper
4 serrano peppers or 1
   jalapeño pepper, seeded
   and chopped
Lettuce leaves
1 avocado, peeled, seeded,
   and sliced

Remove feet from scallops (see p. 192) and slice thinly. Put in nonmetal bowl, cover with citrus juice, and let sit in refrigerator 12-24 hours.

Before serving, combine tomatoes, onion, olives, garlic, parsley, cilantro, tomato juice, oil, oregano, salt, and pepper. Drain juice from scallops, which should look white all the way through. Add scallops to tomato mixture and stir until well blended. Add chopped peppers according to desired hotness. Serve on bed of lettuce accompanied by slices of avocado.

Chilled Scallop Soup

SERVES 4

The perfect prelude to a dinner party.

¾ pound sea or bay scallops
6 tablespoons unsalted
butter
1 large onion, chopped
½ cup dry white wine
3 tablespoons flour

2 cups light cream, warmed
Salt and pepper to taste
Dash of cayenne pepper
Snipped fresh chives or
scallion greens for garnish

Remove feet from scallops (see p. 192). Melt 3 tablespoons of the butter and sauté onion until soft. Add wine and scallops, and poach 3-5 minutes, or until done. Refrigerate until cool to the touch.

In saucepan melt remaining 3 tablespoons butter, stir in flour, and cook 2 minutes. Add cream that has been warmed but not boiled, and whisk until sauce thickens. Season with salt, pepper, and cayenne, then chill.

Purée white sauce and scallop mixture until smooth in food processor fitted with metal blade. Chill thoroughly, then serve garnished with snipped chives or scallion greens.

Batter-Fried Scallops

SERVES 2-3

Use vegetable or peanut oil for frying and heat it to 375°. Before adding the scallops, test the oil with a bit of batter, which should sizzle and turn brown very quickly. Fry scallops in small batches so as not to overcrowd the pieces or lower the temperature of the oil.

1 pound sea or bay scallops
(about 20)
1 cup flour
Salt and pepper to taste
1 tablespoon olive oil

½ cup beer
Oil for frying
2 egg whites
Lemon wedges for garnish
Tartar Sauce (see p. 40)

Carefully dry scallops on paper towels and remove feet (see p. 192). Sift flour into bowl, season with salt and pepper, and mix. With fork, stir in olive oil and beer, mixing until liquid is incorporated. (Don't worry about lumps.) Let sit 1 hour so beer loses its carbonation.

Pour oil to depth of 2 inches in heavy enamel pot and heat to 375°. Beat egg whites until stiff and fold into batter. Drop scallops into batter and mix to distribute. Fry until brown and drain on paper towels. Serve with lemon wedges and Tartar Sauce.

Stir-Fried Scallops   SERVES 2

Cooking in a wok is done very quickly and at the last minute, so it is important to have all your ingredients chopped beforehand and ready to add when needed.

1 pound sea or bay scallops
2 tablespoons rice wine
  (Mirim)
2 tablespoons cornstarch
¼ teaspoon salt
¼ cup plus 2 tablespoons
  peanut oil
1 tablespoon julienned
  gingerroot
1 clove garlic, minced
1 small dried hot chili
  pepper, crumbled

3 scallions, sliced into 1-inch
  width
2 carrots, sliced
⅓ pound fresh mushrooms,
  sliced
¼ pound snow peas, sliced in
  half
1½ tablespoons water
1 tablespoon sesame oil
2 teaspoons soy sauce

Remove feet from scallops (see p. 192). Whisk together 1 tablespoon of the rice wine, 1 tablespoon of the cornstarch, and the salt. Add scallops, stir to coat, and marinate 10 minutes. Heat ¼ cup of the peanut oil in wok until bubbly. Add scallops and fry 3 minutes, stirring constantly. Transfer scallops and liquid to glass bowl and set aside.

Heat remaining 2 tablespoons peanut oil in wok. Add gingerroot, garlic, chili pepper, and scallions, and stir-fry 1 minute. Add carrots, mushrooms, and snow peas, and stir-fry until tender, about 3 minutes. In separate bowl, whisk together water, remaining 1 tablespoon rice wine, sesame oil, remaining 1 tablespoon cornstarch, and soy sauce. Add to vegetables and cook until thickened. Pour scallops and liquid back into wok, tossing to mix, and cook until heated through. Serve with boiled rice.

Coquille St. Jacques

SERVES 4 AS MAIN COURSE,
8 AS FIRST COURSE

This is one of my all-time favorites when entertaining. Rich and delectable, it can be made the night before and reheated right before serving. Half a pound of cooked shrimp may be added for color and texture or to feed the extra guest.

1 ½ pounds sea or bay scallops	Juice of 1 lemon
4 tablespoons unsalted butter	3 tablespoons unsalted butter, softened
1 large shallot, finely chopped	2 tablespoons flour
1 bay leaf	Salt and pepper to taste
½ teaspoon dried thyme	3 egg yolks
1 cup dry white wine	1 cup heavy cream
½ pound mushrooms, thinly sliced	Dry bread crumbs

Remove feet from scallops (see p. 192). If sea scallops are large, cut into bite-size pieces (leave bay scallops whole). Melt 2 tablespoons of the butter in large stainless steel sauté pan. Add shallot and sauté until soft. Add scallops, bay leaf, thyme, and wine. Bring to simmer and cook 3 minutes. Remove scallops from liquid with slotted spoon and set aside. Strain liquid and reserve in separate bowl. Add remaining 2 tablespoons butter to sauté pan and sauté mushrooms until they exude their liquid. Add lemon juice and cook 1 minute more. Remove mushrooms with slotted spoon and add to scallops.

Combine mushroom and scallop juices in sauté pan over medium heat. Make beurre manié by blending softened butter and flour. Whisk this into juices, cooking until thickened. Season with salt and pepper, and reduce heat. Combine egg yolks and heavy cream, and add to sauce, being careful not to let mixture boil. Stir over low heat until sauce is quite thick. Add scallops and mushrooms last, and coat with sauce. Spoon into large scallop shells. Sprinkle bread crumbs over top, broil 3 minutes, and serve immediately. Or do not broil but refrigerate until ready to use. Then bake in preheated 350° oven for 20 minutes and serve.

Grilled Scallop and Shrimp Satay   SERVES 4

You can make the peanut sauce more or less spicy by altering the amount of red pepper flakes.

24 sea scallops   24 medium-size shrimp

MARINADE

3 tablespoons soy sauce   1 tablespoon fresh lime juice
1 clove garlic, minced   1 teaspoon brown sugar
2 tablespoons rice vinegar   2 tablespoons peanut oil
1 tablespoon minced
   gingerroot

PEANUT SAUCE

2 tablespoons peanut oil   1 tablespoon minced
½ cup chunky peanut butter   gingerroot
1 tablespoon fresh lime juice   1 teaspoon brown sugar
¼ teaspoon crushed red   ½ cup hot water
   pepper flakes

Remove feet from scallops (see p. 192). Peel shrimp (see p. 221) but leave tail and last section of shell intact. Mix marinade ingredients in bowl, whisking to blend thoroughly. Add shrimp and scallops, and let marinate 2-3 hours in refrigerator.

Start charcoal fire. Whisk together peanut sauce ingredients until smooth. Alternately thread scallops and shrimp onto wooden skewers and grill over medium coals (those that are not bright red) for about 5 minutes, turning often to make sure all sides cook evenly. Spoon peanut sauce into small ramekins to accompany each serving.

Bay Scallops Sautéed with Sesame-Garlic Butter

SERVES 4

Bay scallops come into market around the first of November when each town on Cape Cod and the islands opens up for commercial scalloping. I have my own personal scalloper, Ned Rice, who goes skin diving along the bottom of Vineyard Sound. He meets me at the store on Sunday nights with his shucked catch, and I pay him a good wage for work he loves to do. During the week he teaches biology at Cambridge High School.

1 ½ to 2 pounds bay scallops
4 tablespoons unsalted
   butter, softened
2 teaspoons minced garlic

2 teaspoons fresh lemon
   juice
1 tablespoon toasted sesame
   seeds

Dry scallops carefully and remove feet (see p. 192). Make compound butter by combining butter, garlic, lemon juice, and toasted sesame seeds. Mix with fork until all has been thoroughly incorporated. Melt in sauté pan and add scallops. Cook over medium-high heat for 3 minutes, or until scallops are just tender. Serve at once.

Scup (*see* Porgy)

Sea Urchins
(Green)

Strongylocentrotus drodachiensis

Sea urchins are covered with fixed spines radiating around their shell-like body, making them look like hedgehogs of the sea. The spines vary in color depending on the species and where they live. Sea urchins are part of the dietary chain of ocean dwellers such as starfish, lobsters, and the tooth-grinding wolffish.

Commonly called sea urchin "roe" or "uni" in sushi bars, this spiny creature's reproductive organs are a desirable taste treat. Both male and female sea urchins can be eaten and are at their peak flavor a month or two after spawning. If they ooze a white, milky fluid, they are very close to spawning and not as desirable. Sea urchins with roe that are small and shriveled have been depleted by spawning and should be passed up.

I use a large, sharp knife and a mallet to open a sea urchin. Laying the urchin on its side and placing the knife blade on the urchin's lower edge, I hit the blade with the mallet and thus remove the bottom quarter of the shell, including the mouth. Inside is a lot of black-green matter that I remove with my fingers, and in the back are the colorful gonads. I use a small demitasse spoon to scoop them out. It might take 10 to 12 urchins to provide enough for one serving, but at $2 a dozen, the cost is not great.

Fresh urchin gonads should have a bright orange or yellow color, contain no brown blotches, and have no unpleasant odor. The simplest way to eat them is raw out of the shell with a squeeze of fresh lemon or lime juice, as their taste is very rich and a little goes a long way. Serve them ice cold with some French bread and a glass of chilled dry white wine.

Sea Urchin Sauce
MAKES 1 CUP

Try this spooned on top of a mild-tasting white fish.

½ cup heavy cream
2 tablespoons dry white wine

½ cup sea urchin roe

Combine cream and wine in saucepan and cook at low boil for 3 minutes. Add roe and stir well until sauce is blended and orange in color.

How to Open a Sea Urchin

Lay the sea urchin on its side. Place a large, sharp knife on the lower edge of the urchin, and hit the knife with a mallet. Discard the bottom quarter of the shell, which includes the mouth.

Place knife blade here

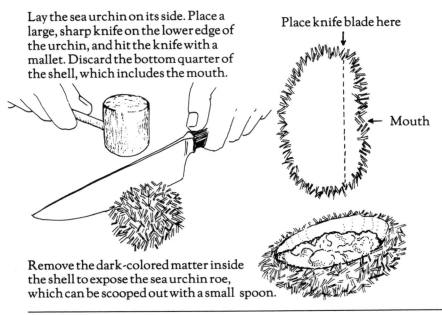

← Mouth

Remove the dark-colored matter inside the shell to expose the sea urchin roe, which can be scooped out with a small spoon.

Seatrout
(see Weakfish)

Shad

Alosa sapidissima

When the Lord made shad,
The devil was mad,
For it seemed such a feast of delight.
So to poison the scheme,
He jumped in the stream,
And stuck in the bones out of spite.

When the strawberry red
First illumined its bed,
The Angels looked down and were glad.
But the devil, 'tis said,
Fairly pounded his head,
For he'd used all his bones on the shad.

Frank Hatch, Sr.

In the Northeast, the appearance of shad signifies the coming of spring. Shad usually becomes available in early February from the rivers around Florida and Georgia. The fish travels upriver through the Carolinas, north into the Chesapeake Bay and Delaware River, and eventually to unpolluted sections of the Hudson and Connecticut rivers by the middle of May. (Shad will neither swim nor spawn in polluted water because of the lack of oxygen.) The parent fish return to the sea after depositing their eggs in the fresh water. In the autumn, the hatchlings find their way to the salt water, not returning to their birthplace until five years later when they are adults.

Shad are a mottled blue or green on the back and creamy white on the belly. A row of large, dark spots extends from behind the gills to the dorsal fin, and they have large, silvery scales. A member of the herring family, shad weigh between 1 and 8 pounds on an average and travel the Atlantic from Labrador to Florida. Their roe is considered a delicacy and is cherished by many New Englanders.

Shad, like herring, is most flavorful when spawning. It has a moderately oily, light cream-colored flesh and is extremely bony. The female, or "roe" shad, is the more desirable, as she is larger and fatter than the male, or "buck," which is milder tasting. The roe is sold in pairs, which, if removed properly from the fish, should be completely intact, held together by a delicate connective membrane. The roe is tastiest when the eggs are small and dark rosy red. As the egg sac enlarges, the eggs become lighter in color and almost white just before spawning and have a less distinctive taste.

A fresh whole shad should be firm to the touch and stiff when picked up, not soft and mushy. The scales should be intact; loss of scales shows the fish has been stored and handled too much. If freshly caught, there should be some evidence of fresh blood around the mouth or gills.

Shad has a rich taste like bluefish but a texture similar to sole or trout. It can be broiled or baked, smoked or grilled, for its natural oil keeps it moist.

How to Bone Shad

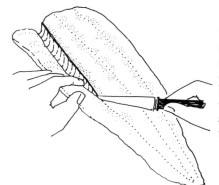

Place the shad skin side down and locate different colorations of flesh. Using a small paring knife, make an incision just on the edge of the darker flesh until you hit a row of internal pin bones. Position the knife as close to the bones as possible and run the blade down along the outer row of bones.

Repeat this procedure on the other side of the row of bones, again holding the knife close to the bone structure. Be careful while cutting not to go so deep as to cut through the skin (bottom side) of the filet.

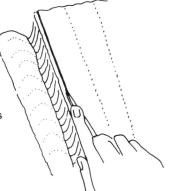

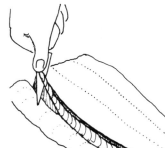

Using the knife or pliers, strip this row of bones from the filet and discard. Repeat this procedure for the remaining 2 rows of bones.

Once the rows of bones are removed, there will be 3 pockets running the length of the filet. These can be filled with a stuffing mixture before cooking the shad.

Steamed Shad   SERVES 6

A dressed fish is one that has been scaled and gutted but still has the head and tail intact. This old East Coast recipe is worth a try, especially when shad is 30 to 50 cents a pound in April. The secret in softening the bones is to make sure the pan's cover fits tightly and the steam is kept in. Add more water as it evaporates if necessary.

1 dressed shad (approximately 4 pounds)	2 ribs celery, chopped
	1 onion, chopped
3 cups water	1 carrot, peeled and chopped
1 cup dry white wine	2 bay leaves, crushed

Preheat oven to 200°. Put shad on rack in deep pan with tight-fitting lid, such as turkey roaster. Add water, wine, vegetables, and bay leaves, making sure liquid just reaches bottom of fish. If not, add more water. Cover tightly and steam in oven 5 hours, basting often. Transfer shad to warmed platter and top with Herb Butter Sauce (see p. 206).

Shad Stuffed with Dates and Almonds   SERVES 4-6

This unusual combination creates a perfect blend of sweet flavors.

2 pounds boned shad filets, cut into 2 equal pieces (see p. 203)	3 tablespoons unsalted butter, melted
2 cups cooked brown or wild rice	Juice and grated rind of 1 lemon
½ cup sliced pitted dates	¼ teaspoon cinnamon
½ cup slivered almonds, toasted	Salt and pepper to taste
1 tablespoon minced gingerroot	2 tablespoons unsalted butter

Check shad for bones. In bowl combine rice, dates, almonds, and gingerroot. Add melted butter, lemon juice and rind, and cinnamon, mixing well. Season with salt and pepper. Stuff pockets in each filet (see p. 203) and spread remaining mixture on top. Put two filets together, sandwich-style, and tie crosswise with twine every couple of inches. Dot top with 2 tablespoons butter and bake in ovenproof dish in preheated oven at 350° for about 50 minutes.

Shad in Parchment

When using parchment paper, you cook the fish naturally in its own juices. The heat goes through the paper, but the steam does not escape, so you have a very moist fish and a beautiful presentation. If you prefer, you can use foil instead, but the effect will not be the same.

1½ pounds boned shad filets, cut into 4 pieces (see p. 203)
Duxelles (recipe follows)
1 lemon, thinly sliced
4 teaspoons dry sherry

4 tablespoons unsalted butter
4 teaspoons fresh lemon juice
4 teaspoons snipped fresh chives

Cut 4 sheets of parchment paper twice the size of each piece of shad, fold in half, and rub butter on half of each sheet to eliminate sticking. Place shad piece on buttered part of paper. Stuff duxelles in pocket of shad filet (see p. 203) and spread extra on top. Place 2 thin lemon slices, 1 teaspoon sherry, 1 tablespoon butter, 1 teaspoon lemon juice, and 1 teaspoon snipped chives on top of each filet. Fold parchment paper over filet and crimp edges together to form neat, tight package.

Put in ovenproof dish and bake in preheated oven at 400° for 15-20 minutes. Remove parchment packages and put on warm plates.

DUXELLES

1 pound mushrooms
3 tablespoons unsalted butter
3 tablespoons minced shallots

1 tablespoon flour
2 tablespoons dry sherry

Clean mushrooms with damp paper towel. Put mushrooms in food processor fitted with metal blade and chop fine. In skillet melt butter and sauté shallots for 3 minutes. Add mushrooms and cook over medium heat until liquid evaporates and mushrooms are browned and pastelike, about 15 minutes. Stir in flour and sherry, and cook 3 minutes more. Remove from heat and cool.

Shad Stuffed with Spinach

SERVES 6

We make this at The Fishmonger and sell it by the slice.

2 pounds boned shad filets, cut into 2 equal pieces (see p. 203)
1 pair shad roe (about ½ pound)
10 slices lean bacon

Salt and pepper to taste
8 ounces chopped fresh or frozen spinach
1 teaspoon minced garlic
¼ cup pine nuts, toasted
2 cups cooked rice

Check filets for bones. Rinse roe and pat dry. Set aside. Cook 4 pieces of bacon in skillet until fat is rendered and slices are crispy. Remove and drain on paper towels. Cook roe in fat for 10 minutes. When done, place in bowl, remove membrane, and break apart roe. Season with salt and pepper. Cook spinach in boiling water for 1 minute and drain, squeezing out all the water. Mix with roe. Add garlic, toasted pine nuts, crumbled bacon, and rice, and combine.

Stuff pockets of each filet (see p. 203) and spread remaining stuffing on top of flesh. Put two filets together, sandwich-style, and put strips of uncooked bacon crosswise on top. Place in baking dish and bake in preheated oven at 350° for 30 minutes. Increase heat to 400° and bake 10-15 minutes more.

Shad with Herb Butter Sauce

SERVES 6

To me, shad is one of the tastiest fish we have in our waters. Its flavor is so mild and sweet that it is best to keep the cooking simple.

3 pounds boned shad filets (see p. 203)

HERB BUTTER SAUCE
¼ cup finely chopped shallots
1½ teaspoons dried tarragon
3 tablespoons white wine vinegar
¼ teaspoon freshly ground black pepper

3 tablespoons dry white wine
½ pound cold unsalted butter, cut into bits
1 tablespoon chopped fresh parsley
Juice of 1 lime
Salt and pepper to taste

Broil shad 7-10 minutes, or until done. Test by inserting fork in its thickest part and pulling back a bit. The fish is cooked if it pulls apart easily and is uniformly tan in color.

Begin sauce by combining shallots, tarragon, vinegar, pepper, and wine in stainless steel saucepan. Bring to boil and reduce to fine glaze. Be careful not to burn.

Over low heat, add half the butter to shallot mixture, whisking it in bit by bit until melted. Do not let boil, or butter will curdle and separate. Add remaining butter in same manner and cook until sauce is shiny and clear. Add parsley, lime juice, and salt and pepper, and stir to blend. Spoon over cooked shad pieces and serve.

Shad with Sorrel Sauce   SERVES 4-6

Sorrel has bright green leaves with an arrowhead shape. Sometimes called sourgrass or sourweed because of its bitter lemon taste, sorrel is low in calories and high in iron and vitamins A and C.

2 pounds boned shad filets (see p. 203)	**4 tablespoons unsalted butter**

SORREL SAUCE

1 pound fresh sorrel	**Pinch of sugar**
4 tablespoons unsalted butter	**Salt and freshly ground black pepper to taste**
2 egg yolks	**Lemon slices for garnish**
½ cup heavy cream	

Place shad on broiler pan, dot with butter, and broil 7-10 minutes or until done. Make sauce. Rinse sorrel under cold running water to remove dirt and grit. Trim leaves off bitter stems. Stack leaves together, roll in tight cylinder, and slice with knife to form grasslike blades. This is called a chiffonade. Melt butter in heavy saucepan, add sorrel, and sauté until wilted, about 3 minutes. Beat egg yolks and heavy cream together in separate bowl. Remove sorrel from heat and slowly add egg yolk mixture, whisking continuously. Return to low heat, add sugar, season with salt and pepper, and cook until sauce thickens. Do not boil, or eggs will scramble. Pour over shad filets and serve at once, garnished with lemon slices.

Shad Roe Pâté

SERVES 8 AS APPETIZER

Shad roe has become an expensive delicacy, for its availability becomes scarcer each year. This recipe makes it easier for everyone to get a taste without overindulging.

2 small pairs shad roe or
  1 large (about ¾ pound)
5 tablespoons unsalted
  butter
2 tablespoons minced onion
2 tablespoons flour

1 cup heavy cream
2 tablespoons fresh lemon
  juice
¼ teaspoon dried tarragon
¼ teaspoon dried basil
Salt to taste

Rinse roe and pat dry, being careful not to break membrane. Melt butter and sauté roe over low heat until done, about 10 minutes, making sure not to burn. Transfer to bowl, break apart roe, and pull off membrane. Mix with fork until cooked roe is separated.

Add onion to butter left in skillet and cook until translucent. Stir in flour and cook 2 minutes. Whisking continuously, add cream in slow, steady stream and cook over medium-high heat until sauce comes to boil. Reduce heat and simmer 3 minutes, or until sauce thickens. Add lemon juice, herbs, and salt. Add sauce to roe and mix with rubber spatula until blended. Cool and refrigerate at least 3 hours. Serve with toast points.

Baked Shad Roe with Salmon Caviar

SERVES 2

One of the rites of passage in my family was being old enough to have shad roe, for it was not a taste every child liked. The old Sanborn's Fish Market near Faneuil Hall in Boston was usually the first to have shad roe in the spring, and my mother would make the long round trip there just to please my father.

2 pairs shad roe (about
  ½ pound each)
6 tablespoons unsalted
  butter
2 tablespoons chopped
  shallots
Salt and pepper to taste

½ cup dry white wine
¼ cup heavy cream
1 teaspoon fresh lemon juice
2 tablespoons fresh salmon
  roe caviar
Finely chopped fresh parsley
  for garnish

Rinse roe and pat dry. Melt 2 tablespoons of the butter in oven-proof sauté pan. Add shallots and sauté until soft. Lightly salt and pepper each roe and lay on top of shallots. Pour wine over top and bring to simmer. Place in preheated 400° oven and bake 5-10 minutes. Carefully remove roe and keep warm.

Place pan on burner and reduce baking liquids to about 3 tablespoons. Add heavy cream and bring to boil. Add remaining 4 tablespoons butter, bit by bit, whisking rapidly until butter begins to melt. Remove from heat, whisking constantly, and add lemon juice. Place each shad roe on warm plate and top with cream sauce. Place tablespoon of caviar on top of each roe and sprinkle with chopped parsley.

Shad Roe
Poached in Butter with Bacon

SERVES 2

If you cook the roe over high heat, the delicate membrane will pop and the tasty eggs will ooze out. To prevent this from happening, many recipes suggest parboiling, but I find this unnecessary. Instead, use a common pin or needle to poke several holes in the roe. This provides a release for the steam and keeps the membrane from breaking.

2 pairs shad roe (about ½ pound per pair)	Freshly ground black pepper to taste
8 tablespoons unsalted butter	4 slices bacon, cooked crisp and drained
2 tablespoons chopped fresh parsley	Lemon wedges for garnish

Rinse roe and pat dry, being careful not to break membrane. Melt butter in skillet with tight-fitting lid. Add roe and cook, uncovered, over very low heat for 3 minutes. Turn roe over carefully with rubber spatula, cover, and let cook 3-5 minutes depending on size. Transfer to warm plates, spoon some of the cooking butter on top, and sprinkle with parsley and freshly ground pepper. Serve with slices of bacon and lemon wedges on the side.

Shark (Mako)

Isurus oxyrhynchus

Of the 63 species of shark in North American waters (300 species in the world), the type preferred most for eating is mako. Averaging 5 to 8 feet long and weighing about 130 pounds, this is a fish of the open ocean feeding on fish sometimes twice its size. Fresh mako is found in the waters from Canada all the way to the Caribbean, and frozen mako is being shipped to the United States from South America. Some people prefer this because the urea smell is eliminated and larger sharks become more tender as a result of freezing.

The flesh of mako shark has a pinkish tinge and is firm to the touch. It is sold in steaks. When cooked, mako shark resembles swordfish and at times has been purposely mislabeled at shady restaurants that then charge top dollar.

Mako shark can be poached, lightly breaded and fried, marinated and grilled or broiled, or stir-fried in a wok with fresh vegetables. Swordfish, tuna, and marlin can be used in place of mako shark.

Mako Shark Salad   SERVES 2

The tang of the Remoulade Sauce adds flavor to the poached shark pieces. For a spicier taste, use cayenne pepper.

1 pound mako shark	Remoulade Sauce (recipe
½ cup water	follows)
½ cup dry white wine	1 head leaf lettuce
1 bay leaf	2 small tomatoes, sliced
4 whole peppercorns	

Place shark steaks in skillet with water, wine, bay leaf, and peppercorns. Gently simmer, uncovered, 10 minutes, or until flesh flakes easily with fork. Transfer to plate and chill in refrigerator. Meanwhile, make sauce.

When fish has chilled, break into pieces. Coat with sauce and serve on platter garnished with leaf lettuce and sliced tomatoes.

REMOULADE SAUCE

1 cup mayonnaise (see
   p. 283)
1 tablespoon minced
   gherkins
2 teaspoons Dijon mustard
2 teaspoons minced capers
2 teaspoons chopped fresh
   parsley

2 scallions, sliced
2 teaspoons chopped fresh
   tarragon (½ teaspoon
   dried)
½ teaspoon anchovy paste
   (more or less to taste)
1 tablespoon ketchup

Combine mayonnaise, gherkins, mustard, capers, parsley, scallions, tarragon, anchovy paste, and ketchup. Refrigerate.

Mako Shark and Vegetable Casserole SERVES 6

Similar to ratatouille, this is equally good served chilled on a bed of lettuce.

2-pound mako shark steak
½ cup olive oil
4 tablespoons unsalted
   butter
2 cups shredded cabbage
1 green bell pepper, sliced
1 red bell pepper, sliced
2 cups peeled, diced eggplant
1 cup coarsely chopped
   onion

2 cloves garlic, minced
2 cups peeled, seeded, and
   coarsely chopped tomatoes
½ pound okra, cored and
   strings removed
½ teaspoon dried thyme
2 bay leaves
½ teaspoon salt
½ teaspoon pepper

Cut shark into 6 equal pieces and set aside. In covered enamel casserole dish heat oil and butter until bubbling. Add cabbage, bell peppers, eggplant, and onion. Mix well and cook 5 minutes. Stir in garlic, tomatoes, okra, thyme, bay leaves, salt, and pepper. Heat until bubbly, then cover and place in preheated 350° oven for 20 minutes. Stir in shark pieces, cover, and bake 30 minutes more. Discard bay leaves and serve with rice or pasta.

Grilled Mako Shark with Teriyaki Sauce

SERVES 4-6

In 1936 Ernest Hemingway caught the heaviest mako shark recorded taken by rod and reel. Weighing in at 786 pounds, the shark was caught off Bimini in the Bahamas.

2 pounds mako shark	⅓ cup brown sugar
⅔ cup tamari	2 tablespoons gin
¼ cup olive oil	1 red bell pepper, cut into
1 tablespoon minced	chunks
gingerroot	1 onion, cut into chunks
2 cloves garlic, minced	8 dried apricots, soaked in
1 teaspoon dry mustard	water for 30 minutes

Cut mako shark into chunks. Make marinade by combining tamari, oil, gingerroot, garlic, mustard, brown sugar, and gin, whisking until thoroughly combined. Pour over shark chunks and let marinate in refrigerator 1 hour.

Start charcoal fire. Put fish on skewers, alternating with chunks of pepper and onion and apricots. Brush with marinade and grill over charcoal, turning frequently, 5 minutes per side. Serve with rice and green salad.

Mako Shark with Fresh Herb Marinade

SERVES 4

This can be made with dried herbs, but fresh are always better.

2-pound mako shark steak,	2 teaspoons minced fresh
1 inch thick	thyme (½ teaspoon dried)
1 cup olive oil	2 teaspoons minced fresh
¼ cup fresh lemon juice	tarragon (½ teaspoon
2 teaspoons minced fresh	dried)
oregano (½ teaspoon	1 tablespoon soy sauce
dried)	¼ teaspoon black pepper

Cut shark into 4 equal pieces and put in glass or ceramic dish. In bowl combine oil, lemon juice, herbs, soy sauce, and black pepper. Whisk well to blend. Pour over shark and marinate 1-2 hours.

Grill mako over charcoal 5 minutes per side, basting with marinade, and serve immediately.

Shark Grilled with Gazpacho Salsa

SERVES 4

Most recipes calling for swordfish can just as easily be made with mako shark, as the two fish are very similar when cooked.

2-pound mako shark steak
2 tablespoons fresh lemon
  juice

½ cup olive oil

GAZPACHO SALSA

1 small cucumber, peeled,
  seeded, and diced
1 medium green bell pepper,
  seeded and diced
1 medium red onion, finely
  chopped
2 tomatoes, seeded and
  chopped
1 clove garlic, minced
3 tablespoons red wine
  vinegar

1 tablespoon Worcestershire
  sauce
1 teaspoon chili powder
1 teaspoon Tabasco
½ teaspoon salt
¼ cup olive oil
2 tablespoons chopped fresh
  cilantro

Cut shark into 4 equal pieces and place in glass or ceramic dish. Combine lemon juice and olive oil, pour over shark, and marinate 1 hour.

Meanwhile, make salsa. Put cucumber, bell pepper, onion, and tomatoes in bowl. Remove half the vegetables and put into food processor fitted with metal blade. Add garlic, vinegar, Worcester-shire sauce, chili powder, Tabasco, salt, and oil. Purée until smooth, about 30 seconds. Return to bowl with other half of vegetables and mix in chopped cilantro.

Grill mako 4-5 minutes per side, basting with marinade. Put on platter and spoon salsa over shark. Serve with accompanying salsa.

Grilled Mako Shark with Orange-Rosemary Butter

SERVES 2

For a different flavor, try lemon or lime instead of orange juice.

1-pound mako shark steak
3 tablespoons unsalted
   butter
3 tablespoons fresh orange
   juice
1 teaspoon grated orange
   rind

½ teaspoon salt
2 teaspoons chopped fresh
   rosemary (½ teaspoon
   dried)
Orange slices for garnish

Place shark in glass or ceramic dish. Melt butter in saucepan and add orange juice and rind, salt, and rosemary. Pour over shark and let marinate 1 hour in refrigerator.

Grill over charcoal 4-5 minutes per side, basting with marinade. Place on platter and garnish with peeled orange slices. Serve with green salad and rice pilaf.

Grilled Mako Shark in Lemon-Tarragon Marinade

SERVES 2

Although the marinating takes time, this is basically a very quick and easy dish to prepare.

1-pound mako shark steak, 1
   inch thick

LEMON-TARRAGON MARINADE

¾ cup olive oil
¼ cup fresh lemon juice
3 scallions, chopped
   (including greens)

2 teaspoons dried tarragon
2 teaspoons Dijon mustard
½ teaspoon salt
¼ teaspoon pepper

Place mako steak in flat-bottom glass dish. Combine all ingredients for marinade and whisk thoroughly to blend. Pour over shark steaks and let marinate in refrigerator 1 hour, turning once.

Start charcoal fire. When coals are ready, place mako on grill and cook 4 minutes per side, brushing with marinade from time to time. When done, remove to serving platter and brush once more with marinade.

Grilled Mako Shark with Sesame Sauce   SERVES 4-5

Mako is an inexpensive substitute for swordfish and is just as tasty.

2-pound mako shark steak,
   1 inch thick

LIME-CILANTRO MARINADE

½ cup olive oil
2 tablespoons fresh lime
   juice
1 tablespoon chopped fresh
   cilantro

1 teaspoon dried thyme
½ teaspoon freshly ground
   black pepper

SESAME SAUCE

¼ cup rice vinegar
¼ cup soy sauce
2 teaspoons Dijon mustard
¼ cup sesame oil

¼ cup peanut oil
1 teaspoon hot chili oil
2 tablespoons toasted sesame
   seeds

Cut shark into 4 equal pieces and place in flat-bottom glass dish. Combine ingredients for marinade, whisking well. Pour over shark pieces and refrigerate, covered, 1-2 hours.

Right before you are ready to grill fish, make Sesame Sauce. In food processor fitted with metal blade blend vinegar, soy sauce, and mustard for 10 seconds. Combine oils and, with motor running, add to processor in slow, steady stream until incorporated. Transfer to bowl and mix in toasted sesame seeds.

Remove shark from marinade and cook over charcoal or under broiler 4-5 minutes per side. Place on platter and serve with Sesame Sauce.

Sautéed Mako Shark   SERVES 2

Here is an easy way to fry fish without all the fuss. Kids love it.

1 pound mako shark, cut into 1-inch cubes	2 tablespoons coarsely chopped fresh basil
½ cup milk	1 egg, beaten
1 cup seasoned bread crumbs	4 tablespoons unsalted butter
¼ cup freshly grated Parmesan cheese	Tartar Sauce (see p. 40)

Soak shark chunks in milk for 30 minutes. Combine bread crumbs, Parmesan cheese, and basil. Dip shark in beaten egg and roll in seasoned bread crumbs. Melt butter in large skillet and sauté shark chunks until browned and cooked, about 10 minutes. Serve with Tartar Sauce.

Stir-Fried Mako Shark   SERVES 2

Shark has a firm consistency and holds together well when stir-fried.

1 pound mako shark	¼ teaspoon salt
½ cup milk	3 to 4 tablespoons peanut oil
2 tablespoons cornstarch	1 tablespoon sesame oil
1 egg white, beaten with a fork	2 teaspoons finely chopped gingerroot
1 tablespoon dry sherry	2 scallions, chopped (including green tops)
1 tablespoon sesame seeds	

Remove skin from mako and discard. Cut fish into 1-inch cubes and soak in milk 1 hour. Remove and pat dry with paper towel to remove excess moisture. Place cornstarch in bowl and add mako, tossing until lightly coated. Combine beaten egg white, sherry, sesame seeds, and salt, mixing well. Add shark cubes and stir until coated.

Heat seasoned wok over high heat for 30 seconds. Add peanut and sesame oils and swirl to coat. Turn down heat if oils begin to smoke. Add gingerroot and scallions and cook 30 seconds. Add fish, tossing constantly with wooden paddles until fish is cooked, about 4 minutes.

Transfer to heated platter and serve with stir-fried vegetables and boiled rice.

Broiled Mako Shark
with Tomato-Basil Sauce

SERVES 4

This recipe can also be made with tuna, swordfish, or halibut.

2-pound mako shark steaks,
   1 inch thick
2 tablespoons unsalted
   butter

Tomato-Basil Sauce (recipe
   follows)
Fresh basil leaves for garnish

Put shark on broiler pan and dot with 1 tablespoon of the butter. Broil 3 inches from heat for 4 minutes. Turn over, dot with remaining 1 tablespoon butter, and broil 4-5 minutes, or until fish flakes when tested with fork.

Ladle some sauce on platter, lay shark on top, and spread more sauce on top. Garnish with fresh basil leaves.

TOMATO-BASIL SAUCE

¼ cup sun-dried tomatoes in
   oil
1 cup fresh basil leaves,
   tightly packed
8 tablespoons unsalted
   butter, softened

1 tablespoon minced shallots
½ cup dry white wine
¼ cup heavy cream

In food processor fitted with metal blade purée tomatoes and basil leaves 10 seconds. Add softened butter and process 10 seconds more, or until well blended. Transfer to small bowl and refrigerate.

Place shallots, wine, and cream in saucepan and boil until reduced to ¼ cup. Whisk in tomato-basil butter 1 tablespoon at a time until creamy consistency is achieved.

Mako Shark with Fettuccine in Fresh Tomato Sauce

SERVES 2-4

If you substitute canned tomatoes for fresh, adjust the amount of salt added.

¾ pound mako shark
2 tablespoons unsalted
  butter
4 tablespoons olive oil
3 heaping tablespoons
  chopped fresh parsley
2 large cloves garlic, chopped
1 tablespoon chopped fresh
  oregano (1 teaspoon dried)

2 tablespoons chopped fresh
  basil (2 teaspoons dried)
½ teaspoon salt
Pinch of crushed red pepper
  flakes
2 cups peeled, seeded, and
  chopped tomatoes
2 teaspoons red wine vinegar
Fettuccine to serve 2-4

Cut shark into cubes. Heat butter and 2 tablespoons of the oil in skillet and sauté shark 5 minutes, turning often to brown all sides. Set aside.

In food processor fitted with metal blade purée parsley, garlic, remaining 2 tablespoons oil, oregano, basil, salt, and red pepper flakes. Transfer to stainless steel saucepan, add tomatoes and vinegar, and cook over moderate heat until sauce thickens.

Meanwhile, bring 4 quarts water to rolling boil. Add fettuccine and cook al dente (about 4-6 minutes for fresh, slightly longer for dried). Drain.

Mix shark cubes with tomato sauce, then toss with fettuccine until well mixed. Serve immediately.

Shrimp

Brown shrimp *(Penaeus aztecus)*
Pink shrimp *(Penaeus duorarum)*
White shrimp *(Penaeus setiferus)*
Cold-water shrimp
(Pandalus borealis)

Shrimp are primarily marketed as either tropical or cold water. Tropical species make up the vast bulk of shrimp and are sold by color (brown, pink, or white) and count (number of shrimp per pound). Most shrimp available in the market are sold flash frozen with their heads removed and shells on. A good brand of shrimp, if frozen quickly after harvesting, should be indistinguishable from the fresh product. Cold water shrimp are smaller in size and usually are sold peeled, cooked, and either frozen or canned.

Most of the shrimp in the United States come from the Gulf of Mexico. Brown shrimp are harvested from North Carolina southward. They are brown-gray to red with tinges of red, green, and orange near their legs and tail. Pink shrimp are harvested from Florida southward. They are pink to brown with tinges of yellow and blue on their legs and tail. White shrimp are similar to the brown in color, but they are gray-green with tinges of green, red, and blue on their legs and tail. Cold

219

water shrimp are red to bright pink in color. They are harvested along the Maine Coast from December through March.

When shrimp are harvested, they are graded by size and the amount it takes to make a pound. The higher the number, the smaller the shrimp and the more shrimp, or units, per pound — U3-9: stuffers (U meaning units per pound); 10-15: jumbo; 16-20: extra large; 21-25: large; 26-40: medium; 41-200: small or tiny.

The shrimp market is as fickle as the stock market, for prices change dramatically throughout the year. Many people are involved in handling shrimp, and everyone has to have a piece of the pie.

Good quality shrimp should be firm to the touch and smell fresh, with no offensive ammonia odor. Don't be afraid to ask your fish broker if you can smell the shrimp before you buy them. When purchasing frozen peeled and deveined shrimp, be aware that preservatives such as sodium bisulfate (illegal in the United States) are added by some countries.

Shrimp can be cleaned before or after cooking. First, remove the shell. Then, with a small, sharp knife, make a shallow incision down the back of the shrimp to expose the vein. With the knife tip or your fingers, remove the vein and discard.

Shrimp can be boiled, steamed, broiled, grilled, sautéed, or deep-fried. Always be careful, however, that you don't overcook them, or they will become rubbery and flavorless.

How to Clean Shrimp

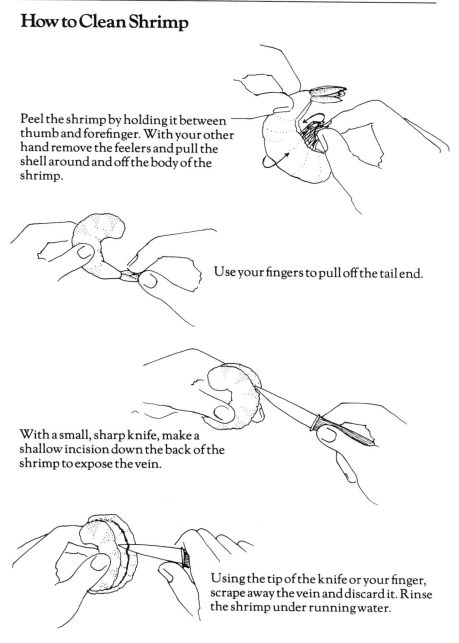

Peel the shrimp by holding it between thumb and forefinger. With your other hand remove the feelers and pull the shell around and off the body of the shrimp.

Use your fingers to pull off the tail end.

With a small, sharp knife, make a shallow incision down the back of the shrimp to expose the vein.

Using the tip of the knife or your finger, scrape away the vein and discard it. Rinse the shrimp under running water.

Shrimp Cocktail   SERVES 4 AS APPETIZER OR FIRST COURSE

Old Bay is a mixture of spices for cooking shrimp or whole crabs that is made in Baltimore.

1 pound extra-large shrimp	1 tablespoon Old Bay seasoning or Shrimp Boiling Mixture (recipe follows)

COCKTAIL SAUCE

1 teaspoon dry mustard	3 tablespoons Worcestershire sauce
½ teaspoon chili powder	
2 tablespoons vinegar	2 teaspoons Tabasco
2 cups ketchup	3 heaping tablespoons prepared horseradish
Juice and grated rind of 1 lemon	

To cook shrimp, bring 2 quarts water and Old Bay seasoning to boil in large pot. Have ready an equally large container of ice water. While you are waiting for water to boil, clean shrimp (see p. 221).

Add shrimp to boiling water and cook 2½ to 3 minutes (no longer). Remove shrimp with slotted spoon and immediately plunge into ice water to prevent further cooking. Shrimp should be pink and slightly curled. Since exact timing depends on size of shrimp, you might want to experiment with one before boiling an entire pound. To test for doneness, make another light incision along the back and pull the shrimp apart slightly. If it is at all gray, it is underdone; if the shrimp is tightly curled and appears tough, it is overdone.

Begin sauce by combining mustard, chili powder, and vinegar, whisking until no lumps remain. Add ketchup, lemon juice and rind, Worcestershire sauce, Tabasco, and horseradish. Blend until smooth. (Extra sauce stored in glass jar with tight-fitting lid will keep in refrigerator several weeks to a month.) Transfer sauce to stemmed glass serving dish and place shrimp over rim.

SHRIMP BOILING MIXTURE

1 bay leaf, crumbled
2 whole cloves
⅛ teaspoon allspice
4 black peppercorns
¼ teaspoon crushed red
   pepper flakes

2 strips lemon peel
4 sprigs parsley
1 teaspoon celery seed

Mix all ingredients until well blended and use as directed.

Shrimp and Artichoke Heart Vinaigrette   SERVES 6

This popular hors d'oeuvre can be served with toothpicks or eaten as a salad on a bed of lettuce.

1½ pounds cooked medium
   shrimp, shelled and
   deveined (see p. 221)
13-ounce can artichoke
   hearts, halved
1 egg
½ cup balsamic vinegar
2 tablespoons Dijon mustard
2 tablespoons chopped
   scallions

1 clove garlic
½ teaspoon sugar
½ teaspoon crushed red
   pepper flakes
½ cup olive oil
½ cup safflower oil
Cherry tomatoes and fresh
   basil leaves for garnish

Combine shrimp and artichoke hearts in crockery bowl and set aside. Place egg, vinegar, mustard, scallions, garlic, sugar, and pepper flakes in food processor fitted with metal blade and blend 10 seconds. Combine oils and, with motor running, add to processor in steady stream.

Pour vinaigrette over shrimp and artichokes, and marinate 3-4 hours. Garnish with cherry tomatoes and basil leaves.

Shrimp Spread

MAKES 2 CUPS

This is terrific to have on hand when guests drop by and can be kept in the refrigerator for up to a week.

1 pound cooked small
   shrimp
3 tablespoons dry sherry
1 teaspoon dried tarragon
1 tablespoon fresh lemon
   juice

½ teaspoon Tabasco
1 teaspoon Dijon mustard
8 tablespoons unsalted
   butter, softened

Thoroughly drain shrimp. In food processor fitted with metal blade blend sherry, tarragon, lemon juice, Tabasco, mustard, and butter for 5 seconds, or until well blended. Add shrimp and combine until coarsely chopped. Transfer to serving dish and chill. Serve with mild crackers such as Bremner Wafers or with toast points.

Shrimp in Beer

SERVES 4-6

Alcohol always evaporates when boiled, but the flavor is left to be absorbed by the shrimp. The taste will vary depending on the brand of beer you use.

1½ pounds large shrimp
4 cups flat beer (not dark)
2 cups water

1 bay leaf, crumbled
1 teaspoon celery seed
½ teaspoon cayenne pepper

To cook shrimp, combine beer, water, bay leaf, celery seed, and cayenne in saucepan and bring to boil. Add shrimp and cook 2½ minutes. Remove and plunge in ice water to cool. Shell and devein (see p. 221). Refrigerate until chilled and serve with salad and French bread.

Shrimp Bisque

SERVES 8

Credit for this recipe goes to Cheryl Williams, who works at The Fishmonger. Her love for cooking comes through in this savory blend of fresh shrimp and spices.

¾ pound small or medium shrimp
½ bunch fresh parsley
1 bay leaf
2 ribs celery, chopped
5 tablespoons unsalted butter
1 large onion, finely chopped
1 carrot, chopped
5 cloves garlic, peeled and minced
1 tablespoon paprika

1 teaspoon dried thyme
4 drops Tabasco
Pinch of cayenne pepper
½ teaspoon salt
½ cup dry white wine
¼ cup white rice (not quick or converted), uncooked
¼ cup brandy
2 cups light cream
Chopped fresh parsley for garnish

Peel and devein shrimp (see p. 221), reserving shells. Coarsely chop shrimp and set aside. Mince parsley in food processor fitted with metal blade or by hand, reserving stems.

Make stock by adding reserved shrimp shells, bay leaf, half the celery, and reserved parsley stems to 6 cups water. Bring to boil, lower heat, and boil gently, uncovered, about 30 minutes, or until liquid is reduced by one half.

Meanwhile, melt 3 tablespoons of the butter in large saucepan. Add onion, carrot, and remaining celery, and cook over medium heat until vegetables are soft. Lower heat and add garlic, paprika, thyme, Tabasco, cayenne, and salt. Cook 10 minutes more, stirring occasionally so as not to let garlic burn.

Strain shrimp stock and discard shells. Measure out 3 cups liquid and add to vegetable mixture along with wine and rice. Bring to boil, reduce heat, and simmer, covered, 30 minutes, or until rice is tender. Add half the chopped shrimp and continue cooking another 5 minutes. Remove from heat, let cool slightly, then purée until smooth in food processor fitted with metal blade. Transfer back to saucepan.

In skillet sauté remaining shrimp in remaining 2 tablespoons butter for 1 minute. Pour in brandy and simmer 1 minute more. Add this and cream to puréed mixture in saucepan. Cook over low heat until heated through, being careful not to boil. Sprinkle with additional chopped parsley just before serving.

Shrimp Salad with Artichoke Hearts in Remoulade Sauce

SERVES 4-6

The flavor of this Remoulade Sauce will improve with time, so make it a day or two ahead if possible.

1 pound medium shrimp
13-ounce can artichoke
  hearts
Remoulade Sauce (recipe
  follows)

1 head Boston lettuce
20 pitted black olives,
  quartered
2 tomatoes, cut into wedges
Paprika

Cook shrimp as described on p. 222. Drain and quarter artichoke hearts. Toss shrimp and artichokes with Remoulade Sauce and divide among 4 to 6 plates lined with lettuce leaves. Garnish with olives and tomatoes, dust with paprika, and serve.

REMOULADE SAUCE

1 cup mayonnaise (see p.
  283)
1 tablespoon Dijon mustard
1 tablespoon prepared
  horseradish
¼ cup chopped fresh parsley
1 rib celery, finely chopped
2 scallions, finely chopped
2 teaspoons fresh lemon
  juice

2 tablespoons capers,
  squeeze-drained
2 anchovy filets, finely
  chopped
¼ teaspoon Tabasco
2 teaspoons paprika
¼ teaspoon cayenne pepper
1 tablespoon ketchup

Combine all ingredients in bowl, mixing until well blended. Cover tightly and refrigerate until ready to use.

The Fishmonger Shrimp Timpano SERVES 4

Combining different-flavored pasta, such as lemon, spinach, and basil, creates a colorful and flavorful dish.

1 pound large shrimp
13 tablespoons unsalted butter (1 stick plus 5 tablespoons)
½ pound fresh mushrooms, sliced
¼ cup flour
2¼ cups light cream
Salt and pepper to taste

Pinch of nutmeg
1½ pounds spinach or basil fettuccine
¼ cup brandy
¾ cup freshly grated Parmesan cheese
Juice of 1 lemon
Minced fresh parsley for garnish

Peel and devein shrimp (see p. 221) and set aside. Melt 2 tablespoons of the butter in skillet or sauté pan. When butter is hot but not brown, add mushrooms. Reduce heat immediately and let mushrooms cook until they release their juice. Remove mushrooms with slotted spoon and save liquid.

Bring large pot of water to boil for pasta. While water is heating, make béchamel sauce by melting 3 more tablespoons of the butter in saucepan over medium heat. Gradually add flour, stirring constantly. Slowly whisk in reserved mushroom juice and cream. Continue cooking until sauce thickens, adding more cream if necessary. Season with salt, pepper (generously), and nutmeg. Add mushrooms to sauce and keep warm while pasta cooks al dente.

Meanwhile, melt remaining 8 tablespoons butter in skillet over medium heat. When hot and foaming, add shrimp and cook 1 minute, stirring constantly. Increase heat, add brandy, and flambé (tip pan to ignite). Shake until flames go out. Remove shrimp with slotted spoon and set aside. Add ½ cup of the Parmesan cheese, lemon juice, and some black pepper to remaining liquid in skillet, then toss with drained pasta.

To serve, transfer pasta to platter or individual plates. Arrange shrimp as next layer and pour béchamel sauce on top. Sprinkle with remaining ¼ cup cheese and garnish with minced parsley.

Shrimp Tempura

SERVES 2

Tempura, a classic Japanese dish, is simply batter-fried food, but in addition to using a good batter, you should use only very fresh ingredients, make sure the oil is very hot, not overmix the batter (it should be quite lumpy), and make the batter just prior to cooking. Tempura is best if served immediately, so it should be made in small quantities. This recipe serves two, but if you increase the portions, cook in batches, drain the ingredients on paper towels, and keep them warm in a low oven, a larger number can be served.

8 to 12 large shrimp	10 snow peas or green beans
1 large onion	4 mushrooms
1 sweet potato or yam	Peanut oil for frying
8 large unblemished spinach leaves	

SOY-GINGER DIPPING SAUCE

¼ cup soy sauce	2 thin slices gingerroot,
¼ cup rice vinegar	julienned (about 1
¼ cup water	tablespoon)

BATTER

1 egg white	1 teaspoon baking powder
1 cup ice water	¼ teaspoon salt
¾ cup flour	¼ teaspoon freshly ground
¼ cup cornstarch	white pepper

Peel and devein shrimp (see p. 221). Make 3 or 4 cuts across belly, turn shrimp over, and gently flatten with side of knife blade. (This will prevent shrimp from curling and accumulating batter while frying.) Cut onion into ½-inch slices, using a toothpick to prevent slices from falling apart into rings. Peel sweet potato and slice crosswise into rounds. Keep spinach leaves and snow peas whole. Quarter mushrooms if they are large and remove stems. All ingredients should be very dry.

In wok heat 2 inches peanut oil until very hot but not smoking (about 375°). Meanwhile, combine dipping sauce ingredients in small bowl, whisking to blend, and set aside to let flavors meld. Then make batter. Whisk together egg white and water. Sift together dry ingredients and add all at once to egg mixture. Stir briefly to combine, leaving batter lumpy.

When oil is hot, dip shrimp and vegetables in batter and fry until golden, turning as necessary for even cooking. Cooking time depends on size and density of ingredients, but nothing should take more than 2 minutes. Do not cook too many pieces at the same time. Doing so lowers the heat of oil and causes coating to become greasy.

Transfer dipping sauce to small individual bowls and serve alongside tempura.

Thai Shrimp with Coconut Milk Sauce   SERVES 4

If you use store-bought coconut milk, make sure you get the unsweetened kind; otherwise you will end up with a dish that tastes more like a piña colada than the Thai-inspired sauce this is intended to be.

1 pound large shrimp
2 tablespoons olive oil
1 onion, finely chopped
1 tablespoon minced
   gingerroot
1 jalapeño pepper, seeded
   and chopped
2 cups unsweetened coconut
   milk* (see page 165)
Juice of 1 lime
1 teaspoon Laos powder*

3 tablespoons fish sauce
   (Nam Pla)* or 1
   tablespoon mashed
   anchovies
¼ teaspoon turmeric
2 tablespoons shredded
   unsweetened coconut
¼ cup chopped fresh cilantro
¼ teaspoon chili paste*
   (optional)
1 scallion, thinly sliced

Peel and devein shrimp (see p. 221) and set aside. Heat oil in large sauté pan. Add onion and cook over medium heat until soft and translucent. Increase heat, add gingerroot and jalapeño, and let sizzle, without burning, about 3 minutes, scraping pan continuously to prevent sticking. Reduce heat and add coconut milk, lime juice, Laos powder, fish sauce, turmeric, and shredded coconut. Stir to combine and continue cooking over low heat, about 10 minutes. (Do not cover, or milk might curdle.) Sauce can be made ahead of time to this point and refrigerated up to 24 hours. When reheating, add some additional fish sauce if mixture needs thinning.

Add cilantro, shrimp, and, if you prefer it spicier, chili paste. Cook just until shrimp turn pink and begin to curl. Garnish with sliced scallion and serve with Saffron Rice (see p. 231).

* These ingredients are available in Oriental markets.

Shrimp Curry with Saffron Rice à la Fishmonger

SERVES 6-8

This is a popular dish at The Fishmonger. The curry is fruity and has a sweet taste. The sauce can be made well in advance and heated at the last minute before final assembly.

2 pounds large shrimp
3 tablespoons unsalted
   butter
2 tablespoons olive oil
1 ½ cups finely chopped
   onion
⅓ cup finely chopped celery
¾ cup finely chopped carrot
2 green apples, cored and
   sliced
Salt and pepper to taste
3 tablespoons curry powder
1 ½ teaspoons tomato paste
1 ¼ cups chicken stock
1 cup water
1 ½ teaspoons currant jelly
¼ cup shredded
   unsweetened coconut

1 tablespoon honey
Pinch of cayenne pepper
1 cinnamon stick
¼ teaspoon ground
   coriander seed
1 bay leaf
¼ lemon, cut in half
Saffron Rice (recipe follows)
Shredded coconut for
   garnish (optional)
Currants or raisins for
   garnish (optional)
Sliced banana for garnish
   (optional)
Mango chutney for garnish
   (optional)

Peel and devein shrimp (see p. 221). Cook in boiling water 2 minutes; shrimp will be a little underdone but will finish cooking when added to curry sauce.

Melt butter in large saucepan and combine with oil. Add onion, celery, carrot, apples, and salt and pepper. Cover and cook over low heat until vegetables and apples are soft. Stir occasionally to prevent sticking. Stir in curry powder and cook another couple of minutes, then add tomato paste, stock, and water. Bring to simmer and add jelly, coconut, honey, cayenne, cinnamon stick, coriander, bay leaf, and lemon. Cook, uncovered, 30 minutes on low heat, stirring occasionally.

Let cool a bit, then remove lemon pieces, cinnamon stick, and bay leaf. Transfer sauce to food processor fitted with metal blade and purée. Return to saucepan and add shrimp. Let simmer 1 minute, or until warmed through. Serve over Saffron Rice and top with garnishes if desired.

SAFFRON RICE

3 tablespoons unsalted
   butter
1 cup chopped onion
2 cups converted rice,
   uncooked

Pinch of saffron
5 cups chicken stock

Melt butter in saucepan. Add onion and sauté 4 minutes, or until soft. Add rice and coat with butter, then add saffron and stir. Heat chicken stock in separate pan and add by the cupful to rice, stirring after each addition until all is used. Cover rice and simmer over low heat until liquid has been absorbed, about 12-15 minutes.

Sautéed Shrimp
in Tomato-Ginger-Cilantro Sauce

SERVES 4

The shrimp should be cooked separately here so they don't get rubbery. Use as a garnish over the sauce and pasta.

1 pound extra-large shrimp
3 tablespoons olive oil
2 cups chopped onion
1 tablespoon minced garlic
2 tablespoons minced
   gingerroot
28-ounce can plum
   tomatoes, with juice

3 tablespoons chopped fresh
   cilantro
Salt and pepper to taste
1½ pounds pasta
2 tablespoons unsalted
   butter

Clean and devein shrimp (see p. 221). Rinse and refrigerate. Heat oil in saucepan, add onion, and cook over medium heat until soft. Add garlic and gingerroot, and sauté 2 minutes. Add tomatoes, breaking them apart with your hands, and simmer 30 minutes, stirring occasionally. Stir in cilantro and turn off heat. Season with salt and pepper. Let sauce sit until just warm. Add in small batches to food processor fitted with metal blade and purée.

Just before serving, boil 2 quarts water and cook pasta al dente. Meanwhile, sauté shrimp in butter until pink, about 3 minutes. Spoon sauce over drained pasta and lay shrimp on top of sauce.

Szechwan Shrimp

SERVES 2-3

Although the Chinese province of Szechwan is landlocked, its aromatic, spicy cooking style is appropriate for many seafood dishes. This recipe has been modified to use American ingredients, but it retains the spicy tradition.

1 pound large shrimp	3 scallions, thinly sliced
2 tablespoons peanut oil	1 tablespoon sesame oil
1 clove garlic, minced	½ teaspoon crushed red
1 tablespoon minced	pepper flakes (or to taste)
gingerroot	2 teaspoons cornstarch
¼ cup soy sauce	1 tablespoon water
¼ cup honey	

Peel and devein shrimp (see p. 221). In wok heat peanut oil until hot. Add garlic and gingerroot, and cook 1 minute. Add shrimp and cook 2 minutes more, stirring often. Remove shrimp to separate bowl to avoid overcooking.

Combine soy sauce, honey, scallions, sesame oil, and red pepper flakes in bowl and add to wok. Cook 2 minutes. Mix cornstarch and water, and add as thickener. Cook about 3 minutes. Add shrimp and toss quickly to coat. Serve over rice or Chinese noodles.

Shrimp and Green Rice

SERVES 4-6

Depending on the chilies you use, you can make this dish wild or tame.

1 pound medium shrimp	1 teaspoon minced garlic
4 fresh Poblano chilies (or	½ teaspoon salt
green Italian peppers)	Freshly ground black pepper
4½ cups chicken stock	to taste
½ cup chopped fresh parsley	¼ cup olive oil
½ cup chopped onion	2 cups long-grain rice,
	uncooked

Peel and devein shrimp (see p. 221). Roast chilies in very hot oven (500°) until skins are burned. Cool 30 minutes enclosed in paper bag. Remove skins, stems, seeds, and white inner membranes. Put chili pieces and 1 cup stock in food processor fitted with metal blade and blend 10 seconds. Add parsley, onion, garlic, salt, and pepper, and continue blending until smooth purée forms.

In heavy casserole heat oil over moderate heat until hot but not smoking. Add rice and stir constantly until coated with oil. Add puréed chili mixture and simmer 3 minutes. In saucepan heat remaining 3½ cups stock to simmer and pour over rice. Bring to boil, cover, reduce heat to simmer, and cook 15 minutes. Add shrimp and press into rice, re-cover, and continue cooking until rice is tender, about 5 minutes more.

Shrimp with Pasta and Pesto   SERVES 4

Pesto is an aromatic sauce that is particularly appealing with a variety of fish and shellfish. Here it is combined with shrimp and pasta, but it can also be spread over broiled bluefish, swordfish, or tuna. Many people like to freeze pesto so it can be enjoyed in the winter when fresh herbs are not as readily available. If you plan to freeze it, eliminate the butter and cheese, adding them after defrosting the sauce.

1 pound extra-large shrimp	3 sun-dried tomatoes packed
1½ pounds pasta	in oil (optional)
Pesto (recipe follows)	

Cook shrimp as described on p. 222 and set aside. Cook pasta al dente and drain, reserving 1 to 2 tablespoons liquid. Mix pesto with reserved pasta liquid, then toss with pasta. Place in serving bowl, top with shrimp, and garnish with thinly sliced sun-dried tomatoes if desired.

PESTO

⅓ cup pine nuts	3 tablespoons unsalted
2 cups fresh basil leaves,	butter, softened
lightly packed (rinsed,	½ cup freshly grated
patted dry, and stems	Parmesan cheese
removed)	2 tablespoons freshly grated
½ cup olive oil	Romano cheese
2 cloves garlic, minced	Salt to taste

Toast pine nuts by placing in pan over medium heat and cooking, stirring continuously, until golden brown. Put nuts, basil leaves, oil, and garlic in food processor fitted with metal blade. Blend until smooth, scraping sides of processor bowl with spatula as necessary to make sure all ingredients are evenly mixed. Add butter and cheeses, and blend 10 seconds, or until mixture is combined. Season with salt.

Grilled Shrimp
with Oriental Barbecue Sauce

SERVES 3

Shrimp are great cooked on the grill, as the smoky flavor of the charcoal permeates the flesh. I prefer to shell the shrimp first because there is less mess when it comes time to eat them, yet they can certainly be cooked with the shells on.

1 pound extra-large shrimp

ORIENTAL BARBECUE SAUCE

3 tablespoons tomato paste	½ teaspoon crushed red
2 tablespoons rice wine or	pepper flakes
dry sherry	2 tablespoons peanut oil
2 tablespoons brown sugar	1 tablespoon minced garlic
1 tablespoon soy sauce	1 tablespoon minced
1 teaspoon molasses	gingerroot
2 teaspoons red wine vinegar	3 scallions, thinly sliced

Peel and devein shrimp (see p. 221), then set aside until ready to use.

To make sauce, whisk together in bowl tomato paste, rice wine, brown sugar, soy sauce, molasses, vinegar, and pepper flakes until well mixed. Heat oil in heavy skillet or wok until very hot. Add garlic, gingerroot, and scallions, and cook about 30 seconds to 1 minute, letting them sizzle but stirring constantly so they don't stick or burn. Lower heat and add contents of bowl. Stir to combine and continue cooking until sauce begins to thicken, about 5 minutes. Remove from heat and allow to cool. Refrigerate in glass container if not using immediately.

Toss sauce with shrimp, mixing until well coated. Cover and let marinate 30 minutes to 1 hour in refrigerator. Meanwhile, prepare coals for grilling. When hot, remove shrimp from marinade and put on skewers, making sure they are not too crowded. Brush more sauce on shrimp and grill just until done, about 3-4 minutes. Serve with boiled rice, grilled vegetables, and remaining sauce on the side.

Skate

Raja ocellata

Skate has had a bad reputation over the years, for it was often substituted for other seafood. In the past, for example, the wings of large skate would be punched out with a pipe-like tool and sold as scallops, even though skate meat bears no resemblance to scallops. Today, skate is being sold under its own name, and as people become more familiar with it, demand for skate in increasing.

Skates harvested for food are generally under 10 pounds, and only the wings, which weigh from 1 to 3 pounds, are eaten. When bought whole, skate wings should be trimmed of their petticoat edges and then skinned so just the white flesh is exposed. Skate wings have a wet gluey film, which can be washed off with cold water, and small barbs that make them difficult to handle. Pliers are needed to strip back the skin; poaching for 2 minutes will simplify this task.

The flesh of the skate, which is ridged, should be firm and light pink in color. When cooked, the flesh turns white and has a sweet flavor similar to that of halibut, although the texture is more like that of crabmeat.

Skate with Black Butter

SERVES 4

At The Fishmonger we trim skate wings so they are ready to cook. Skate is eaten by pulling the rays, or strings of flesh, down off the wing. The taste is sweet and buttery.

4 pieces trimmed skate
  wings, about ¾ pound
  each
1 quart water
½ teaspoon salt

¼ cup white wine vinegar
1 medium onion, peeled and
  halved
1 bay leaf
6 peppercorns

BLACK BUTTER

6 tablespoons unsalted
  butter
2 tablespoons white wine
  vinegar or lime juice

3 tablespoons capers,
  squeeze-drained
Chopped fresh parsley for
  garnish

Rinse skate wings. Combine water, salt, vinegar, onion, bay leaf, and peppercorns in saucepan. Bring to simmer and cook 10 minutes to blend the flavors. Turn heat to low, add skate, and cook carefully so liquid does not boil. Cook 10-15 minutes, or until flesh is white and firm to the touch. Lift skate from liquid, pull off and discard skin, and put flesh on warm plates. Set aside and make Black Butter.

In dry skillet heat butter over medium-high heat until deep brown, being careful not to burn. Add vinegar and capers, and stir to blend. Spoon over individual wings, garnish each with chopped parsley, and serve.

Curried Skate

SERVES 2-3

Instead of using commercially made curry powder, make curry paste, which will keep in the refrigerator for months.

2 skate wings, about 1 pound each
2 tablespoons unsalted butter
¼ cup chopped onion
1 Granny Smith apple, cored and diced
1 tablespoon chopped fresh parsley
2 tomatoes, peeled, seeded, and chopped

1 tablespoon curry powder or curry paste (recipe follows)
½ cup dry white wine
2 cups fish stock (see p. 180)
Salt and pepper to taste
Chopped roasted peanuts for garnish

Place skate wings in pan with enough water to cover. Poach 10 minutes. Remove from water, remove and discard skin, and pull flesh from wings. Set flesh aside while you make sauce.

In saucepan melt butter, add onion, and sauté until soft. Add apple, parsley, tomatoes, and curry powder or paste, and stir to blend. Cook 3 minutes. Add wine and fish stock, and simmer, uncovered, 20 minutes. Let cool and purée in food processor fitted with metal blade.

Return to saucepan and heat. Add skate and season with salt and pepper. Transfer to plates, garnish with peanuts, and serve with boiled rice.

CURRY PASTE

2 tablespoons turmeric
1 tablespoon ground coriander seed
1 tablespoon ground cumin
1 tablespoon ground anise seed
1 ½ teaspoons minced garlic

1 ½ teaspoons minced onion
1 teaspoon salt
¾ teaspoon cinnamon
¼ teaspoon ground cloves
½ cup olive oil
¼ cup white vinegar
1 teaspoon cayenne pepper

Mix first 9 ingredients together and bake in shallow baking pan at 150° for 2 hours. Whisk oil, vinegar, and cayenne together, and add toasted spice mixture, blending well. Pour into glass jar with tight-fitting lid and store in refrigerator.

Poached Skate
with Cilantro Vinaigrette

SERVES 4

For an attractive presentation, arrange skate on a bed of lettuce, spoon on the vinaigrette, and garnish with tomato and cucumber slices.

1½ pounds trimmed skate
  wings, cut into 4 equal
  pieces
1 onion, sliced

2 sprigs parsley
2 tablespoons white wine
  vinegar

CILANTRO VINAIGRETTE

2 tablespoons sherry vinegar
1 teaspoon Dijon mustard
2 tablespoons safflower oil
¼ cup olive oil
2 tablespoons chopped fresh
  cilantro

1 tablespoon sliced scallion
  greens
1 small red onion, thinly
  sliced
Salt and pepper to taste

Place skate, onion, parsley, and white wine vinegar in shallow pan and add enough water to cover. Bring to simmer and cook 15 minutes. Transfer skate to cutting board and remove skin. Refrigerate while making vinaigrette.

In bowl whisk together sherry vinegar and mustard. Combine oils and add, whisking continuously. Stir in cilantro, scallion greens, and onion slices. Season with salt and pepper.

Serve skate drizzled with vinaigrette.

Smelts

Osmerus mordax

These small golden yellow fish are classified as a freshwater fish even though they live and spawn in the sea. They are very closely related to small salmon, and only a trained eye can tell the difference. The most common smelt in our northern waters is the rainbow smelt. Average size for a smelt is about 6 to 8 inches, and a single serving is about six smelts.

Fresh smelts have the aroma of peeled cucumbers. Their shelf life is brief, but they can be frozen whole without hurting their texture (which is soft because of their high oil content) or their taste (which is sweet and delicate like that of most freshwater fish).

Smelts are usually sold whole with head, tail, and innards intact, although larger smelts can be sold dressed, with head and intestines removed. It is not necessary to filet smelts — they are so small that there wouldn't be much left afterward.

Freshness is definitely the key to these little fish, so ask to smell them before you make a purchase. They are most abundant in the markets in midwinter.

Fried Smelts with Fresh Herb Butter   SERVES 4

The important thing about cooking smelts is to get them crispy on the outside yet moist and juicy on the inside. Ask your fishmonger to clean them for you.

16 to 20 smelts, cleaned
(allow 4 or 5 per person)
½ cup flour or cornmeal
½ teaspoon salt
¼ teaspoon pepper
3 tablespoons unsalted
butter

3 tablespoons olive oil
Fresh Herb Butter (recipe
follows)
Lemon wedges for garnish
(optional)

Pat smelts dry with paper towel. On plate combine flour or cornmeal with salt and pepper. Roll fish in mixture to coat lightly. Heat butter and oil in skillet and fry smelts until browned on both sides, about 5-7 minutes total. Dot with Fresh Herb Butter, garnish with lemon wedges if desired, and serve immediately.

FRESH HERB BUTTER

8 tablespoons unsalted
butter, softened
1 tablespoon chopped fresh
parsley
1 tablespoon chopped fresh
chives or scallions

1 tablespoon chopped fresh
basil
2 teaspoons fresh lemon
juice
¼ teaspoon Worcestershire
sauce
2 drops Tabasco

Combine all ingredients in bowl and mix well with fork. Roll any leftover butter into log, seal in plastic wrap, and freeze for later use.

Smelts in Tomato Sauce   SERVES 8 AS FIRST COURSE

Smelts make a fine appetizer. Here they are baked in a lemony Tomato Sauce, then chilled before being served.

24 whole smelts, innards removed	Tomato Sauce (recipe follows)
Olive oil	Chopped fresh parsley and lemon wedges for garnish

Brush smelts with oil and lay side by side in baking dish. Cover with sauce and bake in preheated oven at 400° for 15 minutes. Let cool, then refrigerate. Serve garnished with chopped parsley and lemon wedges.

TOMATO SAUCE

2 tablespoons olive oil	3 tablespoons chopped fresh parsley
½ cup chopped onion	¾ cup chopped fresh basil
3 cloves garlic, minced	¼ teaspoon cayenne pepper
2 cups canned puréed tomatoes	1 teaspoon sugar
¼ cup fresh lemon juice	Salt to taste

Heat oil in skillet. Add onion and garlic, and cook until soft. Add puréed tomatoes, lemon juice, parsley, basil, cayenne, and sugar. Bring to simmer and let cook 20 minutes to blend flavors. Season with salt if needed.

Sole
(*see* Flounder)

Squid

Loligo pealei

Squid, or calamari, are mollusks, but unlike the other members of this group, they have no protective shell. Instead, they have an internal quill that provides stability. Their elongated body, called the mantle, is slightly swollen near the middle and tapers to a blunt point. Two fins work as directional rudders in swimming, and ten arms, called tentacles, surround the head. Each tentacle is equipped with small suction cups to hold prey. Squid propel themselves backward and during propulsion can release an ink, for protection. The dark cloud that results temporarily "hides" them from predators, allowing them to escape to cover.

Fresh squid should be an ivory color with tiny dark blue spots on the translucent skin. It should have no strong odor of chlorine, and the tentacles should be white to pinkish purple. The more pink that is noticeable, the older the squid is. The tentacles are the first to deteriorate and should be kept separate after cleaning until you're ready to use them.

I prefer small squid with bodies no longer than 6 inches. They are thinner and cook more uniformly. Squid can quickly become firm and chewy while cooking. I find it helpful to cook squid 2-3 minutes in boiling water before marinating; this keeps it tender and tasty. When

How to Clean Squid*

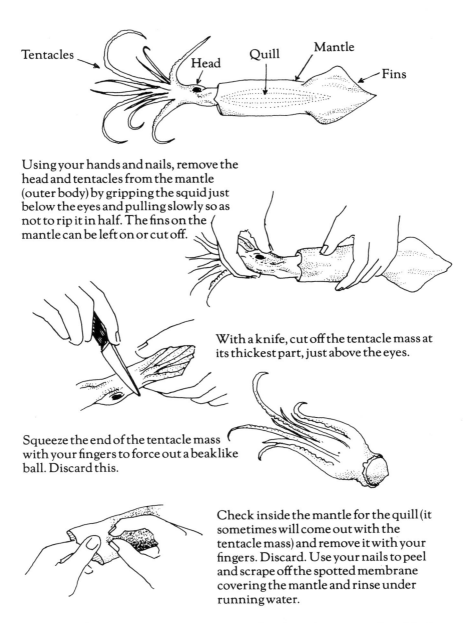

Using your hands and nails, remove the head and tentacles from the mantle (outer body) by gripping the squid just below the eyes and pulling slowly so as not to rip it in half. The fins on the mantle can be left on or cut off.

With a knife, cut off the tentacle mass at its thickest part, just above the eyes.

Squeeze the end of the tentacle mass with your fingers to force out a beaklike ball. Discard this.

Check inside the mantle for the quill (it sometimes will come out with the tentacle mass) and remove it with your fingers. Discard. Use your nails to peel and scrape off the spotted membrane covering the mantle and rinse under running water.

When cleaning squid, the ink sac sometimes breaks and turns everything black, but this is water soluble and can be easily washed off.

stewing or baking, it needs to be cooked 30-40 minutes before it becomes tender.

Squid lends itself to a wide variety of cooking methods: stir-frying, steaming, sautéing, grilling, baking, or braising. It is versatile, very nutritious, and inexpensive. For sautéing, I cut the body into ¼- to ½-inch rings, which makes it cook more evenly; I cut the tentacles in half lengthwise.

Squid freezes very well after it is cleaned, so don't hesitate to buy more than you need. I package it in 1½-pound containers and freeze it until needed. It can be easily thawed in hot tap water.

When cleaning squid, the ink sac sometimes breaks and turns everything black, but this is water soluble and can be easily washed off. The ink is used as a flavoring in Spanish cooking, and today black pasta colored with squid ink is desirable. Like saffron threads, squid ink is becoming very expensive.

Squid and Vegetable Salad   SERVES 4

Squid marinates very well and takes on more flavor as it sits. The julienned vegetables are added mainly for color.

1 pound squid
4 cups water
Juice of 2 lemons
Grated rind of 1 lemon
2 tablespoons chopped fresh
  basil
1 clove garlic, minced
⅔ cup olive oil
½ teaspoon salt
¼ teaspoon freshly ground
  black pepper

½ red bell pepper, thinly
  sliced
1 small red onion, thinly
  sliced
1 carrot, julienned
  matchstick size
2 ribs celery, thinly sliced
Boston or romaine lettuce
¼ pound pitted Greek olives
  for garnish

Clean squid (see p. 243), cut body into ¼-inch rings, and cut tentacles in half lengthwise. Add water to saucepan and heat to boil. Drop in squid rings and tentacles. Cook 2 minutes, or until rings begin to curl and cook through. Drain and plunge squid into ice water to stop cooking.

Put lemon juice and rind, basil, garlic, oil, salt, and black pepper in bowl large enough to hold squid. Whisk until well blended. Add cooked, cooled squid and let marinate at least 4 hours.

One hour before serving, add bell pepper, onion, carrot, and celery to marinade. Continue to marinate 1 hour more, then spoon salad onto Boston or romaine lettuce and garnish with pitted Greek olives.

Squid Risotto

SERVES 4

This recipe uses squid ink as a flavoring for the broth as well as a coloring for the rice.

6 medium squid, about
    ¾ pound total
	1 tablespoon chopped fresh
	    parsley

1 onion, sliced	8 tablespoons unsalted
2 cloves garlic, minced	butter, cut into small
½ cup olive oil	pieces
½ cup dry white wine	Salt and freshly ground black
1½ cups Arborio rice, uncooked	pepper to taste Chopped pimiento for
4 cups fish stock (see p. 180)	garnish
Pinch of saffron	

Clean squid (see p. 243), reserving ink sacs. Cut body lengthwise into strips and chop tentacles. In saucepan sauté onion and garlic in oil until soft. Add squid strips, chopped tentacles, and wine. Cover and simmer 20 minutes. Stir in rice and cook, uncovered, until liquid is absorbed. Heat fish stock to simmer in separate saucepan and stir in squid ink. Add 1 cup of this liquid to rice, stir, and cook until liquid is absorbed. Continue adding liquid by the cupful until rice is tender, about 20-30 minutes. Stir in saffron with last cup of liquid.

Remove saucepan from heat, stir in parsley, and add butter in bits, shaking pan so butter melts down into rice. Season with salt and pepper. Serve garnished with pimiento.

Grilled Squid
with Mustard-Citrus Marinade

SERVES 4

This dish is quick and easy to prepare, but do be careful not to let the squid overcook.

2 pounds medium squid
2 tablespoons Dijon mustard
3 cloves garlic, minced
2 teaspoons dried rosemary
3 tablespoons soy sauce
3 tablespoons fresh lemon
   juice

3 tablespoons fresh lime
   juice
4 tablespoons peanut or olive
   oil

Clean squid (see p. 243) and leave bodies whole. Place in shallow glass dish and set aside while preparing marinade.

In bowl combine mustard, garlic, rosemary, soy sauce, and juices. Whisk in oil, 1 tablespoon at a time, until well blended. Pour over squid and stir to coat. Cover dish with plastic wrap and refrigerate 1 hour.

Prepare charcoal grill. Put squid on skewers and grill 3-4 minutes, turning and basting frequently. Brush with marinade and serve.

Squid in Tomatoes

SERVES 4-6

When I bought into The Fishmonger in 1978, I knew very little about fish and its preparation. This recipe came from a ten-page book titled Recipes from the Fishmonger, *which I inherited with the business. To be writing a cookbook many times that size now seems indicative of what I've learned over the years.*

2 pounds squid
4 tablespoons olive oil
2 cloves garlic, minced
Salt and pepper to taste
1 tablespoon chopped fresh
   oregano (1 teaspoon dried)
1 tablespoon chopped fresh
   basil (1 teaspoon dried)

½ cup dry sherry
32-ounce can peeled
   tomatoes, with juice
1 tablespoon tomato paste
1 tablespoon chopped fresh
   parsley

Clean squid (see p. 243), cut body into ½-inch rings, and cut tentacles in half lengthwise. Heat oil in skillet, add garlic, and cook until golden. Add squid and sauté 3 minutes. Season with salt and pepper, and add oregano, basil, and sherry. Cover and cook 10 minutes over low heat. Stir in tomatoes, breaking them apart with your hands. Add juice, tomato paste, and parsley. Cook, uncovered, 30 minutes, or until sauce thickens and squid is tender. Serve over pasta or rice.

Marianna Lipsky's Squid Sauce   SERVES 6

Karl Lipsky is my own personal elf. He arrives unannounced through the back door of my store once every six months and gets involved with whatever we are doing at the time. He puts on the nearest apron, grabs a spoon, has a few tastes of what we're making, and suggests additions of one kind or another. Then off he goes, leaving behind a package of his famous Jenifer House Ginger-Molasses Cookies. Karl started Jenifer House in Great Barrington, Massachusetts, and is an old and dear business friend of my father's. Karl's wife, Marianna, sent me this recipe, which is a favorite in the Lipsky household.

2 pounds squid	1 bay leaf
4 tablespoons olive oil	1 tablespoon chopped fresh
2 cloves garlic, minced	parsley
2 medium onions, chopped	¼ cup brandy
3 pounds fresh tomatoes,	Pinch of saffron
peeled, seeded, and	½ teaspoon cayenne pepper
chopped	Salt to taste
1 teaspoon dried thyme	

Clean squid (see p. 243), cut body into ½-inch rings, and cut tentacles in half lengthwise. Set aside.

Heat 3 tablespoons of the oil in 2-quart saucepan and cook garlic and onions until soft, about 5 minutes. Add tomatoes, thyme, bay leaf, and parsley, and simmer until sauce is reduced and thickened.

In sauté pan heat remaining 1 tablespoon olive oil and cook squid over medium heat until it has absorbed its cooking juices. Add brandy, heat a bit, and ignite. When flames die down, add to tomato mixture. Add saffron, cover, and cook over low heat about 40 minutes, or until squid is tender. Add cayenne and season with salt. Serve with pasta or boiled rice.

Breaded and Fried Squid

SERVES 2

I never thought I'd cultivate a taste for squid, especially after cleaning 50 pounds of it at a time. When Cheryl Williams served this for lunch one day at The Fishmonger, however, I became an instant convert.

1 pound squid	¼ cup olive oil
Flour for dredging	¼ cup peanut oil
2 egg whites	Lemon wedges for garnish
1 cup Japanese bread flakes (available at Oriental markets)	Soy-Ginger Dipping Sauce (see p. 228)

Clean squid (see p. 243) and cut into rings about ¼ inch thick. Dredge in flour, then place squid in sieve and shake off excess flour — too much makes squid gummy. Beat egg whites with fork until foamy. Dip squid in beaten egg whites, then in bread flakes.

Combine olive oil and peanut oil, and heat in nonstick skillet until bubbly and popping. Add one squid to test; it should start frying immediately. Add other squid in one layer. When browned, turn over with chopsticks. Cook no longer than 3 minutes total and remove to drain on paper towels. Garnish with lemon wedges and serve with Soy-Ginger Dipping Sauce.

Squid Stir-Fry

SERVES 4-6

In April 1987 I took a vacation to Hong Kong and China. The seafood was a sight to behold because it was all sold alive — from turtles to eels. My favorite dish was stir-fried cuttlefish, which is very similar to squid. This recipe is based on that preparation.

2 pounds small squid	2 tablespoons soy sauce
4 tablespoons olive oil	2 tablespoons rice vinegar
1 clove garlic, minced	2 tablespoons dry sherry
3 scallions, sliced 1 inch thick	2 teaspoons cornstarch
2 tablespoons chopped gingerroot	1 tablespoon water
	Fresh chopped cilantro leaves for garnish

Clean squid (see p. 243), remove fins and tentacles, and set aside for another use. Slit open bodies so they lay flat. With small, sharp knife, make diagonal slashes on body ½ inch apart, being careful to stay on top of muscle and not slice too deep. Make similar slashes in other direction so you have diamondlike pattern. Now cut squid into 1½-inch squares.

In wok or sauté pan heat olive oil until bubbly. Add squid, garlic, scallions, and gingerroot, and stir-fry 1 minute. Squid should curl up into a lovely pattern. Add soy sauce, rice vinegar, and sherry, and cook 2 minutes more. Using slotted spoon, transfer squid to serving dish, leaving juices in bottom of pan. Mix cornstarch and water together in cup and stir into juices. Cook until thickened, about 2 minutes, then pour over squid. Garnish with chopped fresh cilantro leaves and serve with colorful fresh vegetables.

Stuffed Squid   SERVES 2-4

The variations for this stuffing are endless. Shrimp can be added to make it more glamorous; mozzarella cheese chunks to create a different texture; slices of carrot, red bell pepper, and black olives to give it more color.

8 large squid or 12 small, about 1 pound total	¼ cup olive oil
¼ cup bread crumbs	Salt and pepper to taste
2 tablespoons chopped fresh parsley	1 clove garlic, crushed
3 tablespoons freshly grated Parmesan cheese	1 cup peeled, seeded, and chopped tomato
2 teaspoons chopped garlic	3 cloves garlic, chopped
1 egg, beaten	⅓ cup dry white wine
	Chopped fresh basil leaves for garnish

Clean squid (see p. 243) and leave bodies whole. Chop tentacles and combine in bowl with bread crumbs, parsley, cheese, 2 teaspoons chopped garlic, beaten egg, and 2 tablespoons of the oil. Blend well. Season with salt and pepper. Spoon stuffing into each squid, being careful not to overstuff, as squid will shrink. Secure each opening with toothpick.

In large skillet heat remaining oil with crushed garlic. Discard clove when browned. Add stuffed squid and lightly brown on each side. Add tomato, 3 chopped cloves garlic, wine, and additional salt and pepper to taste. Cover and cook over medium heat 30 minutes. Garnish with basil leaves and serve with pasta or rice.

The Fishmonger
Red Squid Sauce for Pasta
SERVES 8-10

This sauce freezes well and makes an excellent dish to have on hand for unexpected guests or for an easy meal after a hard day's work.

3 pounds squid
¼ pound salt pork, cubed
  (rind removed)
2 large onions, finely
  chopped
6 cloves garlic, minced
3 tablespoons olive oil
¾ pound mushrooms, thinly
  sliced
2½ pounds tomatoes,
  peeled, seeded, and
  chopped
1 cup dry red wine
12 ounces tomato paste

4 anchovy filets, mashed
1 tablespoon fennel seed
2 bay leaves
½ teaspoon crushed red
  pepper flakes
2 teaspoons dried oregano
1 teaspoon dried thyme
¼ cup chopped fresh basil
1 tablespoon chili powder
½ cup chopped fresh parsley
½ cup freshly grated
  Parmesan cheese

Clean squid (see p. 243), cut body into ½-inch rings, and cut tentacles in half lengthwise. In large sauté pan brown salt pork until fat is completely rendered and pork bits are browned. Add onions and garlic, and cook over medium heat until soft. Add squid and sauté, turning often, until squid curls up at edges, about 5 minutes. When done, transfer contents of pan to large stainless steel pot.

In clean sauté pan heat oil, add mushrooms, and sauté 3 minutes, or until they are soft and exude juice. Add to squid pot along with tomatoes, wine, tomato paste, anchovies, fennel seed, bay leaves, red pepper flakes, oregano, thyme, basil, and chili powder. Simmer, uncovered, 40-45 minutes. Sauce should be thick and squid tender. Just before serving, add parsley and Parmesan cheese. Stir well and serve over pasta.

Striped Bass

Roccus saxatilis

Striped bass are easily distinguished by six to eight predominant, dark lateral stripes, which are not imitated in any other species. The topmost stripes are most distinct, especially in older, large fish, and become less prominent toward the belly. Bass are olive to gray-green on the back, with silvery striped sides fading to silvery white on the belly. In New England they are referred to as "stripers," "greenheads," or "squidhounds" (squid being their favorite food), yet south of New Jersey they are called "rockfish."

Stripers range from Maine to Florida on the East Coast, but most of the catch is taken between the Chesapeake Bay and Cape Cod. Like Atlantic salmon, striped bass are an anadromous species and bear their young in freshwater streams and inlets. Bass were so abundant in the 1600s that they were caught not only for food, but also to fertilize crops.

Today most of the striped bass that are caught are consumed close to where they are landed. The best quality are those caught by rod and reel, yet this accounts for only 7 percent of the catch.

Industrial pollution has sounded what may be the death knell for the once hardy striper. The runs have dwindled, and the fish have shrunk in size. As resilient as striped bass are to contaminants, pollution is affecting their reproductive ability in their natural habitat. The Chesapeake Bay, where most of the Atlantic stock spawns, is in a state of decay. Yet it is here that young stripers stay for up to two years, at which point they begin their migration out into the open ocean in search of more food.

Striped bass are one of the finest tasting fish I have ever eaten. "Schoolies," those fish 2 feet or under, are best poached or stuffed and baked whole. Larger fish are good fileted, then broiled or grilled. A note of caution: Pregnant or nursing women should not eat striped bass because the fish may have a high concentration of petrochemicals, pesticides, and heavy metals. Other fine-flaked fish, such as weakfish, salmon, and red snapper, may be used in place of striped bass.

Baked Stuffed Striped Bass SERVES 4-6

If a whole fish is not available, you can use two equal-size filets, with the stuffing placed between them. Tie filets together with heavy twine, then bake as directed.

4-pound whole striped bass	**Stuffing (recipes follow)**
(or two 1-pound filets)	**½ cup dry white wine**
Salt and pepper to taste	**3 tablespoons unsalted**
Fresh lemon juice	**butter**

Remove scales and gills from fish and clean. Remove center backbone, leaving head and tail intact, and spread open. Season with salt and pepper and squeeze of lemon. Set aside while preparing stuffing.

Spoon stuffing onto one half of fish, fold fish back together, and secure with wooden skewers laced with twine. Place stuffed fish on heavy-duty foil and fold up edges to keep liquids from dripping. Pour white wine over fish, dot with butter, and bake in preheated oven at 400° for 30 minutes, or 10 minutes per inch of thickness.

VEGETABLE AND HERB STUFFING

4 tablespoons unsalted
butter

2 tablespoons chopped
scallions

2 tablespoons chopped green
bell pepper

¼ cup chopped carrot

¼ cup chopped celery

2 tablespoons chopped fresh
parsley

1 large tomato, peeled,
seeded, and chopped

1 tablespoon chopped fresh
basil

½ cup water

2 cups stale bread crumbs

Melt butter in skillet. Add scallions, bell pepper, carrot, and celery, and cook 5 minutes, or until wilted. Add parsley, tomato, and basil, and cook 3 minutes more. Remove from heat, add water and bread crumbs, and mix thoroughly.

WILD RICE AND MUSHROOM STUFFING

½ cup cooked chopped
spinach, drained

2 cups cooked wild rice

3 tablespoons unsalted
butter

½ cup chopped onion

½ cup chopped celery

1 cup sliced mushrooms

¼ cup chopped fresh parsley

Squeeze spinach with hands to remove all liquid. Add to rice. Melt butter in skillet and sauté onion, celery, and mushrooms until soft. Drain excess liquid and add vegetables to rice-spinach mixture. Add chopped parsley and combine.

APPLE-CRANBERRY STUFFING

1 small Granny Smith apple,
peeled, cored, and
chopped

Juice and grated rind of 1
lemon

2 cups cooked wild, white,
or brown rice

½ cup whole-berry
cranberry sauce

½ cup coarsely chopped
walnuts

½ cup diced celery

Dash of allspice

Combine all ingredients and mix thoroughly.

Poached Striped Bass   SERVES 6

Any number of sauces can be used with poached striped bass. Take your pick from the ones that follow this recipe.

5- to 6-pound striped bass	3 sprigs fresh thyme (1
8 cups water	teaspoon dried)
1 cup dry white wine	2 cloves garlic, crushed
1 cup chopped celery	12 peppercorns, crushed
1 cup chopped carrot	⅛ teaspoon cayenne pepper
1 cup chopped onion	Lemon wedges and parsley
4 sprigs fresh parsley	sprigs for garnish
1 bay leaf	

Clean and scale bass, making sure all gills and entrails are removed. Combine next 11 ingredients in large saucepan and boil 20 minutes. Strain, discard vegetables, and pour liquid into fish poacher. Submerge fish in bath so it is barely covered, adding more water if necessary. Bring to slow boil, then simmer about 20-30 minutes. Remove fish from poacher, place on serving platter, and let stand 20 minutes. Remove skin and excess fin bones, garnish with lemon wedges and parsley sprigs, and serve with any of the following sauces.

BEURRE BLANC

4 tablespoons finely minced	4 white peppercorns,
shallots	crushed
½ cup white wine vinegar	8 tablespoons cold unsalted
¼ cup dry white wine	butter, cut into pieces
Pinch of salt	Juice of 1 lemon

Combine shallots, vinegar, wine, salt, and crushed peppercorns in small, stainless steel saucepan. Simmer slowly until liquid evaporates and shallots wilt and are left on bottom of pan. (This takes about 10 minutes.)

Remove pan from heat and add butter piece by piece, whisking constantly. Add each new piece when the previous one has disappeared. Move pan on and off heat so butter does not melt but becomes the consistency of heavy cream or custard. If butter breaks because heat is too high, whisk in 1 tablespoon ice water and add 1 more tablespoon butter. Mix in lemon juice, then strain sauce through sieve into warm sauceboat.

SAUCE GRIBICHE

1 cup mayonnaise (see p. 283)
1 tablespoon chopped shallots
1 tablespoon finely chopped Bermuda onion
1 tablespoon chopped fresh chives or scallion greens
2 hard-boiled eggs, mashed with a fork
1 tablespoon water
1 tablespoon chopped fresh parsley
Salt and freshly ground black pepper to taste
1 tablespoon capers, squeeze-drained (optional)
1 tablespoon chopped gherkins (optional)

Combine all ingredients in mixing bowl and blend well. Chill before serving.

SAUCE VERTE

1 bunch watercress (leaves only)
½ cup chopped fresh herbs (a combination of chervil, tarragon, dill, and parsley)
2 cups mayonnaise (see p. 283)

In food processor fitted with metal blade purée watercress. Transfer to bowl, add fresh herbs and mayonnaise, and mix until well blended.

ORANGE HOLLANDAISE

Make 2 cups of a basic hollandaise sauce, replacing lemon juice with orange juice and adding 1 tablespoon grated orange rind.

MOUSSELINE SAUCE

Make 2 cups of a basic hollandaise sauce and add 1 cup stiffly whipped cream.

Grilled Striped Bass with Fennel   SERVES 4

This past summer I brought a nice piece of striped bass over to my brother Sandy's house for dinner. His son Tim devoured the leftovers in an adolescent feeding frenzy and found bass quite to his liking.

2 pounds striped bass filets	2 bulbs fennel
Salt and freshly ground black pepper to taste	Fennel Butter (recipe follows)
Olive oil	¼ cup Pernod, warmed

Heat charcoal fire until coals are to the white ash stage. Season filets with salt and pepper, and rub skin with oil. Trim fennel bulbs of leaves and stalks, reserving both. Cut bulbs into quarters and put on skewer. Lay reserved fennel stalks on grill to cover an area large enough for filet. Lay filet on top, skin side up. Cook 5 minutes. Lay more fennel stalks on grill and place fish, skin side down, on top of these. Continue cooking until fish flakes easily when tested with fork.

Meanwhile, cook skewered fennel bulbs alongside fish, turning frequently until browned and wilted. Remove fish and fennel from grill and place on flameproof platter. Dot with fennel butter, pour on warm Pernod, ignite, and serve immediately.

FENNEL BUTTER

2 tablespoons chopped fennel leaves	1 teaspoon fresh lemon juice
8 tablespoons unsalted butter, softened	

Mix all ingredients in small bowl until thoroughly blended.

Salade Niçoise

Probably the most traditional dish made with tuna is Salade Niçoise, a variety of freshly marinated vegetables with anchovies and tuna — the French antipasto. This version with fresh poached tuna is superb. Lettuce is not traditional, but I include it on the serving platter.

1 pound tuna	1 pound fresh green beans
¼ cup water	2 hard-boiled eggs
¼ cup dry white wine	1 head Boston lettuce
10 small red-skinned	6 anchovy filets
potatoes	1 red bell pepper, cut into
Tarragon Vinaigrette (recipe	thin strips
follows)	Black olives and chopped
3 ripe tomatoes	fresh parsley for garnish

In skillet with lid, poach tuna in water and wine about 10 minutes. Remove, cool, and break up into bite-size chunks.

Boil potatoes with skins left on until just done and plunge into cold water to stop cooking. Slice into bowl, mix with ¼ cup vinaigrette, and set aside. Drop tomatoes in boiling water for 15 seconds and plunge into ice water. Core, quarter, and remove skins and seeds. Set aside in bowl. Remove stems and strings of beans and blanch in boiling water 30 seconds. Plunge into ice water, drain, and place in separate bowl. Slice hard-boiled eggs into quarters.

Arrange vegetables, eggs, and tuna in separate piles on platter lined with Boston lettuce leaves. Top with anchovies and red bell pepper strips, and garnish with black olives and chopped parsley. Drizzle remaining vinaigrette over top.

TARRAGON VINAIGRETTE

¼ teaspoon salt	¾ cup extra-virgin olive oil
3 tablespoons balsamic	1 tablespoon chopped fresh
vinegar	tarragon (1 teaspoon
1 teaspoon Dijon mustard	dried)
1 small clove garlic, minced	

Combine salt, vinegar, mustard, and garlic in bowl. Add oil in slow, steady stream, whisking until creamy. Add tarragon and blend.

Swordfish

Xiphias gladius

Swordfish is easy to distinguish because of the long, flat, swordlike bill projecting from its snout. The sword is half the length of the fish's body and is used to stun and kill its prey. Swordfish vary in external color from blue to dark gray or brown on the back to white or silver on the belly. They can reach lengths of more than 20 feet and weights of more than a thousand pounds, but they average between 50 and 200 pounds. In the Atlantic, swordfish range from Newfoundland to Florida, with the best fishing in the summer months being off Block Island to the Nantucket shoals and on up to Cape Breton Island.

A whole swordfish is sold as a carcass with no head or tail. Those under 25 pounds are called "rats" and are the least desirable because their steaks are small and rather tasteless. Those in the 26- to 49-pound range are called "pups"; 50 to 99 pounds, "large pups"; and more than 99 pounds, "fish" or "markers," with the latter usually commanding a higher price.

Carcasses over 200 pounds are difficult to handle and are frequently sawed in half. At the fish pier, once you've cut a fish, you own it, so before I commit myself, I test for its firmness (sort of like trying out a mattress), then check the skin color: the whiter the skin, the older the fish. I want one that is a dark steel-gray color.

I check to see whether any blood is coming out of the tail section, as that indicates it has been freshly butchered. Then I look into the body cavity. The belly should be pink and translucent with small veins running randomly. If it is white and faintly pink, I move on to the next one.

So as not to confuse swordfish with mako shark, test the skin of the fish. Shark skin has a rough, sandpapery texture, and swordfish skin is smooth. Also, mako flesh lacks the clear whorls, or "eyes," that appear in the swordfish flesh.

Once the swordfish has been cut into steaks, there is another way you can tell whether it is fresh. Previously frozen or "old" swordfish has more brown than dark red meat and often a brown discoloring around the flesh near the skin. Any swordfish that is especially white and dull-looking should be passed up.

Swordfish is frequently referred to as the "steak of fish." It is rich in flavor with a firm, meatlike texture when cooked. It can be broiled or grilled but should be basted frequently to keep it moist, as it has a tendency to dry out. I like it sliced thin, about ½ inch, and pan-fried briefly over high heat, as in Blackened Swordfish. Half a pound per person is an ample serving.

Stuffed Swordfish in Tomato Sauce   SERVES 6-8

Since most of my customers prefer swordfish cut very thick, I was curious when an Italian lady wanted hers to be only ¼ inch thick. I asked how she was going to prepare this, and she kindly shared this recipe with me.

3 pounds swordfish, cut
  ¼ inch thick

STUFFING

3 tablespoons olive oil	2 tablespoons capers,
2 cloves garlic, minced	squeeze-drained
1 cup finely chopped onion	2 cups flavored bread crumbs
½ cup chopped celery	Dry white wine
½ cup chopped fresh parsley	Water

TOMATO SAUCE

4 tablespoons olive oil	½ cup pitted green olives,
2 cloves garlic, minced	sliced
4 cups peeled, seeded, and	½ cup dry white wine
finely chopped fresh	8-ounce can tomato sauce
tomatoes (about 8 to 10) or	½ cup chopped fresh basil
canned Italian tomatoes	Salt and pepper to taste
6 anchovy filets, mashed	

Remove skin from swordfish and cut into 6 to 8 equal pieces. Refrigerate while making stuffing.

Heat oil in skillet and add garlic, cooking until golden. Add onion and celery, and cook until onion is shiny. Remove from heat and stir in parsley and capers. Transfer to bowl and mix with bread crumbs. Add wine and water by the tablespoonful until mixture holds together. Keep it on the dry side, as fish will exude enough juice to moisten stuffing further while cooking.

Place a portion of the stuffing on one end of each piece of swordfish and roll up. Secure with toothpicks and lay with overlapped side down. Next make tomato sauce.

Heat oil in skillet, add garlic, and cook until golden. Add tomatoes and cook until bubbly. Stir in mashed anchovies, green olives, wine, tomato sauce, and basil. Season with salt and pepper, and cook 10 minutes.

Spread 1 cup tomato sauce on bottom of baking dish. Place swordfish rolls on top and pour on remaining sauce. Bake in preheated oven at 350° for 30 minutes.

Soy Swordfish

SERVES 4

The fish needs to marinate only a short time to absorb the flavor of this marinade.

2 pounds swordfish, cut
  1 inch thick
½ cup soy sauce
2 teaspoons chopped fresh
  oregano (½ teaspoon
  dried)
¼ teaspoon ground cloves
½ teaspoon cinnamon

¼ teaspoon freshly ground
  black pepper
¼ cup dry sherry
2 cloves garlic, minced
2 tablespoons unsalted
  butter, softened
2 teaspoons chopped fresh
  parsley

Cut swordfish into 4 equal pieces. Combine soy sauce, oregano, cloves, cinnamon, pepper, sherry, and garlic in glass bowl. Add fish and turn to coat. Marinate swordfish in refrigerator 1 hour.

Broil or grill fish 4-5 minutes per side. Meanwhile, combine softened butter and parsley. When fish is done, dot with butter and serve with extra marinade, heated.

Swordfish Pie

SERVES 4-6

Thalia Large, a former chef at The Fishmonger, used to love to make this dish. Customers just couldn't wait for it to come out of the oven so they could buy a slice still warm. There are a lot of steps to making it, yet the end result is well worth the effort. You will need an 8-inch spring-form pan with high sides.

ORANGE-PEEL CRUST

2 tablespoons grated orange
  rind
2½ cups flour
¼ teaspoon salt
½ cup sugar
4 tablespoons cold
  shortening

12 tablespoons cold butter,
  cut into pieces
4 egg yolks, slightly beaten
Bread crumbs (used when
  assembling)
1 egg, beaten (used when
  assembling)

Put everything except egg yolks, bread crumbs, and beaten egg in food processor fitted with metal blade. Blend 10 seconds, add egg yolks, and blend 15 seconds more. This is a dry dough and will not ball up. Remove from processor and knead until it forms a ball. Divide into thirds, knead each separately, and refrigerate 1 hour before rolling. Put one ball between two sheets of waxed paper and roll out until a little larger than bottom of springform pan. Make sure there are no cracks in dough. With sharp knife, trace around bottom of pan onto dough. Remove dough scraps and save for top decoration. Repeat procedure with other two balls of dough. Wrap each in wax paper and refrigerate.

ZUCCHINI FILLING

4 pounds medium zucchini, sliced, then julienned
½ cup flour

1 egg, beaten
Olive oil for frying

Toss zucchini in flour, then in beaten egg. Add enough oil to coat bottom of pan. Fry zucchini in small batches until browned, adding more oil before each batch. Drain on paper towels and set aside.

SWORDFISH FILLING

1¼ pounds swordfish, cut 1 inch thick
¼ cup olive oil
1 large clove garlic, minced
½ cup chopped onion
1 tablespoon tomato paste

1 rib celery, finely chopped
½ cup green olives, finely chopped
1 tablespoon capers, squeeze-drained and chopped

Cut swordfish into 1-inch cubes. Heat oil in skillet and add garlic and onion; cook until golden. Add swordfish, tomato paste, celery, olives, and capers. Stir to mix and sauté until swordfish is cooked through, about 6 minutes. Put in bowl and cool, then break fish into small pieces with fingers.

Assembly: Generously butter springform pan and put generous layer (about ¼ cup) of bread crumbs on bottom. Place one circle of dough on top of crumbs and prick with fork. Add layer of half the zucchini and layer of half the swordfish. Do not pack down. Place another circle of crust over this and repeat zucchini and swordfish layers. Place last circle of dough on top and make three slits in it for steam to escape.

Use dough scraps to make shapes such as leaves or fish and lay on top. Brush all with beaten egg and bake in preheated oven at 350° for 45 minutes to 1 hour, or until top is golden brown. Remove from oven and loosen sides with thin, sharp knife. Release spring and carefully remove pan. Let cool on rack and slice like pie.

Swordfish in Orange-Honey Marinade   SERVES 2

This blend of citrus and herbs gives swordfish a special flavor.

1 pound swordfish, cut
   1 inch thick

ORANGE-HONEY MARINADE

½ cup fresh orange juice
3 tablespoons olive oil
2 tablespoons honey
1 tablespoon balsamic
   vinegar
2 teaspoons grated orange
   rind
½ teaspoon dried rosemary

1 clove garlic, crushed
Pinch of allspice
¼ teaspoon ground ginger
1 bay leaf, crumbled
¼ teaspoon salt
Freshly ground black pepper
   to taste

Cut swordfish into 2 equal pieces and place in flat-bottom glass dish. Combine marinade ingredients in glass bowl. Pour over swordfish and marinate 2 hours in refrigerator, turning twice.

Grill or broil fish about 5 minutes per side, basting frequently with marinade. Heat extra marinade and serve along with swordfish.

Swordfish Kebabs   SERVES 6-8
with Saffron and Cilantro

Stir-frying in a well-seasoned wok is a quick and easy way to cook fish chunks, but be sure to choose a fish that holds together and is not flaky. In addition to swordfish, monkfish, tuna, and wolffish work well.

3 pounds swordfish, cut
   1 inch thick
⅓ cup cognac
1 tablespoon ground
   coriander seed
Pinch of saffron
¼ teaspoon salt
¼ teaspoon freshly ground
   black pepper

5 tablespoons unsalted
   butter
2 tablespoons peanut oil
1 pound mushrooms, sliced
½ cup slivered almonds
8-ounce can tomato sauce
2 tablespoons chopped fresh
   cilantro leaves

Remove skin from swordfish and cut into 1-inch chunks. In large glass bowl combine cognac, coriander, saffron, salt, and pepper. Dip swordfish into mixture and coat thoroughly. Cover and refrigerate 3 hours. Remove swordfish pieces and pat dry with paper towel. Reserve marinade.

In wok over medium-high heat melt 2 tablespoons of the butter and combine with oil. Cook swordfish in two batches, tossing continuously until browned on all sides, about 5 minutes. Once swordfish is cooked, transfer to bowl and set aside. Heat 2 more tablespoons butter in skillet and sauté mushrooms until browned, about 3 minutes; drain and set aside. Melt remaining 1 tablespoon butter in clean skillet and toast almonds until browned. Add to mushrooms. Combine tomato sauce and reserved marinade in wok and cook over medium heat 5 minutes, stirring occasionally. Add mushrooms and almonds, and stir. Add swordfish chunks and cook until sauce is hot and bubbly. Stir in fresh cilantro and serve with steamed vegetables and rice.

Blackened Swordfish   SERVES 6

It is important to use only dried herbs and spices in this recipe so they are all the same consistency and coat the filet evenly. Cook in a cast-iron skillet heated as hot as possible. (This creates a lot of smoke, so if you have smoke detectors in your house, disconnect them first.) A gas barbecue turned to the highest heat works well, but charcoal heat is too low. This recipe can be made with other fish steaks, such as tuna, marlin, or shark, also cut ½ inch thick.

3 pounds swordfish, cut ½ inch thick	1 teaspoon white pepper
½ pound unsalted butter	2 teaspoons dried thyme
1 tablespoon paprika (preferably Hungarian)	2 teaspoons dried oregano
2 teaspoons cayenne pepper	2 teaspoons dried basil
1 teaspoon black pepper	1 teaspoon garlic powder
	½ teaspoon salt
	Lemon wedges for garnish

Cut fish into 6 equal pieces and keep well chilled. Melt butter and put in shallow dish for dipping fish. Mix herbs and spices together and put in separate dish. Dip fish pieces in butter first, then in herb mixture. Put on cold plate and refrigerate 15 minutes. Heat skillet to hot. Put individual fish pieces in skillet and cook 1-2 minutes per side. When all fish is cooked, arrange on heated platter, add dipping butter to cooled skillet, and drizzle over fish. Serve with lemon wedges.

Grilled Swordfish with Green Sauce   SERVES 4

Swordfish is quick and easy to prepare and is compatible with a variety of sauces. This sauce is served cold, so you can make it well ahead of time.

2 pounds swordfish, cut 1 inch thick	4 anchovy filets
¾ cup chopped fresh parsley	1 clove garlic, pressed
¼ cup capers, squeeze-drained	¾ cup olive oil
¼ cup minced scallions	¼ cup sour cream
¼ cup watercress leaves	3 tablespoons unsalted butter
	Lemon quarters for garnish

Cut swordfish into 4 equal pieces and refrigerate until sauce is ready.

In food processor fitted with metal blade purée chopped parsley, capers, scallions, watercress, anchovies, and garlic 30 seconds. Add oil in slow, steady stream and blend another 30 seconds, or until all is incorporated. Pour into glass bowl and whisk in sour cream until blended. Chill 1 hour.

Dot swordfish with butter and broil or grill until done, about 5 minutes per side. Transfer to platter, drizzle a little sauce on top, and garnish with lemon quarters. Accompany with remaining sauce.

Swordfish with Pink Butter Sauce   SERVES 4

I see no reason why red wine cannot be used with fish. Its flavor and color enhance a dish that might otherwise be bland or drab.

2 pounds swordfish, cut 1 inch thick	½ cup heavy cream
1 cup dry red wine (such as zinfandel)	3 tablespoons unsalted butter
2 tablespoons minced shallots	8 tablespoons cold unsalted butter, cut into small pieces
1 small bay leaf, crumbled	Thin lemon slices and parsley sprigs for garnish
½ teaspoon dried thyme	

Remove skin from swordfish, cut into 4 equal pieces, and refrigerate. In stainless steel saucepan combine wine, shallots, bay leaf, and thyme. Cook over high heat until mixture is reduced to about 2 tablespoons. Add cream and boil until reduced by one half. Meanwhile, melt 3 tablespoons butter in sauté pan over medium heat and cook swordfish 5 minutes on each side.

With the saucepan over low heat, whisk in cold butter piece by piece, making sure butter does not get hot enough to liquefy. (Move pan on and off heat if necessary.) Sauce should be the consistency of light hollandaise. Serve over swordfish and garnish with thin lemon slices and parsley sprigs.

Swordfish Grilled with Tangy Mayonnaise

SERVES 2

Buying fish for my store was a job I was reluctant to give up. But now Howard Richardson, my fish buyer, carries on the tradition of finding the best and freshest fish available. This is one of his favorite ways of cooking swordfish.

1 pound swordfish, cut
   1 inch thick

TANGY MAYONNAISE

¾ cup mayonnaise (see p. 283)
2 teaspoons Dijon mustard
1 teaspoon fresh lime juice
2 teaspoons Worcestershire sauce

1 tablespoon chopped fresh basil
1 teaspoon cracked black peppercorns
1 teaspoon Tabasco

Cut swordfish into 2 equal pieces and set aside. In glass bowl combine mayonnaise, mustard, lime juice, Worcestershire sauce, basil, cracked peppercorns, and Tabasco. Spread liberally on both sides of swordfish steak. Broil in oven or grill over charcoal 5 minutes. Baste with more mayonnaise and turn over. Cook 5 minutes more, basting top with mayonnaise. Remove to platter, garnish as desired, and serve with extra mayonnaise on the side.

Swordfish with Peanut Butter Marinade   SERVES 4

This versatile marinade can be made with cashew butter or sesame tahina for a subtle change in flavor.

2 pounds swordfish, cut
    1 inch thick

PEANUT BUTTER MARINADE

6 tablespoons creamy peanut
    butter
6 tablespoons warm water
⅓ cup soy sauce
2 tablespoons rice vinegar
¼ cup sesame oil

1 teaspoon crushed red
    pepper flakes
1 tablespoon honey
1 tablespoon toasted sesame
    seeds

Place swordfish in shallow glass dish. Combine peanut butter and water to make thin paste, then whisk in all but last marinade ingredient. Pour over swordfish and refrigerate 1 hour.

Grill fish 5 minutes per side, turning once. Baste with marinade and serve garnished with toasted sesame seeds.

Grilled Skewered Swordfish   SERVES 3-4

Buy the chunks of swordfish that are left after all the steak portions have been cut. These pieces are less expensive and just as fresh.

1 ½ pounds swordfish
2 cloves garlic
¼ teaspoon salt
4 tablespoons balsamic
    vinegar
¼ teaspoon freshly ground
    black pepper
1 tablespoon chopped fresh
    tarragon (1 teaspoon
    dried)

⅔ cup olive oil
1 bay leaf for each piece of
    fish
1 cup boiling water
12 cherry tomatoes
2 green bell peppers, cut into
    pieces
12 mushroom caps
1 medium Spanish onion,
    cut into chunks

Remove skin from fish and cut flesh into random-size pieces. Mash garlic cloves with side of knife blade, then mix with salt until paste forms. Put in bowl and add vinegar, black pepper, and tarragon. Whisk in oil until well combined. Add swordfish to dressing and refrigerate 1 hour. Place bay leaves in boiling water and let soak 1 hour until softened.

Skewer each swordfish piece with bay leaf on one side and alternate with vegetables until all skewers are full. Grill over charcoal, basting with dressing and turning often until done, about 10 minutes total. If broiling in oven, suspend skewers over roasting pan and broil 3 inches from heat. Turn twice and cook 10 minutes total. Serve with rice pilaf and green salad.

Swordfish with Green Peppercorn Sauce   SERVES 2

Green peppercorns are the raw berry of the pepper tree. Once dried, they turn into black or white pepper and become a stronger-tasting spice. Green peppercorns come canned and add a subtle flavor to the fish.

1 pound swordfish, cut 1 inch thick	2 tablespoons unsalted butter

GREEN PEPPERCORN SAUCE

½ slice stale white bread, crusts removed	½ cup roasted pine nuts
2 tablespoons fresh lemon juice	1 shallot, minced
1 cup parsley sprigs, firmly packed	½ cup olive oil
	3 tablespoons sour cream
	1 tablespoon green peppercorns, drained

Cut swordfish into 2 equal pieces. Dot with butter and refrigerate until sauce is ready.

Soak bread in lemon juice until liquid is absorbed. In food processor fitted with metal blade purée bread, parsley, roasted pine nuts, and shallot. Blend 15 seconds, then add oil in slow, steady stream. Add sour cream and blend until no lumps remain. Pour into glass bowl and whisk in green peppercorns. Chill 1 hour.

Grill or broil swordfish until done, about 5 minutes per side. Serve immediately, accompanied by sauce.

Tautog
(or Blackfish)

Tautoga onitis

Tautog is a chunky, blunt-headed, thick-bodied fish that averages 2 to 5 pounds. It has a dark green, almost black, color, suggestive of its other common name, "blackfish," and should not be confused with black sea bass. Tautog range from Cape Cod to the Chesapeake Bay.

Fresh tautog is slimy to the touch, which makes it very hard to hold on to when fileting. The flesh is thick textured, lean, and sweet. It turns white when cooked but has black threadlike specks throughout when raw. Tautog is great in chowders because it holds its shape when cooked and does not fall apart. It can be baked, broiled, or poached, but it should be skinned before cooking.

Broiled Tautog with Guava Sauce ·   SERVES 4

Conant Brewer, a lobsterman in the summer and fisherman in the winter, has been a good friend of The Fishmonger. He frequently brings by fish he has caught, and it was Conant who introduced us to tautog.

1½ pounds tautog filets
2 tablespoons unsalted butter
Salt and pepper to taste
½ cup fresh orange juice
3 tablespoons dry mustard
2 tablespoons soy sauce

1 cup guava or peach jam
2 teaspoons grated lemon rind
½ cup crushed pineapple, with juice
Orange slices for garnish

Check filets for bones and place on broiler pan lined with foil. Dot filets with butter and dust with salt and pepper. Broil 3 inches from heat 6-8 minutes, or until fish flakes when tested with fork.

Meanwhile, heat orange juice in skillet. Whisk in mustard until dissolved. Add soy sauce, jam, lemon rind, and crushed pineapple. Bring to simmer and cook 3 minutes.

When fish is done, remove from pan with wide spatula and put on platter. Spoon sauce over top and garnish with orange slices.

Steamed Tautog with Red Bell Pepper and Saffron Sauce

SERVES 2

Many of our customers are not familiar with tautog, so to drum up interest one day, we had a contest to see who could identify the unknown species in the case. It wasn't until four o'clock that afternoon that a lady said, "Oh, that's a tautog." The prize was taking the fish home free of charge.

1-pound tautog filet

RED BELL PEPPER AND SAFFRON SAUCE

1 medium-size red bell pepper	**½ cup heavy cream**
½ cup dry white wine	**Pinch of saffron**
1 tablespoon fresh lemon juice	

Check filet for bones and refrigerate until sauce is ready. Roast red bell pepper in preheated 500° oven for 10 minutes, or until skin blackens. Remove and enclose in paper bag to cool. Break pepper apart and discard seeds and core. Peel off skin and put pulp in food processor fitted with metal blade. Purée 5 seconds. In saucepan heat wine, lemon juice, and cream to boil and reduce to one half. Let cool. Put in processor with bell pepper and blend 10 seconds. Return to saucepan, add saffron, and heat to simmer. Cook until flavors have blended, about 3 minutes.

Meanwhile, put tautog filet on steamer rack over slowly boiling water. Cover and cook 5-7 minutes, or until filet just flakes when tested with fork. Remove to serving plate and spoon sauce over top. Serve immediately.

Tilefish

Golden *(Lopholatilus chamaeleonticeps)*

Tilefish are found from northern Nova Scotia to southern Florida in deep waters along the continental shelf. They range in size from an average of 10 to 15 pounds to as much as 50 pounds. Their iridescent blue and green coloring is highlighted by bright yellow spots along their sides. They have a blunt-shaped head with a protruding lower jaw, and two fins that run along the upper back.

The flesh of tilefish is white to pink, with a firm, lean texture similar to that of lobster or scallops. This versatile fish is excellent served raw in sushi; broiled, baked, poached, or barbecued; or used in salads, in chowders, or as seviche.

Sautéed Tilefish with Almond Sauce   SERVES 4

Although traditionally served with trout, this almond sauce goes well with any mild-tasting fish, such as tilefish, flounder, or perch.

1 ½ pounds tilefish filets
¼ cup flour
1 teaspoon paprika
¼ teaspoon salt

¼ teaspoon cayenne pepper
4 tablespoons unsalted
   butter
4 tablespoons olive oil

ALMOND SAUCE

3 tablespoons unsalted
   butter
½ cup sliced almonds
1 tablespoon fresh lemon
   juice

3 drops Tabasco
1 tablespoon chopped fresh
   parsley

Cut tilefish into 4 equal pieces and pat dry with paper towel. Combine flour, paprika, salt, and cayenne. Dredge tilefish in seasoned flour. Melt butter in skillet over medium-high heat and combine with oil. Add tilefish pieces and cook 2 minutes per side. Reduce heat to low and continue cooking another 5 minutes, or until fish is cooked through.

Meanwhile, begin sauce by melting butter in small pan. Add almond slices and cook until browned. Add lemon juice, Tabasco, and parsley, stirring to blend. When tilefish is done, transfer to platter and top with sauce.

Grilled Tilefish with Lemon-Ginger Sauce

SERVES 2

The firm flake of tilefish makes it ideal for grilling, and the whiteness of its flesh accommodates just about any kind or color of sauce.

1-pound tilefish filet
Juice of 1 lemon
2 tablespoons olive oil
Lemon-Ginger Sauce (recipe
  follows)

1 tablespoon chopped fresh
  cilantro

Remove skin from fish and check filet for bones. Cut into 2 equal pieces. Pour lemon juice over all and rub oil over flesh. Grill 4-5 minutes per side, transfer to serving platter, and cover with sauce. Garnish with chopped cilantro.

LEMON-GINGER SAUCE

3 tablespoons fresh lemon
  juice
1 tablespoon fresh lime juice
1 tablespoon julienned
  gingerroot

2 teaspoons sesame oil
1 ½ teaspoons cornstarch
¼ teaspoon salt

In saucepan combine lemon and lime juices, gingerroot, sesame oil, cornstarch, and salt. Bring to boil, stirring constantly, and cook until sauce thickens.

Tilefish with Orange-Leek Sauce   SERVES 4

The mild taste of tilefish gets a boost from this rich orange, liqueur, and cream combination.

1 ½ pounds tilefish filets	¼ cup dry white wine
2 tablespoons unsalted butter	

ORANGE-LEEK SAUCE

1 large navel orange	2 tablespoons Cointreau
4 tablespoons unsalted butter	2 tablespoons cognac
1 cup sliced leeks	1 cup heavy cream

Place tilefish in buttered ovenproof dish. Dot with butter and pour wine over filet. Bake in preheated oven at 350° for 15-20 minutes depending on thickness.

While fish bakes, make sauce. Remove rind from orange and cut rind into small, julienne strips. Peel pith and membrane from orange, divide orange into sections, and cut into 1-inch pieces.

In saucepan melt butter over medium heat, add leeks and 2 tablespoons orange rind, and sauté 4 minutes, or until soft. Heat Cointreau and cognac in small saucepan, pour over leeks, and ignite. When flames subside, add heavy cream and half the orange pieces. Cook 3 minutes, or until sauce thickens slightly.

When fish is done, transfer to platter, pour on sauce, and garnish with remaining orange pieces.

Tuna

Bluefin tuna *(Thunnus thynnus)*
Bigeye tuna *(Thunnus obesus)*
Yellowfin tuna *(Thunnus albacares)*

Tuna is the largest of the dark-fleshed fish and can reach weights of well over a thousand pounds. It has an aerodynamic, torpedolike body with a deeply forked tail. Tuna feed on other fish, such as herring and squid, and lay their eggs in the open sea. The United States and Japan catch and consume the greatest amounts of tuna, and Americans eat almost one third of all the tuna caught. Almost a quarter of all the seafood Americans eat is tuna. There are thirteen species of tuna, but only three figure in the fresh market: bluefin, bigeye, and yellowfin.

Bluefin is the largest tuna, reaching more than 12 feet in length and averaging between 80 and 250 pounds, although some weigh in at more than 1,500 pounds. The flesh of bluefin tuna is a dark red with lavender and greenish iridescent highlights. Its mild, delicate taste when raw makes it well suited for sushi.

Bigeye tuna is very similar to bluefin both in flesh color and oil content, which is high. It can be grilled, broiled, or used for sushi.

Yellowfin is the most colorful and abundant tuna in the East. It weighs up to 300 pounds, with 20 to 100 pounds being average. Yellowfin is good for sushi or for grilling. It is mild and sweet, but has a lean flesh, so marinating is recommended.

The skin of tuna is tough and leathery and

should be discarded. We joke at the store that someday someone should start a business making tuna-skin handbags or tuna-skin shoes.

The top half of the tuna is leaner and of better quality than the rest, but, as with all sections, any of the dark reddish black flesh should be cut off and discarded. Unlike other dark-fleshed fish, some tuna has a tendency to cook up dry, so it should be baked or poached with liquids such as wine or water. When broiling or grilling, I like to undercook it and, like rare steak, leave it red in the middle. Tuna is sold in steak form and can be used in most swordfish recipes.

Tuna Tartare   MAKES ABOUT 2 CUPS

This is a modification of the traditional "steak tartare." The tuna must be the freshest available and have a bright red color; yellowfin will look the nicest. Make this right before serving, for tuna discolors very quickly.

¾ pound tuna
1½ tablespoons olive oil
1 egg yolk
3 tablespoons fresh lemon juice
1 tablespoon chopped fresh tarragon (1 teaspoon dried)
1 teaspoon Dijon mustard
1 anchovy filet, mashed
1 tablespoon grated onion
1 teaspoon capers, squeeze-drained and chopped
Chopped scallion greens and whole endive leaves for garnish

Cut tuna into small pieces and put in food processor fitted with metal blade. Pulse-grind to achieve uniform texture. Mix oil, egg yolk, lemon juice, tarragon, mustard, anchovy paste, onion, and capers together in bowl. Add tuna and mix with fork until well blended.

Mound in center of plate and garnish with chopped scallion greens and endive leaves. Serve immediately with pumpernickel bread cut into triangles.

Carpaccio of Tuna

Tuna has the most flavor when eaten raw, but only the freshest fish should be used. This recipe is based on an Italian dish that calls for thinly sliced beef, but tuna works very well.

8 thin slices tuna, 2 ounces each	1 tablespoon capers, squeeze-drained
4 tablespoons extra-virgin olive oil	2 tablespoons chopped broad-leaf Italian parsley
Freshly ground black pepper to taste	Lemon quarters for garnish

Chill 4 plates in freezer for half an hour. Remove and place 2 slices of tuna on each plate. Pour 1 tablespoon oil over top of each, sprinkle with freshly ground black pepper, garnish with capers and parsley, and serve with lemon quarters on the side.

Tuna with Tomatoes and Chilies

Schuyler Grey, my stockbroker, went fishing for tuna off Block Island last summer and hooked a 240-pound yellowtail. A photograph of him and his prize hangs in his office and is titled "The Good Times."

1 pound tuna, cubed	2 red chili peppers, roasted, skinned, and seeded
2 tablespoons olive oil	1 tablespoon chopped fresh cilantro
3 cloves garlic	
4 medium tomatoes, peeled, seeded, and chopped	Salt to taste

Sauté tuna in oil over medium-high heat until cooked, about 7-10 minutes. Let cool, then chill in refrigerator. In food processor fitted with metal blade mince garlic. Add tomatoes and chili peppers, and purée.

Pour tomato-chili mixture in saucepan and simmer 10 minutes, or until liquid evaporates. Add cilantro and season with salt. Flake tuna into smaller pieces, stir into sauce, and cook 3 minutes. Transfer to bowl and refrigerate. Serve as hors d'oeuvre with crusty French bread.

Tuna Salad
with Sesame-Tamari Dressing

SERVES 4-6

This is a favorite salad at The Fishmonger. It is colorful, Oriental in flavor, and perfect for a picnic.

2 pounds tuna, cut 1 inch
  thick
½ cup water
2 tablespoons sesame oil
½ pound mushrooms
½ cup sesame seeds
2 tablespoons minced
  gingerroot

3 ribs celery, finely chopped
2 red bell peppers, thinly
  sliced, then halved
8 scallions, thinly sliced on
  an angle

SESAME-TAMARI DRESSING

1 cup mayonnaise (see
  p. 283)
3 tablespoons tamari

2 tablespoons sesame oil
2 tablespoons fresh lemon
  juice

Cut tuna into 4 or 5 pieces. In saucepan bring water to simmer and add tuna. Cover and steam about 10 minutes. When done, remove from pan, set aside to cool, and break up into pieces.

Heat sesame oil in pan and sauté mushrooms until they exude juices. Keep cooking until juices evaporate and mushrooms are spongy. Cool, then chill in refrigerator.

Meanwhile, toast sesame seeds in nonstick skillet until browned. Place tuna pieces in large mixing bowl. Add gingerroot, celery, red bell peppers, scallions, toasted sesame seeds, and chilled mushrooms. Toss to mix.

Make dressing by combining all ingredients in bowl, whisking until well blended. Add dressing to tuna mixture and toss to coat. Garnish as desired.

Grilled Tuna with Basil-Cucumber Relish   SERVES 6

One of my favorite restaurants in Cambridge is the East Coast Grill, which serves everything from duck to fish and cooks it quickly to perfection. I saw this dish on the blackboard menu and couldn't wait to try it.

3 pounds tuna	4 tablespoons olive oil
4 tablespoons unsalted butter	2 teaspoons hot chili oil or ½ teaspoon Tabasco

BASIL-CUCUMBER RELISH

1 large cucumber, peeled, seeded, and diced	4 tablespoons olive oil
1 large tomato, peeled, seeded, and chopped	2 tablespoons cider vinegar
2 tablespoons chopped fresh basil	½ teaspoon salt

Cut tuna into 6 equal pieces and put in shallow glass dish. Melt butter in saucepan and add olive oil and chili oil. Pour over tuna and turn pieces to coat. Refrigerate 30 minutes.

Meanwhile, start charcoal fire, then prepare relish. Combine cucumber, tomato, and basil. Mix olive oil, vinegar, and salt together in separate bowl and pour over vegetables, tossing to coat.

When charcoal is ready, grill fish 4 minutes on each side, basting often with marinade. Serve immediately, accompanied by relish.

Grilled Tuna with Mandarin Oranges   SERVES 4

This dish can be made in advance and served hot or cold. I prefer it cold because the taste of the oranges and fennel is more pronounced. Grilling over mesquite or hickory chips adds extra flavor.

2 pounds tuna, cut ¾ inch
    thick
4 mandarin oranges,
    tangerines, or navel
    oranges

1 bulb fennel, plus leaves

MARINADE

2 tablespoons tamari
½ cup olive oil
2 tablespoons reserved
    chopped fennel leaves
2 teaspoons chopped celery
    leaves

½ teaspoon dried thyme
1 small bay leaf, crushed
2 teaspoons reserved grated
    orange rind

ORANGE AND FENNEL VINAIGRETTE

Juice of 2 oranges
3 tablespoons balsamic
    vinegar
1 teaspoon Dijon mustard
½ cup olive oil

½ teaspoon reserved grated
    orange rind
2 tablespoons reserved
    chopped fennel leaves
Salt and pepper to taste

Place tuna in shallow dish. Grate rind of oranges and reserve. Peel oranges, separate into sections, and set aside for garnish. Remove leaves from fennel, chop, and reserve. Divide fennel bulb into 4 pieces and set aside.

Combine marinade ingredients in glass mixing bowl and pour over tuna. Marinate in refrigerator 1 hour, turning steaks occasionally.

Right before tuna is ready for grilling, prepare vinaigrette. Place orange juice in saucepan over medium-high heat. Reduce liquid to 2 tablespoons. In glass bowl combine vinegar, reduced orange juice, and mustard. Whisk in oil, orange rind, fennel leaves, and salt and pepper.

Grill steaks and fennel pieces over hot charcoal fire until fish is just springy to the touch, about 3 minutes per side. Cut each steak into 4 pieces and place them and fennel pieces on platter. Cover fish and fennel with vinaigrette and garnish with reserved mandarin orange sections.

Grilled Tuna with Béarnaise Sauce　　SERVES 6

Béarnaise sauce is delicious on a rare piece of filet mignon, but I've discovered that it's equally delectable on rare grilled tuna.

3 pounds tuna, cut into 6
   steaks, each 1 inch thick

Olive oil

BÉARNAISE SAUCE

2 teaspoons dried tarragon
¼ cup chopped shallots
⅔ cup tarragon vinegar
4 sprigs parsley
¼ teaspoon whole black
   peppercorns
1½ sticks unsalted butter
3 egg yolks

1 tablespoon water
2 tablespoons fresh lemon
   juice
Dash of cayenne pepper
1 teaspoon chopped fresh
   tarragon
¼ teaspoon salt (or to taste)

Brush tuna steaks with oil and set aside while starting charcoal fire and making sauce. Combine dried tarragon, shallots, vinegar, parsley, and peppercorns in stainless steel saucepan. Bring to boil and cook, uncovered, until reduced to 4 tablespoons. Remove peppercorns.

Melt butter in clean saucepan without browning. In top of double boiler over boiling water, whisk together egg yolks and water until foamy and warm. Add hot melted butter in slow, steady stream, whisking vigorously until all is incorporated. Cook until mixture thickens. Beat in reduced tarragon-shallot liquid and add lemon juice, cayenne, and fresh tarragon. Season with salt and set aside until ready to use.

Place tuna on grill over hot coals and cook 4 minutes per side. Transfer to serving platter, spoon sauce over top, and serve immediately accompanied by remaining sauce.

Grilled Tuna
with Sesame-Ginger Marinade

SERVES 4

Hans Brisch lives in Lincoln, Nebraska. His daughter Ellen worked at The Fishmonger for three years, and on one of his visits here to see her, I served him fresh tuna, which he'd never had before.

2 pounds tuna, cut 1 inch
   thick

SESAME-GINGER MARINADE

Juice of 1 lemon
Juice of 1 lime
4 scallions, thinly sliced
2 tablespoons minced
   gingerroot

2 tablespoons soy sauce
¼ cup rice vinegar
2 tablespoons Dijon mustard
¾ cup olive oil
¼ cup toasted sesame seeds

Place tuna in shallow glass dish. Prepare marinade by combining citrus juices, scallions, gingerroot, soy sauce, rice vinegar, and mustard. Whisk in oil until creamy. Add toasted sesame seeds and pour over tuna. Marinate 1-2 hours in refrigerator.

Grill tuna 5 minutes per side, basting frequently with marinade.

Grilled Tuna with Ginger-Soy Marinade

SERVES 4

Fish absorbs the flavor of a marinade much more quickly than does meat or poultry, so very little marinating time is needed.

2 pounds tuna, cut 1 inch
   thick

GINGER-SOY MARINADE

¼ cup tamari
¼ cup water
⅓ cup maple syrup or honey
⅓ cup dry sherry

1 clove garlic, minced
1 tablespoon minced
   gingerroot

Place tuna in shallow glass or ceramic dish. Prepare marinade by combining all ingredients in stainless steel saucepan. Bring to boil, then reduce heat and simmer 5 minutes. Cool, then pour over tuna. Marinate in refrigerator 1 hour.

Grill tuna over very hot coals, searing 3 minutes per side and basting often with marinade. Serve with extra marinade on the side.

Tuna with Pasta, Peas, and Mint

SERVES 2-4

Using fresh pasta with this dish makes all the difference, as it is lighter and less filling. Adding smoked tuna gives the dish a slightly salty taste.

¾ pound tuna
3 tablespoons water
3 tablespoons dry white wine
2 cups fresh or frozen peas
4 whole fresh mint leaves
2 tablespoons chopped fresh
mint
1 cup heavy cream
3 tablespoons unsalted
butter

1 pound fresh fettuccine
½ cup freshly grated
Parmesan cheese
Freshly grated nutmeg to
taste
Salt and freshly ground black
pepper to taste
½ pound smoked tuna,
prosciutto, or smoked
turkey, diced (optional)

Poach tuna in covered skillet with water and wine for 10 minutes. Remove tuna, break up into chunks, and set aside. Cook peas in boiling water with mint leaves for 3-5 minutes. Drain, toss with chopped mint, and set aside.

In large saucepan boil cream and butter 2-3 minutes, or until cream has thickened slightly; set aside. Cook fettuccine until just tender and drain. Toss with cream mixture until well coated. Return to low heat and stir in cheese, nutmeg, and salt and pepper. Add peas, poached tuna, and diced smoked tuna if desired, and mix thoroughly.

Tuna with Anchovies and Mayonnaise   SERVES 4

Tuna is particularly nice cooked very quickly over high heat so the center stays red and tender. Anchovies and capers enliven the mayonnaise sauce in this recipe.

2 pounds tuna, cut ½ inch
  thick
2 tablespoons olive oil
2 teaspoons minced garlic
4 anchovy filets, mashed
2 tablespoons capers,
  squeeze-drained and
  chopped

¼ cup dry white wine
1 cup mayonnaise (recipe
  follows)
Chopped fresh parsley for
  garnish

Cut tuna into 4 equal pieces. Heat oil in skillet until very hot and almost smoking. Add tuna and sear 1 minute per side. Remove tuna to platter.

Lower heat and add garlic, anchovies, capers, and wine to hot skillet. Bring to simmer and cook 1 minute. Remove from heat and whisk in mayonnaise. Pour over tuna and garnish with chopped parsley.

MAYONNAISE   MAKES 1 CUP

2 egg yolks
1 teaspoon Dijon mustard
1½ tablespoons fresh lemon
  juice

½ cup olive oil
¼ cup corn oil
1 teaspoon boiling water

It is important to have everything (except water) at room temperature before you begin. Place egg yolks, mustard, and lemon juice in food processor fitted with metal blade and blend 10 seconds. Mix oils together and, with processor running, add 1 tablespoon at a time until ½ cup of oil is used. Then add remaining oil in slow, steady stream. Add boiling water to stabilize emulsion.

Weakfish
(or Seatrout)

Cynoscion regalis

Weakfish is robust and shapely, with distinct speckled markings like a river trout. It got its name because of its rather weak mouth, which would pull out of anglers' hooks when caught. Also known as "seatrout," this fish is found from Massachusetts to Florida.

The flesh of weakfish has a soft texture and is light pink in color. It has a sweet, mild flavor when fresh but deteriorates very quickly. Consequently, top-quality weakfish is not readily available. If you are lucky enough to find it fresh in the market, try weakfish baked, broiled, or barbecued.

Broiled Weakfish with Goat Cheese Sauce

SERVES 2

This delicate, sweet-tasting fish tends to be quite fragile, so the less handling of it the better. Here a tangy goat cheese sauce adds flavor and richness.

1 pound weakfish filets	1 tablespoon unsalted butter

GOAT CHEESE SAUCE

1 cup fish stock (see p. 180)	2 teaspoons fresh lime juice
½ cup heavy cream	2 teaspoons chopped fresh
3 ounces goat cheese,	dill
crumbled	

Place filets on broiler pan lined with foil, dot with butter, and set aside.

In saucepan reduce fish stock to ½ cup by boiling vigorously. Pour in heavy cream and boil 3 minutes. Add goat cheese and whisk to blend. Stir in lime juice and dill, and simmer 2 minutes to blend flavors.

Place broiler pan with filets about 3 inches below heat. Broil 6-8 minutes, or until fish flakes when tested with fork. Carefully transfer filets to serving platter, spoon sauce over top, and serve immediately.

Broiled Weakfish with Watermelon Pickle Butter

SERVES 4

The tangy sweet taste of watermelon pickle enlivens this compound butter, which can be made in larger quantities and frozen until needed.

1 ½ pounds weakfish filets
2 tablespoons unsalted
  butter

Juice of 1 lemon

WATERMELON PICKLE BUTTER

4 tablespoons unsalted
  butter, softened
2 teaspoons fresh lemon
  juice
1 tablespoon chopped
  watermelon pickle

1 tablespoon pickled tiny
  onions
1 teaspoon chopped fresh
  parsley

Place filets on broiler pan lined with foil. Dot with butter and pour on lemon juice. Broil 6-8 minutes, or until fish flakes when tested with fork.

Meanwhile, prepare compound butter. Combine butter and lemon juice with fork. Add pickle, onions, and parsley, blending well. Dot fish with mixture and return to broiler for 30 seconds. Serve at once.

Whiting
(see Hake)

Wolffish

Anarhichas lupus

The wolffish is a fierce-looking creature with a compressed head, elongated body, and single dorsal fin extending the entire length of its body. Its head looks as if it could be used for a battering ram, and its mouth, full of large, gnarled teeth, is an intimidating sight. These teeth are used to grind a variety of mollusks and crustaceans, including whelks, mussels, scallops, clams, crabs, and lobsters, and it is this diet that makes wolffish one of the best-tasting fish in the sea.

The flesh of wolffish has a firm, moist texture and, when fresh, a pink or reddish tinge. The filets are long and lanky like cusk, but when properly fileted, they should be free of internal pin bones.

Wolffish can poached, sautéed, baked, broiled, or grilled. It holds together well while cooking, which makes it suitable also for soups and stews. Wolffish is interchangeable with monkfish, cusk, and hake.

Wolffish and Fruit Salad   SERVES 6

I gave this recipe to Linda Glick Conway for her to publish in The New Carry-Out Cuisine. *It's a nice light salad for a cold buffet luncheon.*

2 pounds wolffish filets
2 cups dry white wine
2 cups water
1 bay leaf
¾ cup slivered almonds
1 tablespoon unsalted butter
¾ pound seedless green or
   red grapes, halved
1 orange, peeled and divided
   into sections

1 grapefruit, peeled and
   divided into sections
1 banana, sliced
1 kiwifruit, peeled and sliced
Lime-Ginger Dressing
   (recipe follows)
1 head Boston lettuce
Snipped fresh mint leaves for
   garnish

Cut wolffish into bite-size pieces. Combine wine, water, and bay leaf in sauté pan. Bring to simmer, add fish pieces, and let simmer 3 minutes after liquid has come back to bubble. Remove from heat and let cool. Drain fish of excess liquid, place in glass bowl, and refrigerate.

Toast almond slivers in small sauté pan with butter until golden. Drain on paper towels and cool. In large bowl combine grapes, orange sections, grapefruit sections, banana slices, and kiwi slices. Toss with chilled wolffish pieces and toasted almonds.

Just before serving, coat fruit and fish mixture with dressing. Lay Boston lettuce leaves on platter and mound with salad, garnished with snipped fresh mint leaves.

LIME-GINGER DRESSING

¼ cup fresh lime juice
½ cup crème fraîche (see p. 16), sour cream, or yogurt
¼ cup mayonnaise (see p. 283)

2 tablespoons honey
1 tablespoon chopped fresh mint leaves
2 teaspoons grated gingerroot

In medium-size bowl combine all ingredients and whisk until well blended.

Japanese Breaded Wolffish   SERVES 2

Because of the firm, nonflaky nature of wolffish, it is well suited for breading and pan-frying in butter. Serve it with Soy-Ginger Dipping Sauce (see p. 228), Tartar Sauce (see p. 40), or lemon wedges.

¾-pound wolffish filet
¼ cup flour
Salt and pepper to taste
2 egg whites

1 cup Japanese bread flakes or any dry stuffing mix or crumbs of your choice
3 tablespoons unsalted butter

Cut wolffish into 4 equal pieces, allowing 2 per person. Combine flour with salt and pepper. Beat egg whites with fork until light. Put bread flakes or crumbs in flat dish. Melt butter in sauté pan over medium-high heat. Dip fish pieces in seasoned flour, then in egg whites, and roll in flakes or crumbs. Fry until browned, about 3 minutes per side depending on thickness.

Cold Poached Wolffish
with Louis Dressing

SERVES 4

Combining mussels, crabmeat, shrimp, or lobster with the wolffish turns this into fancier fare. The dressing lends itself to any combination.

2 pounds wolffish filets
1 cup dry white wine
¼ cup white vinegar

1 cup water
6 peppercorns
1 bay leaf

LOUIS DRESSING

1 cup mayonnaise (see
  p. 283)
6 tablespoons bottled chili
  sauce
3 tablespoons grated red
  onion
Dash of cayenne pepper

½ cup heavy cream
1 tablespoon chopped fresh
  parsley
1 head Boston lettuce
Black olives, tomato wedges,
  and quartered hard-boiled
  eggs for garnish

Cut wolffish into 1½-inch chunks and set aside. In large stainless steel or enamel saucepan combine wine, vinegar, water, peppercorns, and bay leaf. Simmer 10 minutes. Add wolffish and simmer 5 minutes. Turn off heat and let sit 10 minutes, then transfer fish to bowl and chill in refrigerator.

Meanwhile, make dressing by combining mayonnaise, chili sauce, grated onion, and cayenne in bowl. In separate bowl beat heavy cream until stiff peaks form. Fold cream into mayonnaise mixture and add parsley. Chill in refrigerator until ready to dress fish.

Mix fish with enough dressing to coat. Place lettuce leaves on serving platter, spoon fish mixture on top, and drizzle with more dressing. Garnish with black olives, tomato wedges, and hard-boiled egg quarters, and accompany with extra dressing.

Baked Wolffish with Feta Cheese   SERVES 4

This recipe was originally designed for shrimp, but wolffish is a fine substitution at a fraction of the cost. When buying feta cheese, always buy an imported brand because the domestic variety tends to be saltier and less tart.

1 ½ pounds wolffish filets
Salt and pepper to taste
Juice of 1 lemon
3 tablespoons olive oil
3 cloves garlic, minced
1 large onion, chopped
3 cups peeled, cored, seeded, and chopped tomatoes
2 tablespoons chopped fresh basil (2 teaspoons dried)

¾ teaspoon fennel seed, crushed
1 tablespoon sugar
½ pound feta cheese, crumbled
Chopped fresh parsley for garnish

Season wolffish filets with salt and pepper, pour on lemon juice, and refrigerate until ready to cook. Heat oil in sauté pan and add garlic and onion. Cook 5 minutes. Add tomatoes, basil, fennel seed, and sugar. Cook until sauce thickens, about 20 minutes. Season with salt and pepper if desired.

Spread a little sauce on bottom of ovenproof baking dish. Arrange fish filets on top of sauce. Spoon remaining sauce over top of filets, sprinkle with crumbled feta cheese and chopped parsley, and bake in preheated oven at 350° for 15-20 minutes. Serve with rice or noodles and a salad.

Wolffish with Peppercorns

There is no reason why some of the classic steak recipes cannot use fish substitutions, as long as you choose a firm-fleshed fish such as monkfish, cusk, or wolffish. Peppercorns add a lively sharpness to the wolffish but do not overwhelm its sweet flavor.

2½ pounds wolffish filets
3 tablespoons whole black
   and white peppercorns,
   combined
¼ cup flour
2 tablespoons olive oil
5 tablespoons unsalted
   butter

⅓ cup cognac
⅓ cup port
½ cup fish stock (see p. 180)
½ cup heavy cream
Watercress sprigs for garnish

Cut wolffish into 6 equal pieces. Put peppercorns in plastic bag and pound with hammer until crushed but not pulverized. Transfer to plate and mix with flour. Coat fish with this mixture, pushing pepper into flesh with fingers. In large skillet heat oil and 3 table-spoons of the butter to bubbling. Add fish and cook until almost done, about 6 minutes, turning pieces to brown on both sides. Reduce heat to low.

In separate pan heat cognac, pour over fish, and ignite, shaking skillet until flames die down. Add port to fish and simmer 1 min-ute. Pour in fish stock and let simmer 1 minute more. Remove fish to warm serving platter. Rapidly boil down skillet juices to glaze. Add heavy cream and boil until sauce is rich and thick. Cut remain-ing 2 tablespoons butter into bits and stir in, bit by bit, until melted. Pour sauce around fish, garnish with watercress sprigs, and serve at once.

Wolffish with Fennel and Garlic SERVES 4

Fennel, with its subtle licorice flavor, can be used with just about any white fish.

2 pounds wolffish filets
2 bulbs fennel
4 tablespoons unsalted
   butter
2 medium onions, chopped
3 cloves garlic, slivered
Flour seasoned with salt and
   freshly ground black
   pepper for dredging

3 tablespoons clarified
   butter*
¼ cup dry vermouth
Lemon wedges and chopped
   fresh parsley for garnish

Cut wolffish into 4 equal pieces and set aside. Remove stalks from fennel. Wash bulb and slice into quarters, then slice quarters into thin vertical slices. Drop fennel into boiling water and blanch 3 minutes. Melt 4 tablespoons butter in sauté pan, add drained fennel and chopped onions, and sauté until cooked, about 5 minutes.

Make small incisions in wolffish filets with sharp paring knife and insert garlic slivers. Dredge wolffish in seasoned flour. Melt clarified butter in sauté pan over medium-high heat and gently fry fish until browned and cooked through, about 5-10 minutes depending on thickness.

Spread sautéed fennel and onions on warm serving platter, lay cooked fish on top, and use vermouth to deglaze sauté pan in which fish was cooked. Simmer 1 minute, then pour juices over fish. Garnish with lemon wedges and chopped parsley.

* To make clarified butter, cut 1 stick unsalted butter into equal-size pieces, place in thick-bottom saucepan over medium heat, and melt, watching closely. Soon 3 distinct layers will form. Carefully remove pan from heat and cool slightly. Skim off top foamy layer and discard. Then without disturbing bottom layer of sediment, spoon out middle layer of clarified butter. Extra can be stored in securely sealed container in refrigerator for up to 1 month or freezer for up to 6 months.

Seafood Combinations

As demonstrated throughout this book, fish and shellfish provide an endless variety of superb dishes that any cook can master and every palate can appreciate. But when combined with one another, the culinary possibilities become even greater — ranging from short and simple preparations such as Fish Kebabs with Spicy Sauce to elaborate and lengthy endeavors such as Bouillabaisse. Each has its own appeal, whether determined by time constraints, availability of ingredients, or expertise. As you become more familiar with the underutilized species of fish, you may be inspired to concoct your own seafood lasagna, quiche, or stew.

Seafood Crêpes with Scallops and Shrimp SERVES 10

Make the crêpes in advance and refrigerate or freeze until ready to use. It is important that the seafood be drained and patted dry before adding to the sauce. You can use a wide variety of seafood, such as monkfish, crabmeat, wolffish, oysters, or salmon.

CRÊPES

1¼ cups flour	½ teaspoon salt
7 eggs	3 tablespoons unsalted
2¼ cups milk	butter, melted

Put flour in bowl and make well in middle. Break eggs into hole and whisk until batter is shiny. Whisk in milk slowly to work out lumps, then add salt and melted butter. Let sit 1 hour.

Heat well-seasoned 6-inch crêpe pan and add enough batter to just coat bottom, rotating pan so batter is distributed evenly. Turn over crêpe and cook 1 minute. Remove and stack crêpes on large plate as they cook. Cover with plastic wrap.

SEAFOOD

2 pounds scallops
2 pounds medium shrimp
4 cups fish stock (see p. 180)
1 ½ cups dry white wine
2 ribs celery, diced
1 red bell pepper, seeded and
   diced

¼ cup chopped fresh parsley
¼ cup chopped fresh dill
Juice of 1 lemon
Salt and pepper to taste

Cut scallops into bite-size pieces if large. Clean and devein (see p. 221). Heat fish stock and wine in saucepan. Add scallops in batches and poach 30 seconds. Drain scallops in sieve over bowl. Cook shrimp in same stock for 30 seconds. Drain shrimp in sieve over bowl, then cut shrimp in half. Place seafood on paper towels and pat dry. Reserve drained liquid in bowl.

Put seafood in separate bowl and combine with remaining ingredients. Toss well to mix and set aside while you make sauce.

SAUCE

Poaching liquid from bowl
   and saucepan
2 cups light cream
2 tablespoons cognac
8 tablespoons unsalted
   butter

4 tablespoons flour
2 tablespoons tomato paste
Chopped fresh parsley for
   garnish

Heat poaching liquid to boil and reduce to one half volume. Add cream and cognac. In small saucepan melt butter and stir in flour. Cook 1 minute. Add about 6 tablespoons of the roux to reduced poaching liquid, whisking well, and cook until sauce thickens.

Combine 2 cups of the sauce with remaining roux to make sauce really thick. (Reserve extra sauce.) Whisk in tomato paste. Add seafood and mix until well coated.

Place a portion of seafood mixture along length of crêpe. Roll up gently and lay in buttered casserole dish, seam side down. Repeat until seafood mixture is used up. Pour reserved sauce over crêpes, but do not cover completely as crêpes will become too soggy. Bake in preheated oven at 350° for 15 minutes, or until bubbly. Garnish with chopped parsley and serve.

Jamaican Seafood Stew
SERVES 8-10

This spicy stew gets lots of "bite" from the chili peppers. You can reduce the amount of cayenne and chilies if you prefer a milder taste.

1 pound scallops
1 pound shrimp
2 pounds firm fish filets (assortment of monkfish, hake, pollock, and cod)
8 littleneck clams
16 mussels
½ pound bacon, cut into pieces
1 pound okra, tops removed and sliced
2 tablespoons olive oil
2 red bell peppers, cut into ½-inch pieces
1 large onion
6 cloves garlic

32-ounce can tomatoes, with juice
2 hot chili peppers, seeded and sliced
1 tablespoon chopped fresh thyme (1 teaspoon dried)
2 bay leaves, crumbled
1 teaspoon cayenne pepper
6 cups bottled clam juice or fish stock (see p. 180)
4 cups chicken broth
Juice and grated rind of 1 orange
1 tablespoon tomato paste
Chopped fresh parsley for garnish

Remove feet from scallops (see p. 192). Clean and devein shrimp (see p. 221), leaving on tails. Cut fish into 2-inch chunks. Wash clams, and wash and debeard mussels (see p. 141). Refrigerate for later use.

In large soup pot fry bacon until fat is rendered. Add okra and cook until browned. Add oil, bell peppers, onion, and garlic, and cook until soft. Add tomatoes, breaking them apart with your fingers. Add chili peppers, thyme, bay leaves, and cayenne, and simmer 10 minutes to blend flavors.

Add clam juice and chicken broth. Combine orange juice and rind with tomato paste and add to pot. Simmer 20 minutes more. Add clams and cook 2 minutes, then add fish and mussels, and cook 2 minutes more. Add shrimp and scallops, and cook 2 minutes, or until clams open. Serve in large soup bowls garnished with chopped parsley.

The Fishmonger Shellfish Gazpacho   SERVES 6-8

This is a popular summer soup at The Fishmonger. Add a spoonful of yogurt or sour cream on top to temper the spiciness.

½ pound crabmeat, flaked
½ pound cooked small
   shrimp, peeled and
   deveined
1 small cucumber, peeled,
   seeded, and chopped
2 medium tomatoes, peeled,
   seeded, and chopped
1 small green bell pepper,
   seeded and chopped
1 medium-size red onion,
   chopped
3 tablespoons chopped fresh
   parsley
7 cups tomato juice

3 cloves garlic, minced
2 tablespoons Pommery
   mustard
¼ cup olive oil
1 tablespoon chili powder
1 teaspoon Tabasco
1 tablespoon Worcestershire
   sauce
½ cup fresh lemon juice
2 hard-boiled eggs, whites
   and yolks separated
Salt to taste
Garlic Croutons (recipe
   follows)

In large bowl combine crabmeat, shrimp, vegetables, parsley, and 6 cups of the tomato juice. In blender or food processor fitted with metal blade place remaining 1 cup tomato juice, garlic, mustard, oil, chili powder, Tabasco, Worcestershire sauce, lemon juice, and hard-boiled egg yolks. Blend 20 seconds, or until smooth. Pour into bowl with seafood and vegetables, and stir to blend. Season with salt, then ladle into bowls and garnish with chopped hard-boiled egg whites and garlic croutons.

GARLIC CROUTONS
6 slices French bread, cut
   into ½-inch cubes
1 clove garlic, minced

¼ teaspoon salt
4 tablespoons olive oil

Place bread cubes on cookie sheet and bake in 350° oven for 10 minutes to dry out. On cutting board with back of spoon mash garlic and salt together until paste is formed. Put into skillet and combine with oil over medium heat. Add bread cubes, tossing to coat all sides. Sauté 5 minutes, or until golden brown. Cool and serve as garnish for gazpacho.

Bouillabaisse

SERVES 6

The secret to success with bouillabaisse is in making the base, which must simmer for 45 minutes to meld the flavors. The fish and shellfish are added at the end according to their cooking times and cooked only for a few minutes. Adding the rouille to the individual bowls allows the diners to have as much garlic as they want. Let the fun begin!

⅓ cup olive oil
2 cups sliced leeks, white part only, washed and drained
½ cup grated onion
2 cloves garlic, minced
4 tomatoes, peeled, seeded, and chopped
1 rib celery, diced
1 bay leaf
½ teaspoon dried thyme
1 teaspoon fennel seed
Pinch of saffron
1 teaspoon grated orange rind
2 tablespoons tomato paste
10 cups fish stock (see p. 180)
2 to 3 pounds fish frames (haddock, bass, or flounder)
6 littleneck clams, washed

12 mussels, cleaned and debearded (see p. 141)
1¼-pound lobster, cut into 6 pieces (intestines and craw behind eyes removed)
½ pound haddock, cut into 1½-inch pieces
1 pound monkfish, cut into 1½-inch pieces
½ pound swordfish, tuna, or marlin, cut into 1½-inch pieces
½ pound pollock, cut into 1½-inch pieces
½ pound squid, cleaned (see p. 243) and sliced into rings
½ pound scallops, feet removed (see p. 192)
12 large shrimp, with shells
Rouille (recipe follows)

In large soup pot heat oil until hot. Add leeks, onion, and garlic, and cook until soft, about 5 minutes. Add tomatoes, celery, bay leaf, thyme, fennel seed, saffron, orange rind, and tomato paste. Stir and cook 2 minutes. Add fish stock and fish frames. Bring to simmer and cook 40-45 minutes. Strain to remove all solids and discard. Broth may be frozen or refrigerated at this point.

Return broth to pot and bring to simmer. Add clams, mussels, and lobster, and cook 5 minutes. Add haddock, monkfish, swordfish, and pollock, and cook 3 minutes more. Add squid, scallops, and shrimp, and cook 2½ to 3 minutes. Ladle into large soup bowls, top with a bit of rouille, and serve with warm bread for dipping. Set out an extra bowl for discarded shells and supply lots of napkins.

ROUILLE*

2 whole red bell peppers	½ teaspoon salt
3 egg yolks	½ teaspoon crushed red
9 cloves garlic	pepper flakes
Pinch of saffron	1¾ cups olive oil
½ cup bread crumbs	1 tablespoon boiling water

Roast red peppers in preheated 500° oven for about 10 minutes, or until skin begins to turn black. Remove and enclose in paper bag to cool down. When cool enough to handle, pull in half, remove seeds and pulp, and peel off outer skin.

Put all ingredients except oil and water in food processor fitted with metal blade and blend 30 seconds. With motor running, add oil 1 tablespoon at a time until 1 cup has been used. Then add remaining ¾ cup in slow, steady stream. When mixture has the consistency of mayonnaise, add boiling water to stabilize emulsion so it will not separate later on.

* It is very important that all the ingredients be at room temperature before making rouille, which has the consistency of mayonnaise, a red color, and a strong garlic flavor. Add a small amount to each bowl of bouillabaisse right before serving. Rouille can be stored in the refrigerator for up to 2 weeks without spoiling.

Fish Kebabs with Spicy Sauce

SERVES 4-6

I enjoy combining different types of fish when cooking on the grill, choosing fish that have a similar texture and will not fall apart when turned.

½ pound swordfish	2 tablespoons fresh lemon
½ pound tuna	juice
½ pound shrimp	Salt and pepper to taste
½ pound mako shark	Spicy Sauce (recipe follows)
½ cup olive oil	

Cut fish into 1½-inch chunks, removing skin from swordfish and dark center from tuna. Leave shrimp whole in shells. Put alternating types of fish on skewers. Combine oil, lemon juice, and salt and pepper, and brush over seafood. Cook on grill (or under broiler) 8-10 minutes, turning often and basting with olive oil mixture. Remove to serving platter and accompany with sauce.

SPICY SAUCE

3 tablespoons peanut oil	2 tablespoons rice wine
4 cloves garlic, minced	(Mirim)
1 tablespoon minced	2 tablespoons rice vinegar
gingerroot	1 tablespoon sugar
3 scallions, sliced	1 tablespoon sesame oil
1 teaspoon crushed red	2 tablespoons peanut oil
pepper flakes	2 teaspoons cornstarch
½ cup chicken broth	2 teaspoons water
2 tablespoons soy sauce	

Heat 3 tablespoons peanut oil in saucepan and add garlic. Sauté 3 minutes, add gingerroot and scallions, and sauté 1 minute. Stir in red pepper flakes.

Combine chicken broth, soy sauce, wine, vinegar, and sugar in bowl. Add to saucepan and heat to simmer. Combine sesame oil and 2 tablespoons peanut oil, and add to pan. Mix cornstarch with water and stir into sauce, cooking until thickened.

Shellfish Sauce for Pasta

SERVES 3-4

The key to this recipe is making sure all the bivalves are cleaned completely so the sauce won't be gritty. To me, few things are more delicious than pasta decorated with a variety of fruits from the sea.

½ pound baby squid
¾ pound medium shrimp
(about 20)
16 mussels
8 littleneck clams
6 tablespoons olive oil
4 cloves garlic, minced
⅓ cup dry white wine
1 cup peeled, seeded, and
chopped tomato

3 tablespoons chopped fresh
basil
1 cup crème fraîche (see
p. 16)
Freshly ground black pepper
to taste
Linguine to serve 3-4
Chopped fresh parsley for
garnish
Freshly grated Parmesan
cheese

Select smallest squid available. Clean well (see p. 243) and set body and tentacles aside. Remove three quarters of shell from shrimp, leaving tail intact. Devein (see p. 221) and set aside. Clean and debeard mussels (see p. 141) and set aside. Scrub clams and set aside.

In skillet heat 3 tablespoons of the oil over medium-high heat. Add half the minced garlic and cook 1 minute. Add squid and shrimp, and sauté 2 minutes. Remove seafood with slotted spoon and set aside.

In same skillet heat remaining 3 tablespoons oil and add remaining minced garlic. Cook 1 minute. Add mussels and clams, and stir to coat. Add wine, cover, and simmer 4-5 minutes, or until shells open. Remove shellfish with slotted spoon and put with squid and shrimp. Strain broth through 2 layers of cheesecloth and return to saucepan. Add tomato and basil. Simmer until reduced by one half. Add crème fraîche and simmer until thickened. Season with freshly ground black pepper.

Cook pasta in 2 quarts boiling water until al dente, about 4-5 minutes. Drain and put on large serving platter. Put seafood in warm cream sauce and coat well. Spoon over pasta, garnish with chopped parsley, and serve with freshly grated Parmesan cheese.

The Fishmonger Seafood Quiche SERVES 4-8

Make the pie dough 24 hours in advance so it has a chance to rest before being rolled out. Prebake the pie shell before filling so the crust will not become soggy. This type of quiche is popular at The Fishmonger. We make it only on Thursday and by Friday all are sold or reserved.

PIE DOUGH

9 tablespoons cold unsalted butter, cut into pieces
2 tablespoons solid shortening

½ teaspoon salt
Scant 2 cups flour
Scant ½ cup ice water
1 egg, beaten

FILLING

⅓ pound scallops, sliced
6 medium shrimp, peeled and deveined (see p. 221)
⅓ pound crabmeat
2 tablespoons unsalted butter
½ cup chopped onion
2 teaspoons dried dill

3 eggs
4 cups light cream, scalded
½ teaspoon salt
¼ teaspoon black pepper
½ cup grated Swiss cheese
2 tablespoons chopped fresh parsley

Make dough. In food processor fitted with metal blade add butter, shortening, salt, and flour. Turn on machine and let mix 10 seconds. With motor running, add ice water in steady stream. Wait for dough to ball up, then remove. Knead dough a bit and form into flat circle. Wrap in plastic wrap and refrigerate 24 hours.

Working from center, roll dough into circle larger than pie plate. Put in pie plate, fold under edges, and make high, fluted crust. Prick holes with fork in bottom of crust, line with foil, and cover with dried beans or rice. Prebake crust 20 minutes in preheated 400° oven. Remove beans or rice and foil, and bake 5 minutes more. Remove from oven and brush well with beaten egg.

Prepare filling. Poach scallops in 2 cups water for 1 minute. Remove with slotted spoon and set aside. Cook shrimp in same cooking water for 1½ minutes. Remove with slotted spoon and slice in half lengthwise. Check crabmeat for shell pieces and drain thoroughly. Melt butter in sauté pan, add onion, and cook until soft. Stir in dill.

Begin custard by whisking together eggs. Add scalded cream slowly, whisking continuously. Add salt and pepper.

Line bottom of pie shell with onion-dill mixture and spread scallops over top. Distribute shrimp evenly and spread crabmeat over shrimp. Sprinkle with grated cheese and then chopped parsley. Fill with custard, reserving a portion to add later. Bake in preheated oven at 350° for 20 minutes. Add more custard to center to make quiche puffy and full. Bake 20-25 minutes more, or until knife inserted in center comes out clean.

Shellfish Ravigote   SERVES 4-6

The sauce has more flavor if fresh herbs are used. It is a classic dressing to use with any shellfish or cold poached fish. Garnishing the platter with avocado, cherry tomatoes, cucumber slices, and various fresh herb sprigs enhances the presentation.

1 pound fresh crabmeat **½ pound cooked lobster meat, chopped**	**½ pound poached scallops**

RAVIGOTE

2 tablespoons white wine vinegar	**2 tablespoons finely chopped scallion greens**
2 tablespoons fresh lemon juice	**1 tablespoon finely chopped fresh tarragon**
6 tablespoons olive oil	**1½ cups mayonnaise (see p. 283)**
1 tablespoon finely chopped red onion	**2 teaspoons Dijon mustard**
1 tablespoon chopped shallots	**1 anchovy filet, chopped to a paste**
2 tablespoons chopped fresh parsley	**1 hard-boiled egg, finely chopped**
2 tablespoons capers, squeeze-drained and chopped	

Combine crabmeat, chopped lobster, and scallops in bowl and refrigerate. In mixing bowl whisk together vinegar, lemon juice, and oil. Whisk in remaining ingredients and chill. Pour some sauce over shellfish and toss to coat. Serve on platter, garnished as desired, and accompany with extra sauce.

Seafood Lasagna   SERVES 8

This is a great company dish. It can be assembled the night before, refrigerated, and baked when the guests arrive.

6 lasagna noodles, cooked
7 tablespoons unsalted butter
1 cup chopped onion
10-ounce package frozen chopped spinach, thawed and squeeze-drained
3 ounces cream cheese, softened
1 cup cottage or ricotta cheese
1 egg, beaten
1 tablespoon minced shallots
¾ pound raw shrimp, peeled and deveined (see p. 221)
1 pound scallops, feet removed (see p. 192)

½ cup dry white wine
2 cups thinly sliced mushrooms
¼ teaspoon nutmeg
2 cups Béchamel Sauce (recipe follows)
1 cup crushed canned tomatoes
½ teaspoon cayenne pepper
2 pounds flounder filets (about 8 filets)
½ cup freshly grated Parmesan cheese
Chopped fresh parsley for garnish

Cook lasagna noodles in boiling water until done, about 8-10 minutes. Drain, cool, and reserve.

In skillet heat 3 tablespoons of the butter over medium heat. Add onion and cook until soft. Add spinach, cook 2 minutes, and transfer to bowl. Add cream cheese, cottage cheese, and beaten egg, and mix well with hands.

In same skillet melt 2 more tablespoons butter and add shallots. Cook 2 minutes, or until soft. Add shrimp, scallops, and wine, and simmer until shrimp are pink, about 2-3 minutes. Remove seafood with slotted spoon to bowl and save liquid for sauce.

In same skillet melt remaining 2 tablespoons butter, add mushrooms and nutmeg, and cook until soft, about 3 minutes. Remove mushrooms and add juices to other reserved liquids.

Make Béchamel Sauce and add tomatoes, cayenne, and cooked mushrooms, blending well. Add reserved cooking liquids to thin sauce, if necessary, to the consistency of heavy cream.

BÉCHAMEL SAUCE

4 tablespoons unsalted butter
4 tablespoons flour

2 cups milk, scalded
Salt and pepper to taste

Melt butter in saucepan, stir in flour, and cook 2 minutes. Add scalded milk, whisking as you add. Season with salt and pepper.

Assembly: Butter baking pan large enough to accommodate width and length of 3 strips of lasagna. Spoon a little sauce in bottom to cover. Spread with half the spinach-cheese mixture. Lay 4 pieces of flounder on top. Spread half the shrimp-scallop mixture over flounder. Generously spoon half the sauce over all. Lay down 3 lasagna noodles to cover. Repeat once again, ending with sauce on top, sprinkled with Parmesan cheese. Bake in preheated oven at 350° for 30-35 minutes, or until sides are bubbly and top is browned. Garnish with chopped parsley.

Paella
SERVES 6

This can be assembled on top of the stove and then put in a hot oven to cook for 30 minutes. Be sure not to overcook the shellfish.

½ cup olive oil
½ teaspoon ground coriander seed
½ teaspoon black pepper
1 clove garlic, minced
2 chicken breasts, each cut into 6 equal pieces
1 onion, chopped
3 hot Portuguese sausages (linguiça or chorizo)
2 cups rice, uncooked

6 artichoke hearts, halved
1 pound monkfish, cut into 1-inch pieces
4½ cups chicken broth
1 cup frozen peas
2 cups canned tomatoes
Generous pinch of saffron
1 bay leaf, crumbled
12 mussels, cleaned and debearded (see p. 141)
12 shrimp, in shells

Combine ¼ cup of the oil, coriander, pepper, and garlic, and rub over chicken pieces. Heat remaining ¼ cup oil in Dutch oven, add chicken, and brown. Remove and reserve. Add onion and sausages to Dutch oven and cook 5 minutes. Add rice and artichokes, and cook 7 minutes. Add monkfish and stir to incorporate. Stir in chicken broth, peas, tomatoes, saffron, and bay leaf, and bring to simmer. Put pot in 400° oven and cook, uncovered, 15 minutes.

Remove from oven, push mussels and shrimp down into mixture, and return to oven, cooking 15-20 minutes more, or until mussels open and shrimp are pink.

Caviar and Other Salted Fish Roe

As defined by the Food and Drug Administration (FDA) in 1966, only the eggs of the sturgeon can be classified as true caviar; all others must have the name of the fish included — for example, salmon caviar, whitefish caviar, or lumpfish caviar. Sometimes the country of origin must be included, too, because each country has a different processing method.

The Soviet Union and Iran provide the finest and most expensive caviar, made from the roe of the beluga, the largest of the sturgeons and that with the largest "berries," or eggs. Other sturgeons used include the osietr (osetra) and sevruga.

The processing of caviar is a fine art. In the Soviet Union, the female sturgeon is brought to the plant still alive if possible, and her belly is slit open to remove the egg skeins. These are put on a large mesh grid or screen with holes large enough to allow the eggs to pass through individually and fall into stainless steel buckets for washing and cleansing of unwanted matter. Next, they are salted by someone who has the expertise to determine just the right amount of salt to add. This is critical because too much salt will discolor and shrink the berries and too little will not retard their spoilage. Once the salt is added, it takes only 15 to 30 minutes before the caviar is ready to be packaged in tins and stored at 26°F. to 30°F. (The salt prevents it from freezing.) The tins are turned periodically to relieve the pressure on the bottom eggs and to let the natural fat from the eggs be distributed throughout. Fresh caviar has a shelf life of up to one year, but six months is safer. It should always be stored between 26°F. and 30°F.

Pressed or compressed caviar is a combination of eggs from the beluga, osietr, and sevruga that have been culled from the top of the line. The berries used for this might be too small, bruised, cracked, overripe, or the wrong color. The berries are gathered together in a cheesecloth sack and placed in a machine that compresses them. The gelatinous mass that is left is salted lightly, packaged in jars or tins, and sold as pressed caviar.

In U.S. waters, sturgeons have been overfished and are endangered species. Some states have recently established programs to replenish these river dwellers, but progress is slow because it takes a sturgeon about 20 years to reach maturity.

Fresh salmon caviar, or "red caviar," is a very reasonably priced substitute for sturgeon caviar and is available fresh or pasteurized. The fresh is a deeper orange color and must be refrigerated or frozen. (Unlike true caviar from sturgeon, freezing does not hurt the eggs or the flavor.) The pasteurized type is found on the grocery shelf in 1-ounce jars; it is saltier than the fresh and has less flavor.

Whitefish caviar is made from the roe of the lake whitefish, a small, slow-growing fish that is a member of the salmon and trout family. Marketed as "golden caviar" or "golden white-fish," the eggs have a sturdy membrane and also freeze well.

Lumpfish, sold in grocery stores, gourmet shops, and supermarkets, is the most commonly available caviar substitute. Its natural color is unappealing — somewhere between dark green and brown or gray — but someone came up with the idea of dying it to make it more attractive. Now you can get bright green for St. Patrick's Day, red for Christmas, or the more traditional black.

As elegant as caviar is, it should never be served with a silver spoon, for it reacts with the silver and takes on a metallic taste. Use bone, stainless steel, mother of pearl, or even small plastic utensils. Place the caviar in a glass bowl set on a bed of crushed ice to preserve its freshness and accompany with unbuttered toast points or unseasoned crackers. Ice-cold vodka, a fine champagne, or even a quality-grade bottled water goes well with this treat. A squeeze of lemon is sometimes needed with a more heavily salted caviar. Other preparations include chopped egg, capers, onion, and lemon wedges. Blini, small buckwheat pancakes rolled up like crêpes, are often served with a generous dollop of sour cream topped with caviar. And to raise the ordinary to the sublime, heap a spoonful on top of a baked potato — a meal in itself.

Nutrition Chart
(Figures based on 3½-ounce raw portion)

Seafood	Protein	Cholesterol	Calories	Omega-3*
Anchovies	28.89 g	85 mg	210	H
Black Sea Bass	18.43 g	41 mg	97	L
Bluefish	20.04 g	59 mg	124	M
Caviar	24.60 g	588 mg	252	nd
Clams	12.77 g	34 mg	74	L
Cod	17.81 g	43 mg	82	L
Crab	18.06 g	78 mg	87	L
Cusk	18.99 g	41 mg	87	L
Eel	18.44 g	126 mg	184	L
Flounder	18.84 g	48 mg	91	L
Haddock	18.91 g	57 mg	87	L
Hake	18.31 g	67 mg	90	L
Halibut	20.81 g	32 mg	110	L
Herring	17.96 g	60 mg	158	H
Lobster	18.80 g	95 mg	90	L
Mackerel	18.60 g	70 mg	205	H
Mahi-Mahi	18.50 g	73 mg	85	L
Marlin	21.10 g	nd	86	L
Monkfish	14.48 g	25 mg	76	L
Mussels	11.90 g	28 mg	86	L
Ocean Perch	18.62 g	42 mg	94	L
Oysters	7.06 g	55 mg	69	L
Pollock	19.44 g	71 mg	92	L
Porgy	18.88 g	52 mg	105	L
Red Snapper	20.51 g	37 mg	100	L
Salmon	19.84 g	55 mg	142	M
Scallops	16.78 g	33 mg	88	L
Sea Urchins	10.03 g	nd	120	L
Shad	16.93 g	72 mg	197	H
Shark	20.98 g	51 mg	130	M
Shrimp	20.31 g	152 mg	106	L
Skate	19.20 g	nd	88	L
Smelts	17.63 g	70 mg	97	L
Squid	15.58 g	233 mg	92	L
Striped Bass	17.73 g	80 mg	97	L
Swordfish	19.80 g	39 mg	121	M
Tautog	18.10 g	nd	88	L
Tilefish	17.50 g	50 mg	96	L
Tuna	23.33 g	38 mg	144	M
Weakfish	16.74 g	83 mg	104	M
Wolffish	17.50 g	46 mg	96	L

Source: Human Nutrition Information Service/USDA, National Fisheries Institute Food Science Division

*L = low; M = moderate; H = high; nd = no data available.

Recommended Reading

Bigelow, Henry B., and William C. Schroeder. *Fishes of the Gulf of Maine.* Cambridge: Museum of Comparative Zoology, Harvard University, 1964.

McClane, A.J. *The Encyclopedia of Fish Cookery.* New York: Holt, Rinehart & Winston, 1977.

Davidson, Alan. *North Atlantic Seafood.* New York: Viking Press, 1979.

Montagné, Prosper. *The New Larousse Gastronomique.* New York: Crown Publishers, 1977.

Index